Advance Praise f

"I was particularly struck by the words in Antonio's new book, 'If any leader tells you that they are serious about developing themselves, their team, and their company—but they don't journal, don't believe them.' To change results, you first have to change yourself. That's why I believe that many more leaders would journal, if they knew what to write, when to write, how much to write, and had a clear development path to follow: this book gives us leaders exactly that. If you are serious about building yourself, your team, and your organization, *My Daily Leadership* is the missing piece."

—Mark Crisp, CEO, Helm Bank USA

"This latest book from Antonio is jam-packed with wonderful new tools and techniques designed to help every leader quickly reach the next level of their development no matter the size and complexity of the organization. This book gives the reader a clear and structured leadership development framework to follow, and the various examples of leadership insight are worth the cover price alone. If you're a leader who cares about self-development and making a really positive impact, this book is definitely for you."

—Tracy Hernandez, SVP, Kaseya

"Every leader has a clear responsibility: the responsibility to maximize their own personal leadership potential, and to become the best leader that they can possibly be. This highly-interactive, engaging, and inspirational book is long overdue and the exercises in it give the reader a clear step-by-step roadmap to extraordinary leadership and business development. Leaders are lifelong learners, and leaders are readers. I urge leaders everywhere to read and learn the lessons of this new book and to establish the daily habits of leadership and business success."

—Bruce Hanson, CEO, AWT

"Leadership development is extremely important to me and my organization, and that's why *My Daily Leadership* is such an important book. The very best leaders are on a journey of self-improvement—and that journey requires daily focus and attention. Antonio's book is a roadmap, a daily reference, and guide for those leaders serious about improving the performance of themselves, their teams, and their business. At its heart, *My Daily Leadership* is written for those wanting to develop winning daily habits of self-evaluation and leadership excellence."

—JIM HUNTER, CEO, PeopleBest

"The commercial world is increasingly complex and the demands placed on executive teams are more challenging than ever. What most leaders need now, is a clear framework for strategic and tactical success. Leaders need to futureproof their business, by futureproofing themselves. This book gives leaders across the whole commercial spectrum: from small to large, from simple to complex, from new to old, a clear daily leadership guide—a clear and powerful daily leadership template to follow. If you are a leader, or if you have aspirations to be the best leader that you can possibly be, I urge you to read this book—your future you (and your future team) will thank you for it."

—DENISE KEE, CEO, Xtremax

"Anything of any real value takes focus, effort, and intentionality—especially leadership. And that's why I am delighted to recommend Antonio's latest book to any leader who wants to take a more thoughtful and considered approach to developing themselves and those around them. I am confident that this book will become a regular and trusted point of reference for those looking for a daily guide to help them develop leadership insight and ongoing growth and inspiration. This book is more than a 'must read,' it's a 'must do.'"

—CROMWELL LITTLEJOHN, CRO, Northrop & Johnson

My Daily Leadership

A POWERFUL ROADMAP FOR LEADERSHIP SUCCESS

CONCILIO ET LABORE

ANTONIO GARRIDO

Post Hill
PRESS

A POST HILL PRESS BOOK
ISBN: 978-1-63758-180-3
ISBN (eBook): 978-1-63758-181-0

My Daily Leadership:
A Powerful Roadmap for Leadership Success
© 2022 by Antonio Garrido
All Rights Reserved

Post Hill Press
New York • Nashville
posthillpress.com

Published in the United States of America
1 2 3 4 5 6 7 8 9 10

Julie.
You help make me better every day—
and you help make every day better.

CONTENTS

. . . .

INTRODUCTION
. . . .

You may be checking out this introduction trying to figure out whether this book is for you:

If you are a business leader, C-suite executive, divisional manager, entrepreneur, or solopreneur[1]...

...and...

...you're someone who wants to significantly improve your leadership skills and success...

...and...

...you are the kind of person who recognizes that to achieve something worthwhile likely requires some effort, application, and intention...

...then yes, this book is likely for you.

Now ask yourself: "Do I want to be a *good* leader, or do I want to be a *great* leader?"

To help you answer, consider:

Good leaders help people do better at work; great leaders help people do better at life.

If you want to be a great leader, not just a good leader, again, this book is for you.

---

[1] ...or if you're planning to become any of these things in the future. Good stuff. Keep at it, and don't get discouraged. We're all with you. ☺

Good leaders want their people and company to develop, and to grow, and to improve, and to thrive, and to be happy, and to prosper—of course they do.[2] The thing is, good leaders can only become great leaders once they come to the realization that they must also grow by improving and develop their own personal competencies, skills, beliefs, and habits.

If this also sounds like you, then yes, this book is for you.

So many "self-help" books are designed to light a fire under you.
They say:

"Don't do that, do this..."
"Rest."
"Don't eat that, eat this..."
"Run."

"Don't think that, think this..."
"Carbs."
"Don't say that, say this..."
"Fast."

"Don't listen to that, listen to this..."
"Yoga."
"Don't read that, read this..."
"Meditate."

"Don't go here, go there..."
"Save."
"Don't ask him, ask her..."
"Spend."

---

2   Possibly why you're still reading these words.

"Don't sleep in, sieze the day."
"Take."
"Don't wish that, wish this..."
"Give."

"Don't watch that, watch this..."
"Read."
"Don't invest in that, invest in this..."
"Write."[3]

This book is different from all of those books. It is not a "self-help" book intended to tell you what to think, nor what not to think.

It's not intended to tell you what to believe or not to believe.

This book is not designed to light a fire *under* you, it is intended to light a fire *within* you that grows, and grows, and spreads to others, now and for decades to come.

Lighting a fire within yourself and others is a cornerstone of great leadership, after all.

To evoke and slightly misappropriate B. K. S. Iyengar, leadership journaling is a light, which once lit, will never dim. The more you journal, the brighter the flame.

> If you want to learn how to light and build fires within and not under people, and you want to learn how to light and build a fire within yourself, then yes, this book is definitely for you.

The good news is that the "effort" you have to put in to "light all of these inspirational fires and keep them stoked" is not a monstrously heavy lift; rather it's a series of small but regular, interesting, thought-provoking loads. These loads compound over time to make significant and lasting improvement in your

---

3   All as clear as ditchwater.

leadership development, your people, and the success of your company or division.

This book and the daily habits it develops are designed to reveal and strengthen your own unique and powerful leadership style—to maximize your innate leadership potential.

Your success as a leader is determined by the intentionality and thoughtfulness of your daily agenda. And this book will help you significantly fast-forward your leadership development. All current and future leaders must take personal responsibility to improve their own leadership skills, habits, and capabilities.

Remember:

Leaders lead whether they want to or not.
Leaders communicate whether they want to or not.
Leaders set examples whether they want to or not.
Leaders are responsible whether they want to be or not.

...and, most of all...

Leaders encourage what they tolerate in themselves and others.

Some leaders, recognizing that they have perhaps hit a ceiling in either career, or self-esteem, or self-development, look outside themselves for help: they seek out leadership accountability groups, they appoint a mentor, or they even pay handsomely for executive coaching not realizing that the very best way to improve is, quite simply, to spend some time with their journal—their Leadership Journal, that is, but more on that later.

Sounds a little too simple, right?

Well, most worthwhile things do sound simple; take this simple groovy "health" list example:

quit smoking, cut down on bad carbs, exercise more, limit alcohol, drink more water, get an annual medical checkup, and get more and better quality sleep.

They all sound simple enough, right?

So why then, are we as a nation all so sick and so over-weight? Why do we have raging hypertension, sleep issues, and other more serious ailments? Since we all know what we *should* do, why are we all dropping like flies?[4]

The fact is, in order to improve at anything, you simply have to do the work—pound the pavement, lift the weights, get outside your comfort zone, challenge, stretch, say "no" to that extra slice of pie, and resist finishing that bottle of wine just because "Well, it's open now, isn't it?"

Some things, the best things, perhaps, are "simple, not easy."

Leadership Journaling is simple, not easy—but it is the most efficient and effective way to build self-awareness, increase knowledge based on self-evaluated experience, and plan your own development path as well as what's next for your people and the company.[5]

If you believe that "doing the work" has real lasting value, this book is certainly for you.

CONCILIO ET LABORE

This should be the official motto for all the leaders who journal with regularity.

It is the first motto of *My Daily Leadership*.

It translates from the Latin as:

By wisdom and effort.

---

4   Flies, in my experience, tend not to "drop," they tend to fly—hence the name, I suspect. Why people think that flies "drop like flies" is quite beyond me. Entomologists, answers on a postcard, please.

5   Hoorah!

Some will be put off by it, and others will be inspired by it.

Leaders have a responsibility to lead with intentionality and clarity: to be unclear is to be unkind. It is impossible to be a great leader if you are wooly or unclear. One of the key benefits of Leadership Journaling is that it helps bring clarity of thought, vision, and purpose.

Some leaders tell us that they would consider journaling, if only they knew what to write.
Good news, we'll tell you what to write.

Some leaders tell us that they're not sure when to write.
Good news again, we'll tell you that too.

Some leaders say that they're unclear about why they should journal.
It's your day, we'll explain that too.

Some leaders tell us they're not sure how much to write every day.
Again, we've got your back.

Some leaders say they're not sure how a Leadership Journal is different from any other journal.
Yes, we'll cover that for you too.

Some leaders tell us they don't know how to measure and track their progress.
Yes again.

WHO THIS BOOK IS NOT FOR:

This book is *not* for you if you believe:

"Do as I say."
...not as I do!

"I judge people by their actions."
...but I judge myself by my intentions.

"Everyone in the company has an Annual Performance Review and Development Plan."
....oh, except for me, of course, I'm the boss and I'm already close to perfect.

"No pay raises this year, I'm afraid."
...I don't want the increased overhead to impact my stock options.[6]

If these kinds of thoughts are yours, it might be best to put the book down and check out some of these titles: *What the Roman Army Can Teach Us about Leadership*, or *What the MMA and Leadership Have in Common*, or *When Your Boardroom Becomes a Battleground*.[7]
...well, you get the idea.
A final few thoughts before you finally make up your mind:

❖ Anyone who says he is committed to being successful but doesn't journal, don't believe him.

❖ All who truly excel in any field from sales, management, leadership, entertainment, and sports to politics...journal.

---

6   Don't you dare!
7   You might also want to consider taking up yoga and meditation. De-stress. Take five deep breaths. Relax. Smile, just for once—you might enjoy it. I know your team will. Have you ever considered making decaf a more regular beverage choice? Herbal tea can be nice too.

✧ Journaling has been around for more than five thousand years, and things that have that kind of resilience and persistence are usually valuable and worthy of attention—fads change, fashions change, styles change, but the very best, most worthwhile things persist. It's that simple.

So, it's "make your mind up" time. Are you in, or out? If you're in we'll see you on the next page and the first step to lasting leadership greatness.
Onward!

"No man can lead others, who cannot lead himself."
—Socrates

READY TO MAKE A START?

· ·

Look at you, you made it all the way here; well done! Happy to have you with us. It's going to be quite a ride—strap yourself in. ☺

One of the first imperatives of Leadership Journaling is to furnish yourself with a really nice journal, of course. A really splendid one. A really, really, really splendid one. You know, all leather-bound and imperious looking. Something that you'd feel proud to have sitting front and center on your desk.

"Hold the phone!" I hear you cry. "You don't seriously mean to tell me that I'm going to have to write, do you? By hand? With an actual pen? On real paper? We're not still living in the Dark Ages, you know?"[1]

Yes, I do mean that—on real paper, with an actual, real pen.

Yes, I have heard of apps, and computers, and the internet, and AI, and everything.

And yes, I do realize that you practically live on your smartphone.

And yes, I do recognize that you can type much quicker than you write.

And yes, I do understand that you haven't used a pen since high school.

And yes, I do know that some people don't think in straight lines.

And yes, I do appreciate that you might just get a nasty blister.

...but none of those things can change the overwhelming fact that the adult learning model dictates that the process of

---

1   Our first argument. Has the magic gone already? Is it over?

writing on paper significantly increases understanding, retention, and application.

The research conducted by Pam Mueller of Princeton University and Daniel Oppenheimer of University of California, Los Angeles argues that when we write in a notebook by hand, as opposed to typing on a laptop, our understanding and memory retention is significantly increased. Typing, it seems, is best suited to surface-level understanding and retention, whereas writing longhand requires the individual to process the issue much more deeply, and it forces them to be extremely selective with what to commit to paper and what to discard—the selectivity process is critical to the difference since we simply cannot write by hand as quickly as we can type.

Writing by hand creates a positive feedback loop whereby the outputs become the reinforced inputs—much more so than typing. Writing by hand is much more involved than typing.

When writing on paper, our brain must first consider the issue.

We then have to filter out the less-critical elements.

We then decide what to include, what to exclude, and what to record.

Our brains then instruct our muscles what words to write as well as how to write them.

While we do this, our eyes perceive the pen moving across the paper trailing the required words behind it.

As we read the words that the pen reveals, our brains then repeat these words back to ourselves confirming that those words were indeed our intended words.

In this way writing by hand creates a continuous feedback loop, connecting the thinking, the editing, the telling, the moving, the seeing, and the reinforcement of repeating and validating.

The researchers explain, "There is something about typing that leads to mindless processing, and there is something about ink and paper that prompts students to go beyond merely hearing and recording new information."

Now that we have gotten over the shock and disappointment of all of that, shall we move on? Thank you.

Your brand new, bright and shiny journal should have at least two hundred pages of good, high-quality paper—your new leadership thoughts should sit somewhere worthy of them.

A4 size if you're in the UK, "letter size" if you're in the US[2]; nothing smaller, please. You and your new thoughts will need space to stretch out, put their feet up, and breathe.

Ideally it should be leather-bound, handmade, and something that deserves engaging with every day. Think Rolls-Royce, Bentley, Hermes, Louis Vuitton. Why do your thoughts and your development deserve any less than this level of quality and perfection?

Try: www.mydailyleadership.com

Keep this swanky new journal with you as you read this book—you can write in it as we go along—there will be lots of important prompts for you along the way.

By the time you get to the end of this book, your Leadership Journaling journey will already be off to an amazing start, and you'll have begun to notice a significant difference in yourself, your company, and others around you. It will already have become a life-changing, lifelong habit. Marvelous.

As mentioned, get your hands on a good, high-quality pen too. Again, something that would look splendid sitting on top of the journal that you'd feel proud to have sitting front and center on your desk. Your pen and journal should be something that deserves attention and intentionality every day.

A fancy calligraphy pen with lots of clever nibs?

Umm, no.

Colored gels and scented highlighters?

Again, no: you're not nine, and this isn't arts and crafts.

---

2 Australia? India? Azerbaijan? No idea. Look it up.

A #2 pencil with a brightly colored, monster-shaped eraser at the end?

Look, if you have to ask....

A plastic ballpoint chewed at the end?

** sigh** Can we move on?

All joking aside, developing your leadership abilities is an important, serious, and worthwhile pursuit. Leadership Journaling is a serious and worthwhile pursuit too—you need a good journal, with good paper, and a good (serious) fountain pen. This is the start of a lifelong journey of development; let's give it the level of importance that it, you, your people, and your company deserve.

If you don't want to make the investment personally, is it your birthday soon? Christmas, maybe? Mother's Day? Father's Day? Leader's Day?[3]

#TRUSTTHEPROCESS

"Trust the Process" is another cornerstone of Leadership Journaling. The phrase was coined by fans of the NBA's Philadelphia 76ers. It was first used during a particularly rough patch for the team. It basically means, "Sure, things may look tough now, but we have a plan in place to make it better: and if we do what we said we were going to do, we are 100 percent confident that things will get better. We trust ourselves, and we trust our action plan."

#TrustTheProcess is the second motto of the serious journaler.[4] Find somewhere splendid near the beginning of your journal to write this one down too.

---

3   Leader's Day? There isn't one? There jolly well should be! Who's with me? Chaaaarge! Wait, who do we ask?

4   We did consider having this motto represented in Latin also—"Processus Habeat Fiduciam" if you're keeping score. But, after some debate, we decided that it seemed overly precocious, too pretentious, and a little bombastic. Grandiloquent, you might even say. Sorry again.

Remember, always trust the process because the process is the thing that's going to get you from A to Z, from good leader to great leader. So, keep going, keep the faith in the process, and don't ever give up.

As Sherpa Tenzing likely said to Edmund Hillary as Edmund was struggling to put one foot in front of the other trudging up Everest with nothing but mountain ahead of him and no sight of the summit, half starving, frozen to the core in the teeth of a blizzard, and fighting for every breath, "Edmund, old stick, don't give up. Keep going. Trust the process."

As Hannibal, the ancient Carthaginian general and founder of military strategy said[5] to his lead elephant musher who was bemoaning the perils of taking elephants (yes, real life, gray, wrinkly, big, lumbering pachyderms) across dangerous rifts and perilously unstable and narrow ravines over the Alps, "Keith,[6] don't give up. Trust the process."

As Thomas Edison doubtless said to his assistant, William Hammer, after yet another disappointment in an extensive list of failed attempts at finding the perfect filament for his new incandescent lamp doohickey thingy, "William, we have to trust the process. I know, let's try human hair next."

The world is littered with countless such examples: you probably already have your favorite story of persistence, grit under pressure, and dogged determination to succeed—if not, they're easy to find. Use the memory and lesson of your favorite "determination" story when things get tough, and you only have the process to fall back on. The process, if it's a good process, will *always* carry you through and win the day.

Remember, when things get a little tough, trust the process.

When you'd rather not bother journaling today, trust the process.

---

5   Probably.
6   Not his real name, I am positive.

When your leadership development progress seems a little slow, trust the process.

When you forget to remember the commitment that you made and think you've slipped too far to start over again...well, you've got the message by now, I'm sure.

Make a commitment.

Make a start.

Trust the process.

If it's a good process, the process will always save you, but it must be followed to have any value. Process leads to progress—always.

So, dear reader, are you yet ready to take the plunge, dedicate yourself to the Leadership Journaling process, and make a firm and lasting commitment? Come on, get your natty new swimsuit on and dive in; the water is quite lovely.

If so, grab your journal and your pen and do your best to follow each of the prompts and exercises as we transition through the book. The exercises are intended to increase your self-awareness as well as have you explore your understanding and appreciation of the most privileged position in the world: leadership. As you complete the exercises, your journal will chart your progress and will act as a wonderful record of your development over the first six weeks or so of your amazing new journey of self-discovery and improvement.

Tremendously exciting stuff.

"The more you sweat in practice,
the less you bleed in battle"
—*Chinese Proverb*

To read more and to download free Leadership Journaling resources including a thirty-day journaling template, as well as download a list of all of the prompts in this book, visit: www.mydailyleadership.com/resources

Shop our handmade, leather-bound journals and exclusive carbon-fiber fountain pen and specially formulated inks. Subscribe to our daily journaling prompts. Basically, pop along to find all manner of helpful leadership development advice, self-development paraphernalia, and what have you.

CHAPTER 1

Would you have employed you?

How well are you doing?

HOW WELL ARE YOU DOING?

Imagine that in some sort of parallel, Willy Wonka, Marty McFly, quantum universe, you had the opportunity to go back in time and interview *yourself* for the position that you currently hold. How well would you have fared in the interview all those years ago, I wonder? Would you have given the applicant that you interviewed (you) the role, or would you have chosen another candidate?

It's really easy to say, "Yes, of course I would have given me the role. After all, I was perfect for the job. I mean, I have the role now, don't I? And I've held it for twelve years, and I'm making a pretty handsome fist of it, aren't I?"

Well, maybe, maybe not. I do know one thing for sure, though, you're not perfect—no one is.

Since you're not perfect, what would have been your main concerns in offering you the position? And would you have been right to be worried?

As the interviewer, what would your interview notes have looked like?

How would you have debriefed the candidate's performance to the HR director when she asked about your top three concerns following your interview?[1]

What would you have said the candidate's biggest areas for development and improvement were?

...and now back in the present tense, have you done anything about reducing those weaknesses and areas for development lately?

What about your next role; would you employ you to do that if you had the chance to interview you for it right now, or do you still have some way to go to be "ready" for it?

---

1   The candidate we're talking about is "past" you—if you're following the rather tricky and convoluted thread. ☺

What about the role that you ultimately aspire to; would you (or anybody else, for that matter) employ you to do that role today, I wonder?

What I'm talking about here is the extent to which you have a well-developed capacity for honest self-introspection and self-evaluation, and do you possess a high degree of self-awareness? The best leaders most certainly do—and it's at the seat of self-development, improvement, and change.

Here's the catch—almost everyone who has low self-awareness is entirely convinced that they have a very well-developed sense of themselves. And almost everyone who possesses a very well-developed self-awareness skill knows that they do not. Ouch!

NEWSFLASH

Leaders who have a well-developed sense of self-awareness typically do very well at developing their leadership skills; those who don't, invariably don't.

YOUR FIRST JOURNAL ENTRY

Quick, go get it—I will wait!

Consider this: How would you rate your overall leadership performance over, say, the last two quarters? Give yourself a score from 1 to 10.[2]

In fifty to one hundred words, write down in your Leadership Journal specifically where have you excelled these last sixty days or so, and specifically where have you fallen short, and why.

You will be encouraged to read back on this, your first entry, in around a month, so be sure to make sure that your answer is thoughtful, considered, and worthy of the future leader that

---

[2] Hint—it's not ten. It's not even nine!

you are to become. This first exercise should take you around ten minutes to complete.

If you're struggling to give yourself honest, specific, frank (to the point of brutal) feedback, you will likely not develop your leadership skills nearly as quickly as you should...nor as diligently as you could. A lesson for us all.

Self-awareness is like a muscle—use it to build it, leave it to lose it.

Increasingly large numbers of leaders understand, rate, measure, and develop their self-awareness muscles in their Leadership Journaling: it's one of the main benefits of journaling, after all.

For reasons that we will explore later in this book, successful leaders need to have a very acutely developed self-awareness muscle, not least because honest feedback is often in very short supply. Again, more on this later.

Congratulations, by the way, for making your first serious entry in your journal, you're already on your way to self-awareness mastery and leadership greatness. Hoorah! ☺

Whilst we have just considered whether or not you would have employed you, let's spend a few moments considering whether I might have employed you too.

WOULD I HAVE EMPLOYED YOU?

Throughout my career, I have interviewed countless candidates for a variety of roles from executive leadership positions to entry-level interns and everything in between.

In my current role as executive coach and business consultant, I am often asked to help our clients find exceptional candidates. I have a very established interview process that includes a fixed set of interview protocols; one of which includes being sure to ask each candidate the same set of critical questions.

Depending on the specifics of the role, the set of questions varies, of course; but each candidate for the particular role would receive the same set of eight to ten questions during the interview. The answers and responses to each of these questions are graded and recorded, which makes it easier to compare and contrast skill sets, attitudes, and abilities of candidates when preparing shortlists.

An interview is, at its heart, a three-C assessment: Capability, Credibility, and Chemistry.

Capability:

Does the applicant have the skill sets, competencies, and wherewithal to successfully execute the demands of the role—and the role that could potentially follow it? Basically, is the person *capable* of doing an excellent job?

Credibility:

Do the candidate's work history, experiences, results, and achievements suggest that they would be a natural and suitable person for consideration? Would it be obvious to all of the new-hire's work colleagues why this person was given the role? Would you feel comfortable with this individual out and about representing you and your company with your logo on their lapel?

Chemistry:

Would the candidate fit easily into the company structure and culture—basically, is there core value alignment on both sides?

Depending upon the particular challenges of the role, the manager, the team, the company position, the goals, and so on, one of the three Cs inevitably takes priority over the other two: and this has to be also factored in, of course.

In order to explore the most important of the three Cs above, the interview questions I ask are focused on that particular area, and they are intentionally very tough. They are questions that really stretch the candidate's thinking, appropriateness, and fit. But, and here's the million-dollar trick, they are questions designed to get to the heart of the candidate's levels of self-reflection, self-analysis, and self-awareness. These questions and the process that surrounds them are designed to really separate the wheat from the chaff.[3]

Here's how the process works:

Let's imagine that somewhere along the interview, I ask the candidate one of these important self-awareness-revealing questions.

I would, for example, ask the applicant to take a moment to define the word "quality" as it pertains specifically to light engineering, pet-food manufacturing, the hotel sector, SAAS, middle management, cost-accounting, or whatever market or vertical that the business operates in and/or for whatever particular role the candidate is applying for.

Now then, "quality" is a tricky concept to be able to extemporaneously describe with any real precision, especially under the pressure and confines of a job interview. Give it a quick go now; how might you answer the "quality" question? It's a slippery concept, is "quality," and no mistake.

I would often hear things like "standards," and "price," and "warranties," and "guarantees," and "brand," and so on. But most of the time the answers would be rather weak, confused, and lacking in precision. As I said, "quality" is a tricky concept.

As the candidate sets about defining the particular concept in question, I would rate their offering from 1 to 10 depending upon the "quality" of their answer.[4]

1 = Dreadful. Too ghastly for words. "Beam me up, Scotty."

---

3   Or the sheep from the goats. Or the cats from the dogs. Or the boils from the bunions. Well, you get the idea.
4   Did you see what I did there?

    10 = Quick, call the nice folks at Websters, we have a brand-new submission for them.

Once they finish their thought (or they run out of steam[5]), I would then ask them to rate the answer that they had just given from 1 to 10.

Once the candidate offers their self-assessed rating I would, of course, ask them for their reasoning to support their self-evaluation score—as a failsafe just to check that I fully understood their answer as well as their foundational logic.

Now then, and here's the critical piece, let's imagine that the applicant in front of me has given what I consider to be a rather poor answer, which I had rated a generous 3 out of 10. And let's pretend that the candidate self-assesses their answer and reported it to be a 3 or 4 out of 10 in their own estimation; phew, congruence. Good self-awareness. Alignment. Happy days. Let's move on to the next question.

But, what if I had scored their answer as 3 out of 10, and the applicant reported it as a 9 out of 10? Now, Houston, we have a problem.

Why? The question and self-assessment mechanism are asked not to assess the candidate's understanding of the principles of "quality." Let's be honest, who cares? No, these questions are asked in order to specifically understand the candidate's level of self-awareness and the extent to which they can dispassionately review their own performance. I'm perfectly OK with hearing a poor answer so long as the candidate also recognizes that it's a poor answer and can articulate why, and has the professional humility to acknowledge it. Because, if they don't or can't or won't when under the microscope of the interview, what hope do they have for doing so when they're chairman of the board with very little daily oversight?

---

5   Which is often the same thing, I find.

To gauge and fully understand the candidate's ability to self-reflect with some level of accuracy, I would repeat the exercise by asking for further definitions of other tricky concepts, say, "marketing," or "democracy," or "leadership." I would ask them to describe what is meant by the word "justice" as it applies to work, or to explain what "doing your best at work" might mean, for example.

The process looks like this:

> The interviewer asks a tricky question relating to the role in some abstract or slightly esoteric way.

> The interviewer rates the answer privately.

> The applicant is asked to self-rate their answer and to share their thoughts in support of their number.

> The interviewer shares their score and their supporting "logic."

> Significant differences in scores are explored.

There are two additional nuances to consider:

> When exploring the differences in ratings to a particular answer, did the candidate push back and challenge the interviewer's rating? Did they agree or disagree with the premise? Did the candidate defend, justify, or rationalize?[6]

> Candidates' responses to significant differences of opinion are always very telling also.

---

6   The Holy Trinity of the ineffective leader.

Finally, let's pretend that there were similar gaping chasms across six or seven of these questions where I scored the candidate low, and they scored themselves unexpectedly high.

At the end of the interview, I would then ask the applicant this revealing question, "When you speak to your significant other in around twenty minutes to discuss the interview experience, and they ask you how the interview went, what will you tell them?"

If they give a very favorable account of how things went and of how optimistic they were for a call-back, there would be red flags, fireworks, claxons, and alarms sounding all over the place.

If, however, they report that their biggest concerns center around the differences between our gradings, there would still be some hope for our beleaguered and hopeful applicant since their self-awareness muscle had just had a rather good workout on the asymmetric bars, and a semblance of it was finally presented.

Time for Our First Story

Around twenty-five years ago, I was having an early dinner with my chairman following a board meeting which ran a little late. This inspirational and visionary gentleman was one of the most developmental and insightful managers I have ever had the pleasure of working for and learning from.

"Tell me," he asked, with his customary warm smile. "Did you earn your money today, and did you do your best?"[7]

Hmmmmm. A spankingly-good question, right? I had always admired his extremely well-honed questioning skills, and this one was no exception.

---

7   Yes, well spotted—one of the questions that I subsequently inserted into my interview process. Have a celebratory slice of cake. Go on, a big one. ☺

Before answering, I considered a few facts...

I knew that I had arrived very early to the office that day because I had a mountain of work to tackle.

I knew that I had been working hard all day, with hardly a moment to even have lunch or a cup of coffee.

I knew that I had made some important and far-reaching decisions.

I knew that I had fixed some short-term problems, and had found time to coach a couple of my managers.

I knew that I had attended a couple of meetings and had given some useful input.

I knew that I had contributed well to the direction of the board meeting, and I knew that, on balance, I had helped make our world slightly better and so was feeling pretty confident that the answer was yes.

"Yes, I think so. I've been working hard all day, so I guess so." I said, hopefully.

"To which one?" he asked.

"Um, to which one? To which one, what?" I inquired.

"Yes, you earned your money today; or yes, you did your best?"

Recognizing that this was two questions and not one, and recognizing, too, that the guy asking, in effect, paid me every month, I thought it wise to declare that I did indeed earn my money today. I wouldn't want him spending too long thinking about that answer at the next check-run.

"Oh, I see. Yes. Yes, to both."

Phew. Terrific. Bullet dodged. Tick one down for me.

"Oh?" He replied somewhat quizzically. "What makes you say that?"

Oops! Belay that "tick"!

"And what about you?" I asked, ignoring his new question. "Did you?"

Brilliant, I thought. Deflection.

He thought and then offered, "I'd say yes, and no." A few more seconds' thought, and then, "It's nearly always a 'yes,' and it's nearly always a 'no,' I find."

"Oh? Tell me more." I said.

Double brilliant.[8]

He went on to explain that he thought it important for every leader to ask themselves these two questions every day. "It really helps develop self-awareness," he would say. "Self-awareness is the very foundation of great leadership development."

He believed that all leaders worth their salt should be able to look themselves in the mirror at night (every night) and know that they had made the world that their company occupied a little better. "That's what you're paid to do," he would argue. "Earning your money is a perquisite of the job; a 'minimum standard.'" More on minimum standards later.

"The answer to that question should nearly always be 'yes,'" he explained. "Otherwise, you're a fraud and should go work somewhere else." Deep.

"'Trying your best' is a completely different proposition altogether." He said. "What is your 'best,' anyway?"

"Best," he argued, is an extremely high bar. It's five gold medals at the Olympics. It's the 185 lb. mother lifting a car to free a trapped child. Best is walking unaided to the South Pole in the teeth of a twenty-day blizzard. "Best" is overcoming incredible and overwhelming challenges. No Olympic athlete gets personal bests every single day that they train—so why should we expect the CEO, the COO, or the CRO hit "best" every single day? "Best" is really, really tough.

---

8   "Tell me more..." has been my number one go-to question for the last twenty-five years when talking to chairmen of the board, CEOs, important clients—and any one of my four children—especially when that bottle of rather special thirty-year-old South African red inexplicably goes missing, and their friends are all effusing on social media about what a great Sangria they all had at the party over the weekend, Emily. Grrr. Anyway, I digress.

"The answer to 'best' is almost always 'no,'" he argued. "And a 'no' to the 'best' question begs the critical supplementary question, "Well, since it's a "no", what would, or could, or should I have done, or failed to do today, in order to have done better—in order to have come *closer* to my "best"?'"

Brilliant!

Time for our second journal entry.

Find somewhere deliciously self-aware in your journal, copy and write the answers to these thorny little gems:

Did I earn my money today?   Yes.   No.
Did I do my very best today?   Yes.   No.

Here's why I circled those answers:

Specifically, to have come closer to being my "very best" self as a great leader today, I should have said, tried, included, excluded, done more of, done less of these things...

I will do better tomorrow.

Congratulations: you're *still* on your way to self-awareness mastery and leadership greatness. Hoorah![9]

---

[9]   It's easy, right?

Now that we've taken a look at you from your own perspective and we have introduced the principle of "every day I will work hard to get better," let's give some thought to what your people think of you. You might want to sit down for the next bit; our leaders often find this next segment rather unsettling.

WHAT WOULD YOUR LEADERSHIP REPORT CARD LOOK LIKE?

Are you yet a "straight-A" leader in the eyes of those you lead?

If your people were to write your report card right now, would it say that you're a straight-A student, or would your Leadership Report Card be mostly Bs with a couple of As? Would it show straight-Bs, perhaps? Some Bs with a couple of Cs? Or would it be largely Cs? Would there even be a disappointing F or two? Would you be supremely proud of what you would read about yourself?

We would all like to imagine, of course, that our Leadership Report Card would declare that we are all straight-A leaders: individuals with enormous integrity and vision, extraordinary drive and passion, blessed with unsurpassed strategic and tactical prowess, practically effervescing with unrivalled self-awareness and commercial insight...basically, an all-round good-egg and person voted most likely to win a Nobel Peace Prize for leadership[10] before the year is out.[11] That's what "best" looks like, right?

But, if your people were really asked to complete it completely honestly, would your report card really say those splendid things about you every day, I wonder? What about the day you tried giving up coffee and were as crotchety and ornery as a tired and hungry baby cutting its first tooth and sat in a cold, wet diaper?

---

10 No, there isn't one.

11 Charming too. Devilishly dishy, probably. Witty as a stick...and such lovely teeth.

You might think (hope) they would say things like, "Well, he's firm, but fair." Or, "She's a real tough-cookie, a hard-ass, but she knows what she's doing." Or, "His methods are brutal, but his record speaks for itself."

In other words, sure, you're a terrible leader, but you get things done—and the ends always justify the means.

But, dear leader, the ends *do not* justify the means—or rather, they do for cruddy leaders, but they do not for great ones.

"Style," how you get things done, is as important as the results you generate—more so, perhaps.

Do you lead with "style": charm, and wit, and intelligence, and self-deprecating humor, and panache?[12] Or are you an ogre who "does what needs to be done to get things done?"

...and don't fool yourself with the answer.

You could outright ask them for their heartfelt thoughts, of course. You could send a company-wide leadership appraisal and employee engagement survey. You could explain that you are looking for a true and honest 360, asking everyone to grade you from 1 to 10 against a complete set of critical leadership attributes. The company could assure all participants that the responses to the survey were entirely anonymous. You could spend a small fortune and bring in consultants to ensure even-handedness in the question sets and guarantee an unbiased assessment of the feedback.

Ah, but here's the rub: if you're not quite as glorious as you maybe think, nor as approachable as you like to believe, nor as supportive or developmental as you hope to be, nor as tolerant as you suspect; what are the chances that they'd tell the truth, the whole truth, and nothing but the truth? Slim. Very slim. Problem.

---

12   There's a world shortage of panache these days, don't you think? Bring back capes, that's what I say. Who's with me?

You could forgo the consultants and have all your people line up outside your office and simply invite them in one by one to ask them what they think of your leadership prowess. I wonder what they'd say to your face as they sat across from you at your big and imposing desk.

But, before you pay too much attention to their "frank and honest" feedback, just remember who is asking them, who pays their wages every few weeks, who hires and fires around here, who decides the promotion schedule, who assigns the parking spaces, and who approves the annual pay raises. Bearing all of that in mind, would the truth, the whole truth, and nothing but the truth be their uppermost thought?

No, it wouldn't. So, don't bother inviting them. More on this in Chapter 5.

There would, of course, likely be lots of saccharine-laced compliments for at least one of your recent initiatives that didn't stink too much.

There would likely be some slightly polished recollections of half-decent advice you doled out one time or another.

You'd hear some cautiously positive platitudes about some inspiring speech you gave somewhere once, I am sure.

There would be so much equivocation, vacillation, hesitation, and procrastination[13] that I wouldn't even bother asking them: it would, after all, be a bit like asking turkeys to vote for Thanksgiving...and, let's not forget, turkeys tend not to want to do that if they can at all avoid it.

That's the bad news.

The good news is that, if approached correctly, your Leadership Journal will become your brutally honest Leadership Report Card, as well as the mechanism for significant improvement.[14] All it requires is self-awareness, a smattering of self-re-

---

13   '-ation' would need a lie down if things didn't quiet down soon.
14   Hoorah!

flection, a soupçon of time, a smidgeon of self-regulation, and a splash of consistency. But lots more on all these things later.

Having said all of that about your Leadership Report Card, remember this:

> Great leaders don't lead in order to make themselves look really smart, they lead in such a way as to make those they lead look really smart.

In reality, therefore, you want all of those you lead to score all straight As across the board on *their* report cards. And that's your *real* Leadership Report Card, isn't it? You get straight As when they all do. And if they're not, neither do you. And if they're not, whose fault is that?

If your last round of employee appraisals has them "averaging" at 3 out of a maximum 5 (or whatever your equivalent is of, "Good in parts, but could do better") then the very same can be said of you since you're leading this team, right? That's a "B" at best, right? QED.

More on this later too.

Time for Another Story

My business coach once asked me a tricky question.

I should explain that before he was my coach, he used to be the captain of a nuclear submarine—one in a long line of submarine captains—in fact, he was a fourth generation submarine captain. Smart family. Good underwater genes, I suspect.

As you might imagine, nuclear submarines are extremely complex, expensive, and dangerous places; literally chock-a-block full of things that could seriously hurt you—hard surfaces, sharp edges, and pipes carrying liquids and gasses under enormous temperature and pressures. Don't forget the fact that sometimes the floor slopes down...or up, or to starboard, or to port. Oh, and they also have a bunch of those pesky intercontinental ballistic missiles on board to think of, and simply masses of high-explosive ordnance too. Did I mention the fully functioning nuclear reactor at the back of the boat? Not a place to kick back, rest, relax, and unwind.

On top of all this, nuclear submarines are a veritable hive of activity 24/7, 365, and every single element of their running and functioning has to be super-smooth, incredibly precise, and ultra-efficient—it's simply the very best way not to get blown to smithereens and waste literally billions and billions of tax payers' dollars—to say nothing of the lives of the 150 or so submariners on board.

Anyway, my coach told me about a time that his sub was on maneuvers somewhere underneath the Arctic Circle. They had been submerged for almost three months and were tracking other "red" submarines across that part of the globe while endeavoring to remain hidden from detection—a difficult, protracted, and oftentimes stressful exercise.

One night, my coach, the captain, was asleep in his quarters at around 4:00 a.m.—statistically the most dangerous time of the day, coincidentally.

At the other end of the boat, a twenty-four-year-old technician somehow electrocuted himself while welding to repair a metal pipe. He died almost instantaneously.

Now, here's the question: Whose fault was it that the unfortunate young submariner died that particular night?

Before you answer, here are some options for you to consider:

> Was it the individual's fault for doing something stupid or dangerous, or for not checking that both his equipment and the environment were safe?
>
> Was it his manager's fault for not ensuring that he had been properly briefed?

Was it his trainer's fault for not ensuring that he had been properly trained and certified?

Was it the fault of the person on watch that night for not supervising the work?

Was it the fault of the person who asked him to fix the pipe at 4:00 a.m.?

Was it the captain's fault?

Was it someone else's fault?

Was it no one's fault?

Tricky.

Give it some thought. Answer before moving on. And no vacillating, please: no "either-or"; put your bum on a horse—remember, as a leader, you only have one bum, and it can only go on one horse.[15]

According to my coach, the captain of the submarine that fateful early morning, it was 100 percent his fault—the captain's fault. And let us not forget that he had been soundly asleep at the other end of the boat and rightly had no idea that the unfortunate young submariner was even attempting to repair that ruptured pipe.

When I asked him why he thought that the accident had been his fault since he had been asleep at the time, hundreds of feet away, he simply replied, "I was the captain. It was my boat. *Everything* that happens on the boat is the captain's responsibility. When I took on the responsibility of the captain's role," he continued, "I took on the responsibility for everything that happened on the boat—the good, as well as the bad."

And, well, who could argue with that logic?

The best leaders, it seems, accept complete responsibility for all of the shortcomings—from themselves and their teams.

---

15 If you're an "either-or" leader, stop it! Decisiveness is important. If you choose wrong, course correct. Learn the lesson. Remember: one bum, one horse.

What's more, they widely praise the victories, and they individually shoulder the responsibility for all the failures.

Captains of nuclear submarines, it seems, are selected for their high level of self-awareness, among other things. They recognize which things are in their sphere of control, and which things are outside their sphere of control, and they act and lead accordingly.

ARE YOU AN "INNIE" OR AN "OUTIE"?

No, not belly buttons, issues. Do you internalize or externalize your issues?

It's very easy to blame whatever disappointing circumstances are dogging us on a variety of external factors: the bad economy, the inclement weather, the lack of management support, the uncaring government, the global pandemic, a disadvantaged childhood, and so on. And while those difficulties and others certainly contrive to make progress difficult at times, it's simply not good enough to have them account for the long-term differences between where you (and the company) are and where you (and the company) want to be.

The danger with "externalizing" our problems in this way is that it is too easy to be passive in the resolution of them. "Some people are lucky," these people contend. "They get all the breaks; things always go their way. It's easy for some; they didn't have to deal with all of the nonsense of my problems."

However, the world is littered with literally countless stories of people overcoming enormous hardships, difficulties, and tribulations and beating all odds to emerge victorious.

It seems that the people who externalize their problems are forever destined to be defined and limited by them, while those who internalize their problems and take full responsibility for solving them somehow develop the fortitude, creativity, and dogged determination to do something about flipping the script and making a winning hand out of even the crappiest cards they might have been dealt.

The poor unfortunates who habitually externalize their problems are forever bemoaning the good fortune of those who find a way to succeed, the "lucky" ones.

The "lucky" ones, however, have, more often than not, realized that whether or not they have contributed to their current predicament, they take responsibility for it as well as the future. Self-accountability is powerful leadership stuff—it's as powerful as self-awareness.

Find somewhere suitably responsible to write this critical leadership principle down in your spankingly-new journal:

The First Principle of Leadership:

It's *always* my fault!

Refer back to this foundational principle every day until you 100 percent accept it.

You are 100 percent responsible for where you are conceptually right now regardless of the path that got you to this exact spot. The great news is that you are also responsible for where you will be in six weeks, six months, six years from now: so, decide that wherever you will be in the future, you will be there because you chose to be there, and you will accept full responsibility for it. Why? Because it's always your fault—and most of the time, that's an amazing and uplifting thing!

THE RECIPE FOR SELF-DEVELOPMENT

Self-development requires self-awareness. Self-awareness requires self-reflection. Self-reflection requires self-accountability.

As it is in many other critical areas of life, accountability (self-accountability), lies at the heart of self-development. If you don't track and keep score of your own plans and behaviors, who will?

Just like my coach the ex-submarine captain, and nearly every single inspirational leader whom I have ever worked for, argue, the best leaders work on daily development and daily improvement recognizing that they are the author of their own destiny. Internalization, it seems, requires a high degree of self-awareness.

To start building your self-awareness leadership muscle, you need to take a regular look in the leadership mirror and start grading your own performance—yes, on a daily basis.

It's simply not good enough to live your leadership life by the words of the incorrigible Gloria Gaynor in her song from the Fierstein and Poiret musical, *La Cage aux Folles*, "I Am What I Am," nor the words of the incomparable and irrepressible Dr. Seuss when he espoused:

> *Today you are you,*
> *That's truer than true.*
> *There's no one alive*
> *Who is youer than you!*

Sure, there is no one as good at being you than you. And, sure, you are one of nature's glorious sunbeams but, let's be honest, you've got a lot of work to do.

It's time to become an expert in the kind of leader you want to be. Find an intentional spot in your journal to write:

The Second Principle of Leadership:

I am becoming an expert in the kind of leader *I want to be.*

Good. And now another question:

> Who is, or has been, ultimately responsible for all the successes and all of the failures in your team, division, or business: you or your people?

Your people, right?

Wrong.[16]

You personally are also 100 percent responsible for all the failures in your team, division, or business.

Drat!

Collectively, you and your team are all responsible for the successes.

Hurrah!

To put it another way, "It is amazing what you can accomplish if you do not care who gets the credit." Nice one, Harry Truman. Good internalized and low-ego thinking.

More on this in Chapter 3.

IF ONLY I'D HAVE SAID...

How many times have you looked back on an argument that you perhaps shared with a loved one, only to find yourself saying things like this: "When he said that, I should have said this...."? Or, "If only when she did that, I had mentioned that

---

16   We just covered this above. Pay attention.

time when she did this..."? Or, "When they suggested that, I should have suggested this..."?

It's infuriating, right?

And doesn't it always seem to be the case that these pearls of retrospective wisdom and insight come to us in a flash of inspiration...typically three hours too late? Grrrr.

Sure, you're still seething about the whole affair, but unfortunately the world and everyone else in it has already moved on: and if you were to offer your nugget of rhetorical genius now, three hours later, it would sound childish, or sulky, or unnecessarily argumentative.

If only you had thought of the amazing pithy comeback, or the remarkable suggestion, or "helpful" thought in the heat of battle! Well, the world doesn't always work like that, does it?

The same is true for leadership skill. There doesn't have to be an argument, or friction, or heated debate for us, some hours later, to wonder how we could have done better. We can apply the exact same reflective habit to everything that we do every day—in fact, it is to be encouraged—no, it is much more than that, it is mandatory for leadership self-improvement.

Ask yourself not only, "Did I earn my money today?" and "Did I try my best today?" but also...

How well did I write that important e-mail?
How well did I respond to that question?
How completely did I consider that challenge?
How objectively did I approach that task?
How supportive was I with that colleague?
How efficient was I with my time?
How well did I delegate?
How creative was I with that new initiative?
When I managed that issue, should I have taken the time to coach someone instead?

...you get the idea, I am sure.

Self-reflection builds self-awareness. It's how we get closer to our "best," remember?

THE MAGIC QUESTION OF LEADERSHIP:

"Where and how could I have done better today?"

As mentioned, all great leaders have developed a daily habit of self-reflection.

The best of the best actually consider that question every single day, and they write the answer to this question in their journal—every day.

Oh, you haven't been doing that the last twenty years? Hmm, I wonder what that says about your level of responsibility for the improvement of your own leadership skill?[17]

At the end of the day (yes, every day), great leaders take a moment to take stock: it's their Evening Evaluation. They review the day (yes, every day) to ask themselves these types of questions:

✧ How would I rate my overall performance today?

✧ Would my Report Card today show A+? A? A-? B+? B?

✧ Where *specifically* could I have done better?

✧ How could I do better next time in order to make that A- into an A+?

---

17   Answers on a postcard to:
      Maybe I'm Not Quite The Effervescent Leader That I Thought Myself To Be
      Must Try Harder Industrial Estate,
      Disappointed House,
      Sad Face Drive,
      It's a Sad Sad World.
      BOO HOO

Once you start to embed this high-level, high-functioning daily (yes, daily) self-reflection habit, writing these specific thoughts down in one, easily-accessible place, your leadership skills start to improve enormously—very quickly.

Remember, wisdom only comes from evaluated experience. Wisdom does *not* simply come from time served!

So, let's make a good, no, a great start. For the rest of the day, pay enormous attention to everything you do and everything you fail to do. Everything you say and everything you fail to say. Everything you think. Everything you read and everything you write. Every decision you make, and every time you kick the decision-can down the road.

Then, tonight, take a couple of minutes to review your leadership performance from the day. Write down your important thoughts, as well as record your "leadership score." Where to record it, I wonder? Yes, your Leadership Journal. ☺

Find a perfectly self-aware spot in your Leadership Journal to jot down and complete this sentence...

> I could have been a better leader today if only I had...

Go on, I'll wait....
Done it?
Well done, you.
You've continued to make a good start.
Gold star.
Go to the top of the class.

Now take a moment to think about what you have written. Was your leadership performance below the standard that you should expect of yourself—the standard of a *great* leader? Don't berate yourself too much. Recognize it, accept it, move on. The good news is that tomorrow you will have a do-over. Decide to fix what needs fixing—whether a situation, a relationship, a problem that maybe you made worse (or caused). Go to bed with your subconscious working on the issue—it's going to be whizzing away all night in the background anyway, so give it something worthwhile to chew on—you'll be amazed at how creative a problem-solver your subconscious can be when you're intentional about nudging it in the right direction.

The rule is simple:

Recognize where you have fallen short.
Forgive yourself for having fallen short.
Learn the lesson.
Resolve to get better.
Fix it tomorrow.
Move on.

If you don't accept it, and you don't find a way to move on, you won't sleep very well, I'm afraid. And, if you've taken a good look in the mirror lately, you could really do with a good night's sleep.[18]

Remember what Ralph said:

> *"Finish each day and be done with it. You have done what you could. Some blunders and absurdities, no doubt crept in; forget them as soon as you can. Tomorrow is a new day. You shall begin it with serenity and with too high a spirit to be encumbered with your old nonsense."*
> —*Ralph Waldo Emerson*

---

18 A good night's coma? Shut your face.

Nice one, Ralph.

ARE YOU THE SORT OF LEADER NOW THAT YOU WISH YOU HAD BACK THEN?

Time for Another Story

There was once a brand new, bright-eyed, freshly minted CEO[19] who was given his first leadership position with a large British publicly traded company—a big role, and a big step up for this particular individual. He arrived at work for his first day to discover a handwritten note[20] on his desk from this boss, the chairman of the group. The note asked the new CEO to pop along to see the chairman of the group "once he had settled in."

As soon as he was able, the new CEO arranged to meet with his boss. After the usual pleasantries, the chairman asked the new CEO whether or not he had ever worked for a terrible manager. "Of course," he said, "I mean, who hasn't, right?"[21]

With a nod, the chairman reached across his desk to take a blank sheet of paper from his printer. He removed a rather expensive looking fountain pen from his jacket pocket, and he placed it on top of the piece of paper and proceeded to slide both across the highly polished desk towards the CEO.

"Do me a favor," said the chairman. "Write me a list of all of the attributes and characteristics of a truly terrible leader."

"Okaaaay," said the CEO, slightly quizzically. And with that he picked up the pen and started to write.

We can all imagine that his list looked something like:

A micromanager, inconsistent behaviors, command and control style, someone who leads by fear, ego-

---

19   Well-intentioned, well-suited, and widely experienced. A foil-packaged, carefully folded, beautifully moist and lemon-scented towelette of a new CEO. Lovely.

20   No, not an e-mail. Posh.

21   Word.

tistical, poor communication skills, inability to create developmental company culture, no strategic thinking skill, inflexible.[22]

Having written eight or nine attributes of managerial woe and dreadfulness, the CEO replaced the cap of the pen, placed the pen back on top of the piece of paper containing the list, and slid everything back across the desk again toward the chairman.

The chairman read the list and nodded. With a smile, he slid everything back across the desk towards his new recruit accompanied by the words, "Precisely. Now, write down some more for me. Imagine someone truly, truly terrible. Get creative."

Thinking this exercise rather odd, the CEO, intrigued, took up the pen and wrote a few more. Perhaps:

> Unpredictable, closed-minded, slow to adapt, fearful of change, not customer-oriented, poor at dealing with conflict, promotes cronyism.

Everything was then slid across the desk once more.

After reading the expanded list, the chairman, slid everything back across the desk again with the request to try to add just a few more items.

A few more items were added. Probably:

> Selfish, fails to give credit, poor delegator, no self-regulation, low self-awareness, bully.

Everything was slid across the desk once again.[23]

---

22 Bad breath too. Probably.
23 The desk was knackered.

"Perfect," said the chairman having read the final list. Putting away his pen, the chairman slid the piece of paper across his desk one final time.[24]

"You're right," he continued. "That's *exactly* what a terrible manager and a dreadful leader looks like. Do me a favor, will you?"

"Of course."

"While you are the boss around here, promise me that you'll never, ever, ever, do any of the terrible things on that list!"

"Err? OK?"

"That's the spirit. Fold up that piece of paper, put it in your pocket, and carry it with you at all times: I will likely want to ask you about it at some time or other. Treat that piece of paper as your new job description. Semper vigilans."

"Errr?"

"Be ever vigilant."

"Oh, yes. Semper that thing. Vigilant. Right."

"And welcome aboard."

...and with that, a hearty handshake was exchanged, and the rather obscure and profoundly unusual meeting was over.

Unsurprisingly, the new CEO worked very hard over the next few years to live up (or not live down to) to the ideals hidden in that uniquely powerful list. He carried it with him every single day. The piece of paper became rather ragged after a while: it was typed up, printed, and photocopied often. The list was revised occasionally to become a new list—The Manifesto of Extraordinary Leadership Dreadfullness.

Over the years many people read the list, and it was passed around the company quite freely. It was pinned to noticeboards. It was pinned up in the canteen. Managers who reported to the CEO were given the list along with a request to point out to the CEO if ever he was displaying any of the characteristics on the list. Every manager or leader who joined the company was

---

24 The desk needed a lie down and a few days off work.

invited to write their own list of leadership dreadfulness and carry it with them at all times too.

Eventually, the key elements of all of the Manifestos went to form parts of the Company Operational Handbook. It was, unsurprisingly, a very well-managed company, profitable, solutions-oriented, developmental, and most people stayed working there happily till they retired.

How do I know the details of this story so well? I was the freshly minted CEO in the story.

More on this story in Chapter 7.

MANIFESTO OF LEADERSHIP DREADFULNESS: YOUR TURN...

Find a deliciously clean page or two in your wonderful new journal to create your own list of Leadership Dreadfulness: base it on the characteristics of all of the terrible bosses you ever worked for[25] and finish it off by resolving never to stoop so low.

Refer back to this important list often (every few days, why not?)—you'll be amazed how quickly you improve as a leader and as a person. Your company, your family, your friends—heck, even yourself—will thank you before too long.

This important exercise starts to reveal your leadership Core Values. Core Values are the fundamental principles, ideals, commandments, ethos, and beliefs that are really important to you and that define who you are as a person.

The exercise above is similar to taking a Leadership Core Values assessment—but in reverse. For some, this exercise is significantly more visceral and powerful than for others—but all at least agree that it is a very enlightening and worthwhile leadership drill. The list should be reviewed regularly (quarterly) with a quick self-check measuring how well or badly you are doing!

---

25 If you've never worked for one—good for you, you've been lucky. Get creative: let your imagination run riot.

If you want to save some time and better understand and reveal your own personal leadership core values, discover the self-assessment tool which can be found at www.mydailyleadership.com.

ARE YOU A GOOD DRIVER, REALLY?

Of course, you are, right?

Most of us believe that we're pretty good drivers, don't we? In fact, according to a recent report, around 80 percent of Americans believe not only that they are good drivers, they believe that they are actually an "above-average" driver.[26]

Most of us like to think that, when driving, we make really sensible decisions about weather conditions, speed and direction, and are great at anticipating the sometimes-unexpected decisions of all of the other drivers, cyclists, and pedestrians around us.

We tend to believe that our point of view, our ability to react, and the condition and performance of our vehicle is likely superior to most other road users.[27]

How it might be that around 1.35 million people die in road crashes each year, on average 3,700 people lose their lives on the roads every day, and an additional twenty to fifty million suffer non-fatal injuries, often resulting in long-term disabilities—well, how any of that happens is a mystery. That's obviously all the other drivers around me, right? They're menaces, they are, but not me; I'm well above average, I am, so there!

Just like our opinion of our elevated driving prowess, lots of leaders think of themselves as "above average" leaders too. In fact, more than half of them tend to think themselves exemplary leaders and managers. Note: they don't consider themselves good leaders, they consider themselves outstand-

---

26 Think about that for a second—mathematically, it can't possibly be true.

27 I guess that's why we feel able to speed, drive tired, drink coffee, listen to the radio, put makeup on, and text all at the same time—and that's just a Monday morning!

ing leaders, despite the recent poor performance of their business, division, or team. Well, that's all of the other people around me, right? They're terrible leaders and managers, they are, but not me.

Daily journaling has a two-fold benefit: it helps us to identify problematic issues that we might not be fully aware of as well as giving us the tools to address them. Daily self-reflection gives us a much keener sense of self-awareness, and self-aware-ness lies at the heart of self-development—so let's continue to make a start. Remember, wisdom comes from evaluated experience—without the evaluation, there is no wisdom.

Any good doctor will tell you that she can't begin to proactively fix a problem until the issue has at least been well identified and defined, so you'll likely have a range of tests and x-rays:

Like all good doctors who can't attempt to fix a problem until it is well diagnosed and understood, it's probably high time for a steaming-hot, hearty mug of leadership self-awareness.

Give yourself another rating for your current leadership skill and competency 1 to 10 over, say, the last six weeks.

> 1 = Truly, truly terrible. Embarrassing, really. It's the naughty-step for me, and no mistake. How I even got here is a mystery—it probably helps that the chairman is my uncle.

> 10 = As close to perfection as is humanly possible. They'll be building me a statue soon, I'm pretty sure.

Hint: It's absolutely not a "10," I'm afraid.[28]
If it isn't a 10 (and it definitely isn't), it means there are some gaps. QED.

---

28   No, it's not a "9" either—try again. Heck, it's probably not even an "8," but "7"? Statistically unlikely.

CLOSING THE GAPS

But where are the gaps? How serious are the gaps? How long have the gaps been there? What caused the gaps, and how can I close them? Will the gaps seriously limit me, my people, and my business? Sounds like it's maybe time for a Leadership Health Check.

So, how do we take a Leadership Health Check? Where do we go in order to get our leadership blood test, MRI, and x-ray? ...and that weird back-tappy-thing that doctors sometimes do?

And then, what would our daily prescribed (Leadership Journaling) medicine look like? All good questions: and the answer is easy. In fact, it's as simple as 1, 2, 3.

1. **Take a Leadership Assessment.**

   There are lots to choose from.

   Some assessments measure personality types, while others measure communications styles, and others are designed to measure strengths, aptitudes, attitudes, and so on.

   You could do a lot worse than to go to:

   www.mydailyleadership.com/leadershipassessment

   The *My Daily Leadership* assessment is specifically designed to explore the most critical twenty leadership building blocks. See Chapter 2 for details.

   Whichever assessment you plump for it is incumbent upon you to pay very close attention to the results and resolve to make some fundamental changes—otherwise, well, why even bother taking the test(s) in the first place, right?

And please don't be like any of those dreadful leaders with crushingly-low self-awareness scores who wholeheartedly agree with all of the positive comments that the assessment reveals, and then, when reading the not-so-positive comments say things like, "Bah! Nonsense. I mean, how accurate are these things anyway?"

If you choose the right assessment, it's accurate. Please pay close attention to the results and its recommendations.

To intentionally adulterate and misappropriate the genius of Tom Landry of Dallas Cowboys fame:

"A leadership assessment is something that tells you what you don't want to hear, which has you see what you don't want to see, so you can be who you always knew you could be."

2. Start your leadership journal.

Journal every day—yes, every day.[29]

Journaling is a bit like daily flossing for the leadership mind.

Sure, flossing seems to make some theoretical sense, but, let's be honest, no one wants to really floss every day do they? It's a bit of a drag, and it can sometimes seems like a waste of time—so, I mean, why even bother?

Yes, yes, every single dentist on the planet implores us to floss every single time we see

---

29 Yes, really. We've already covered this. Get used to the idea. Yes, Sundays too. Yes, I know you have Little League. Well, find the time.

them—but, hey, what do they know, they're only extremely highly-trained and well-paid teeth experts, after all.

We surely know better, right? I mean I didn't floss yesterday, and all my teeth didn't fall out did they?![30]

Use your Leadership Journal to specifically develop your strengths, and, significantly more importantly, to intentionally ameliorate your weaknesses. Your job is to use your journal to work on the particular issues that the assessment identifies. It's how great leaders grow.

3. **Take another Leadership Assessment six months later.**

   The same assessment as the first assessment.

   Track the differences.

   Act accordingly.

Rinse and repeat...
...well, forever, I'm afraid.

WHAT IS LEADERSHIP ANYWAY?

It's time for a definition.
   We all love "rules," and "secret hacks," and "Top 10" lists, right?

   "Top 10 reasons for this..."

---

30   Have patience, they will. ☺

"Top 3 secrets of that..."

"What they don't want you to know about this..."

"19 things I wish I knew when I was 19..."

....you get the idea.

Go to any bookstore[31] and pop along to the business section. There you will discover miles upon miles[32] of books on leadership theory and development—all good stuff, of course, but none of it really makes the topic any clearer. In fact, the more leadership books you read, the more confused and conflicted you are likely to become.[33]

The good news is that today's your day since we are going to demystify "leadership" for you in one fell swoop. When you boil it all down to its absolute constituent parts, its absolute basics (the fundamental particles, as the physicists would say), there are only two foundational rules of leadership—yes, just two—in all those miles and miles of books!

And, since we love our rules and lists so much, here they are. **Find a charmingly simple and elegant page in your Leadership Journal to write them both down:**

Leadership Rule #1:   It's not about you!

Leadership Rule #2:   It's 100 percent all about you!

Wait, what?

---

31 Please. They need the business, and you'll receive a warm welcome, I am sure. And likely you'll find another great book on a topic that you hadn't even realized you were interested in—and then pass the book on. It helps to make the whole world a little bit better, you'll see. ☺

32 Yes, Captain Pedantic, not literally "miles." I'm speaking figuratively—just for dramatic effect, you understand. Honestly, some people!

33 Apart from this one. Obviously.

At first glance, it might seem that these two foundational leadership rules must conflict with one another. However, they coexist perfectly harmoniously. Let's break them down for now, but we will cover them both in much more detail as we canter through the rest of the book, of course.

Rule #1: It's not about you!

Most leaders can engage with this rule fairly easily, right? It's self-evidently and patently a good leadership rule. It's an obvious starting point, if you think about it. Straightforward, simple, and self-contained. A gem of a rule, I'm sure you agree.

The rule argues that the leader's job is to focus more on the needs of the people they lead, rather than their own personal needs. OK, got it. They succeed when their teams succeed as mentioned earlier. The leader should spend his or her time helping others. It's a basic principle of servant leadership, and we all agree with that philosophy, after all. So, it's 100 percent not about you, it's 100 percent about them. Got it?

OK, swiftly on to Rule 2.

Rule #2: It's 100 percent all about you!

See, now it seems to get a trifle tricky, because of Rule 1, right?

Well, think of it like this...if you want your people to allow you to be their leader, you had better get your leadership shit together and give them something really worthy of followship.

Ouch! Physician, heal thyself.[34]

Or, to paraphrase the very wise and erudite Nelson Mandela, you can't help change others, till you first change yourself.

Nice one, Nelson.

So, you need to work on getting yourself 100 percent prepared to be a great leader.

---

34   Gospel of Saint Luke. Word!

More on these two rules later.

Perhaps now might be the perfect time to start to define Leadership Success.

HOW DO *YOU* DEFINE LEADERSHIP SUCCESS?

Give this a few moments of thought—go on, I'll wait.

Most leaders and managers are likely to say, "Leadership Success is reaching your and your teams' goals."

The rest tend to argue that success is one of these three things: "Success is being happy," or "Success is a good work-life balance," or "Success is dying with the most toys."[35]

But, what about the person who sets himself very low goals: The person who, through adversity perhaps, has a poor self-image and who doesn't believe he can achieve very much, therefore sets his goals intentionally low for fear of further disappointment? What about the person who has had very limited opportunity to even get on the success ladder? What about the person who has had a boss deliberately hold them back? What about the leader who has inherited a great team and does nothing more to help them?

We need another definition of success, it seems.

Try this one out for size, see how it fits:

Success is *reaching one's full potential.*[36]

You are a leader, therefore, success is measured by reaching your own full potential while helping others achieve the same. Back to Rule 1 and Rule 2 again. It's almost as if all of these things are connected, isn't it? ☺

Reaching one's full potential takes some intentional effort, of course. Reaching one's full leadership potential takes some

---

35 Word.

36 YES!

work and some dedication too—but, with a little guidance, it is eminently feasible and hugely rewarding.

Eleanor Roosevelt said that a good leader can inspire confidence in the leader, a great leader can inspire confidence in others.

Doesn't getting closer to reaching one's full potential fill oneself with confidence and positivity about dealing better with the inevitable vagaries of the future?

SUCCESS IS NOT AN EVENT, IT'S A HABIT.

Your daily agenda over time determines your level of success. As any engineer will tell you, the quality of the output of any system is determined by the quality of the inputs as well as the quality and integrity of the processes.

The good news is that if you make good decisions and take appropriate actions, you can expect good things to happen.

The not so good news is that your life will never change until you change something that you do daily. Or, to put it another way, if you always do what you've always done, you'll always get what you've always got.

So, if you want something different, something better as a result, you have to do something different, something better early on.

When you look at successful people, those closing the gap to their full potential, you will notice how they do something every day in order to be successful—success doesn't suddenly occur by magic out of the clear blue sky for some and not for others: for that matter, neither does failure.

Both success and failure are the inevitable result of the quality of the inputs and the quality of the process.

What you become, what you will be six months from now, or a year from now, or a decade from now, is determined by what you do today and every day in between. In other words, you are preparing for something every day—you're either preparing for success, or you are preparing for failure. It's a decision, it's an every-single-day decision, and the decision is yours to make every single day.

Find somewhere rather delightfully insightful in your journal and write a few critical words that will have an enormous impact (positive or negative) on the quality of your future and those you lead:

I am preparing myself and others for success when I...

I am preparing myself and others for failure when I...

How you answered that question will be a good predictor of your future success.

...And, if you didn't say that you're preparing yourself for success when you journal every day—or, if you didn't say that you're preparing yourself for failure when you fail to journal every day, please go back and fix that now—it seems that you may have completely missed the point that I was trying to make.[37]

Thanks. ☺

According to Aristotle,[38] we are what we repeatedly do. Excellence is, therefore, not an event, it is a habit—so long as

---

[37] My fault—I should have been more overt and a little less subtle. Naughty author! Basket! ☺
[38] And who among us has the gumption to argue with Aristotle? Not I.

the habits are "excellent," of course. Success is, therefore, not an event, it is a habit—so long as the habits are "successful."

We are all defined by our habitual behaviors and rituals—all of us. Yes, even you.

Good rituals and habits help us reach our full potential, bad rituals and habits take us in the opposite direction.

Good thoughts help us reach our full potential, bad thoughts do not.

Good beliefs help us reach our full potential, bad beliefs do not.

Good behaviors help us reach our full potential, bad behaviors do not.

Good skills help us reach our full potential, bad skills do not.

Good self-awareness helps us reach our full potential, poor self-awareness does not.

Habits, like interest rates, compound at an alarming rate. Good things beget more good things, bad things ultimately beget more bad things and, ultimately, your mugshot on *America's Most Wanted*: it's just how the world works.

Think of any exceptional, world-class sports personality who is still participating competitively. This person is among the very elite in their field, right? They are talented and determined individuals. They have worked hard, made enormous sacrifices, and practiced and practiced and practiced some more—often beyond the point where most others have given up: the blisters, the weather, the timing, the effort, and so on, it seems, contrived to get the better of them. The really successful ones endured the things that most others in their sport were not prepared to. They trained and studied and persisted to the point where they became recognized as among the crème de la crème in their chosen field.

Once they reached the pinnacle of excellence, then what did they do? Relax? Take it easy? Goof off for six months? No, they kept on practicing and training and working at self-improvement, sometimes concentrating on the most minute detail and nuance till the laws of diminishing returns had diminished never to return. They certainly didn't think, "Well, here I am, now at the peak of my skill and prowess with a five-year contract and juicy sponsorship deals: it's high time to take a break and to rest on my laurels. What's more, I will fire my coach, my nutritionist, my agent, my physio, my publicist, and order in pizza with the cheesy crust for the rest of the month. Pass me the TV remote, my training days are over!"

Why then is it that some leaders[39] get to a point of relative career success and think, "Well that's it, I am now fully-baked in my leadership and career gloriousness; it's time to step off the learning and developing gas and 'coast' as far as self-development is concerned. What got me here will definitely get me there. What's on TV? Cheesy-crust pizza anyone?"

A short list of things all leaders habitually do every single day:

Brush their teeth.
Floss their teeth.[40]
Breathe.
Think.
Eat.
Drink.
Sleep.
Communicate (even if only with themselves).
Make decisions.

A shorter list of things that really great leaders also do every day:[41]

Get intentionally better at leading by journaling every day!

---

39   Not you, dear reader, I'm referring to the slightly cruddy ones. ☺
40   But, as mentioned, only the ones they want to keep.
41   Including weekends and holidays? Yes. Birthdays too? Yes. Valentine's, surely not Valentine's too? Yes. What about Thanksgiving? Yes! What about...YES!

...Oh, and one more thing!
   ...Well, two things!
      ...Well six things, really—see chapter 3.

THE TWO THINGS:

We have already covered the importance of reflection—it leads to self-awareness, remember? We will cover this again in more detail as we continue through the book, of course, but now's a good time to think about reflective and reflexive practice, and the key similarities and differences.

Reflective Practice

Journaling is a reflective practice. It is the engagement in a process of continuous learning and development. In its simplest form, it requires us to think about what we have done recently, or to explore what we typically do under similar circumstances, and what would/could we have done better, and how we might do better next time. This kind of self-reflection requires intentionality and conscious effort.

We see so many leaders who imagine that they can simply rely on "experience" or "time served" in order to improve—but neither of these things work; all they serve to do is make you more like the you that you already are—there's no tension, no growth, no change.

We are talking about more than simply learning from experience—only to the extent, though, that you take the time to dissect the experience and your involvement in it. This is how "insight and wisdom" are developed, and both are critical leadership attributes. Remember, wisdom comes from evaluated experience. The evaluated experience we refer to here is found in reflective and reflexive intentionality.

More of this in Chapter 4.

To illustrate what we're talking about in terms of reflective practice, an example in your journal might look like:

Today, when Bill told me that his team was going to miss the quarterly numbers, instead of putting more pressure on him by telling him how extremely disappointed I was, and that he had better figure out a recovery plan by first thing tomorrow morning, I should have taken more time to figure out...

...what resources, training, and support I should have brought to bear in order to better help him achieve his goals.

...what I can do now in order to help him and his team recover the gap by the end of the next quarter.

I reacted to this issue as if it was Bill's fault when, in reality, it was really my fault.

I'm the leader and it's therefore always my fault.

I will call him now and tell him not to worry, and that he and I can meet tomorrow to better discuss and understand the issues.

Bill and I can jointly create a credible and well-costed recovery plan with clear KPIs along with early milestones for success, as well as potential course correction items if necessary. In this way I will take some responsibility for the ultimate result which is, after all, my deliverable too.

Nice. No, not nice, gorgeous! Self-awareness. Growth. Teamwork.Intentionality.Wisdom.Accountability.Collaboration. Responsibility.

Gorgeous with tonic, ice, and a twist of lemon. ☺

Reflexive Practice

Reflexivity is a different skill—an even more difficult skill to master. But, like all developing skills, it takes some intentionality, repeated drills, and determination in order to master them.

Reflexivity is looking for ways to question our own attitudes, core values, beliefs, assumptions, commandments, ethics, ethos, and habits in so far as they impact others. Hmmm, sounds like something a good leader should do more of, right?

To illustrate what we're talking about in terms of reflexive practice, an example in your journal might look like:

> *Today, when Bill told me that his team was going to miss the quarterly numbers, I became instantly annoyed and aggravated. These sort of things trigger me enormously. I realize that I nearly yelled at him again, and I certainly said some unhelpful, and probably hurtful and unsupportive, things.*
>
> *I need to take time to figure out how to improve my self-regulation in these kinds of tricky circumstances—it's really easy to be helpful and Mr. Nice Guy when things are going well, but I need to figure how to be more helpful and more agreeable when things are difficult.*
>
> *I wonder whether Bill might have told me earlier that he was going to miss his numbers, if I were better at controlling my emotions whenever he brings me disappointing news. If he had felt able to come to me earlier, the "fix" might now be much easier.*
>
> *This really is my fault.*
>
> *I'm going to work on figuring out how to be more consistent, even tempered, and resilient in the face of adversity.*

*I'm going to call Bill right away and give
him permission to point out whenever I'm
being an unhelpful bombastic jerk!*

Brilliant. No, not brilliant, sensational! Self-awareness. Growth. Honesty. Vulnerability. Courage. Intentionality. Wisdom. Accountability. Responsibility.

Sensational with tonic, ice, and a twist of lime. ☺

Your journal, if well-constructed, well-attended to, and well-formatted, is the space for both of these critical "reflective" and "reflexive" practices since both are essential to self-understanding and exacting self-change. A detailed daily Leadership Journaling practice should find ways to have the journaler do both of these things with some regularity. See Chapter 17 for examples of the kinds of daily questions that develop both of these separate (but connected) critical skills.

Remember, these reflective and reflexive skills help you in life generally, not only at work. Improving these skills will naturally lead to better relationships with family, friends, and strangers. Also, and this is key, they will lead to a much better relationship with yourself—and what could be more gorgeous than that?

Is legendary status a choice, therefore? Is it a decision?

Yes it is. It's a daily choice. It's a daily decision.

Success as a leader, therefore, is habitually working on reaching your own full potential while habitually helping others achieve the same.

Look, it's back to Rule 1 and Rule 2 again, folks.[42]

And all of this just by giving your leadership development journey as much time and attention as we give to our weekly groceries. Nice.

---

42   I can't stand how gorgeous that is!

Once Leadership Journaling becomes a habit, so too does intentional development—more on this in Chapter 3.

BUT FIRST, ANOTHER QUESTION, ANOTHER STORY, AND AN ANCIENT RIDDLE.

The question:

> Will Leadership Journaling change me for the better as a person, as well as change me for the better as a leader?

Great question. The answer is 100 percent yes, it will definitely change you—you will be a completely new and better person and leader. And 100 percent no, you'll still be exactly you. It's Rule 1 and Rule 2 again, folks. It seems that leadership is a pursuit of contradiction: which, of course, it is...and then again, no, it isn't.

Some leaders we train worry that by journaling daily, they will change, and maybe not in "a nice way." You see, they want to change, they acknowledge that, but they worry that they might change too much, or change in unpredictable and unexpected ways—and the fear of who they might become worries them. Some worry that they will become way too driven, or way too single-minded, or way too preoccupied by leading and success that their private life, for example, might suffer.

Of course, none of these concerns ever come to pass since daily journaling is a sure-fire way to 100 percent manage and control the person they are and ensure that the person they want to be is the person that they will become. In other words, journaling will change them completely, and at the same time, it won't.

Let me try to explain all of this with a 2,500-year-old philosophical headscratcher—and it's all about a famous Greek ship named, we think, the Argo.[43]

Theseus was the Argo's captain in ancient Greece around 500 BC.

After winning a tremendous battle near Crete, it was decided that Theseus's ship should be kept as a museum piece in safe harbor for the prosperity of the Greek nation.

The Greek citizens would flock from near and far to marvel at the beautiful lines of the victorious vessel and hear tales of battles, victories, high jinks, and seafaring derring-do.

As the years passed, some of the wooden parts began to rot, and they were, of course, replaced with identical "new" pieces.

Imagine then after, say, a century or so, with every single part of the Argo having been replaced: Would the ship in the harbor still be Theseus's battle-winning ship?

Most people say that yes, it is the same ship: same shape, same name, same design, same material, and so on. It hasn't moved from its moorings all of these years. Ergo, it's the same Argo, the same ship.[44]

Well, dear reader, riddle me this then. Imagine that every piece of the Argo that had been taken from the original ship had been kept in a warehouse and completely restored—piece by piece. Then, instead of replacing these pieces back in the original ship, they went to construct a whole "new" Argo—a ship made of exactly the same pieces (the very original pieces of wood) that the Argo was made of. This "new" ship arguably has more of a claim of being the original Argo than the ship now in port calling itself the Argo. Can two completely separate things be the exact same thing?

Tricky. Answers on a postcard, please.

---

43   No, not Jason's, another one—we (historians) think.
44   Heraclitus and Plato discussed this one at length. It's tricky, and no mistake.

So, yes, dear reader, Leadership Journaling will change you, slowly over time like the Argo—and, although completely changed, you will still be completely you. Nice.

Another question:

What kind of leader do you want to be: World-Class, Best-In-Class, Exceptional, Good, Average, Below Average?

Despite the amazingly competent and glorious leader you are right now,[45] we should all strive for constant and consistent improvement, right? Of course!

I imagine when you read the question above, you thought, "Oh, world-class, definitely." Or, "best-in-class" at least—any less and you should hand over your leadership badge and take up knitting, perhaps. Or wood turning. Or cheese making. Or Morris Dancing, perchance.[46]

However, confession time: it was a trick question.

The answer must be none of those things. The real answer, the only possible answer, is, "I want to become the very best leader I can possibly become," and that's it. It's not a race against other leaders, or a race to achieve some sort of medal or certificate of competence since there isn't one. The race is you, against you—trying to become your best you.

Don't compare yourself to others—ever.

The best that you can ever be is the best that you can be. Your job is to try to be the very, very, very best that you can be—always.

Find a gloriously determined spot in your journal and write:

---

45   Pink, and moist, and glorious, and fluffy.
46   Yes, Morris Dancing is a real thing...but don't. Just don't.

> "I am determined to reach my maximum leadership potential in order to be-come the very best leader that I can possibly become!"

We're all on a journey.

We all have our own limits, of course, and we should work hard to reach the very boundaries of them. None of us can be better than we can be. But what we should all do, if we love our people, is love ourselves and strive to be the best leader that we can be in order to help the people we lead love themselves and what they do too.

WHAT DOES REAL DETERMINATION REALLY LOOK LIKE?

When you find that your journaling is becoming a little repetitive, tiresome, and slow, I want you to think of what real determination looks like: it looks like Kendo.

Kendo is a Japanese martial art descended from ancient swordsmanship. The practitioners wear protective armor and basically try to knock the livin' bejesus out of their opponent with a bamboo "sword."[47]

Like all martial arts executed to a high and competitive standard, there is a very strict grading system. The proponents move up in levels of skill and competence from complete novice level—1st Kyu, all the way to master level—8th Dan.

Progress in Kendo takes an extraordinary level of intentionality and dedication since there is a minimum age in terms

---

47 They don't really; they try to score quite sophisticated and technical points; but "knock the livin' bejesus" sounded more, well, dynamic. Artistic license. Sorry. Let's move on.

of eligibility to be graded, and there is a minimum time delay between gradings.

Progressing from 7th Dan to 8th Dan is a study in absolute intentionality, determination, and single-mindedness.

When a 7th Dan Kendo enters the 8th Dan examination, guess what the average pass-rate is? Go on, guess...

No, it's typically around 0.5 percent or less! Gasp.

A little more than 99.5 percent of all entrants fail—it's how they keep the standards and the integrity level of graded skill at a truly exceptional level.

This means that almost every single 7th Dan trying out for their 8th Dan knows with almost absolute certainty that they're likely to fail the examination. And yet they turn up in droves to do their best.

So, imagine you're a 7th Dan, and you've just failed to pass your 8th Dan examination—highly likely, remember? Failure is almost guaranteed.

But, one mustn't allow oneself to become too despondent: better luck next time, right?

But wait, hold fast! What do you imagine is the MINIMUM amount of time before you are eligible to reapply for a failed 8th Dan test? Go on, guess.

Six months? Ha! Not even close!

A year? Pah! I scoff at your measly year.

Two years? You wish!

No, it's ten years minimum!

Whaaaat? Ten more grueling years of dedicated work, study, training, and hardship.

And then, a full decade later, when you take the test again, what's the average pass rate from 7th Dan to 8th Dan the second time around? It's exactly the same as before; it's still less than 0.5 percent. Aaaargh!

The minimum time between 6th and 7th Dan is six years, and five years between 5th and 6th Dan. Kendo is tough!

Get your head around all of that. Get your head around the dedication that these individuals have in their pursuit for dueling perfection.

Now, am I asking you to have the same level of determination and dogged pursuit of perfection in your daily journaling practice as the Kendo 8th Dan? Well, no, of course not, but I am asking you to make a very real and determined commitment to it—at least the same level of commitment you gave to other things that you really wanted to master—those really, really tricky things you accomplished when your level of determination was sufficiently aroused:

Walking, talking, reading, tying your shoelaces, and using a fork, remember?

These are all extremely tricky things for the determined infant, and they take years, sometimes, to get right. And you accomplished most of these things without too much of a to do, I'm guessing.

"Ah, yes, Antonio," I hear you cry. "But things were different when we were young infants; we simply hadn't learned to accept failure at that early stage in our life, but when we get older, things get trickier, and we all become less determined!"

Oh, what about driving a car? How old were you when you took your test, two years old? I think not. I bet you worked hard to get your driver's license—I know that I did—I know that my four kids certainly did.

What about when you graduated from college—was that easy?

What about when you saved for your first mortgage deposit?

What about when you first learned how to set the clock on the VCR or set up Apple Pay?[48]

It seems that if we want something enough, we put in the work.

---

48   No, I never did either. But that's why we have kids, right?

And remember, when journaling gets tough (and it will), it could be worse—you could be trying to achieve 8th Dan Kendo. Here's what we notice about 8th Dan Kendos—they try to get better at Kendo every day, in almost every conceivable way.

Let's try to be as intentional as an 8th Dan Kendo leader, shall we?

More on this in Chapter 3.

In 1975, the All Japan Kendo Federation developed and published "The Concept and Purpose of Kendo." The following is taken from their Purpose Statement and applies well enough to journaling and leadership if you mentally squint just a little:

> To mold the mind and body.
> To cultivate a vigorous spirit
> And through correct and structured training,
> To strive for improvement in the art of Kendo.
> To hold in esteem courtesy and honor.
> To associate with others with sincerity.
> And to forever pursue the cultivation of oneself.
> Thus will one be able:
> To love one's country and society;
> To contribute to the development of culture;
> And to promote peace and prosperity among all people.

As a very final word: if you actually are an 8th Dan Kendo master—well done, you. Exceptional. Kudos. Much admiration, honor, and respect.

Back to journaling....

WHAT GREAT LEADERS DO EVERY DAY

As stated above, the great ones try to get better at leading every day, in almost every conceivable way.

They...

...intentionally follow a self-development plan.
...adopt a positive attitude by focusing on gratitude and a positive vocabulary.
...are solutions-oriented and use tools to help them make better decisions.
...evaluate their experience and focus on lessons learned.
...work to reveal, and then eliminate, their leadership blind spots.

As we wrap up this chapter, let's agree to...

...take a good long daily look at yourself in the brutally frank and honest mirror of self-awareness.
...be ultra-intentional about what you're learning.
...become the best leader you have the potential to become.

And then let's finally agree to really, really persist with it, even though sometimes it's difficult. Let's be determined little soldiers—like you were when you learned to walk, and talk, and write, and read, and tie your own shoelaces, and use a fork, and ride a bike, and drive a car. When you want to do something, really want to do it, you always find a way—you're a determined blighter, and you always find a way.

Find a particularly wonderfully honest space in your Leadership Journal. Copy and complete this exercise:

Give yourself a grade, A+ to F, for your leader-ship performance over the last, say, 30/60/90 days. _____

Now, resolve to improve the score over the next ninety-days. Write a few words pertaining to that new and determined resolution.

And then, finish off this sentence...

To dramatically improve my report card over the next ninety days, as a minimum I need to start, stop, and continue the following: _____

"You can't determine your future, but you can determine your habits. And your habits determine your future."
—F. M. Alexander

Congratulations! You have reached the end of Chapter 1 and, if you have followed all the journaling recommendations so far, you will have made a really great start to becoming a significantly improved leader.

Onward! ☺

CHAPTER 2

What Is a Leadership Journal?

We need a better definition.

WOULD A LEADERSHIP JOURNAL BY ANY OTHER NAME SMELL JUST AS SWEET?

Now that we have defined "successful leadership" in terms of potential, let's define what a "Leadership Journal" is.

A journal, from the Old French "journalier" (meaning "daily"), can refer to several things. In its original meaning, it refers to a daily record of activities, but the term has evolved to mean any record of activities, regardless of time elapsed between entries. It's perhaps high time to explore the differences between the various types of journal.

There are eight main types of journals—seven of which are definitely not what we are aiming for:

1. **Chronicle of events.**

   A record of news or personal events over the course of a day or other period.

   > "Dear Diary,
   > Today I went to...."

   This is not what we're going for.
   You're not Ernest Hemingway nor Samuel Pepys—you're simply not that interesting.[1] Sorry.

2. **Stream of consciousness.**

   Letting your random and meandering subconscious thoughts bubble to the surface for later psychoanalysis. Aimless automatic writing allowing the subconscious try to express whatever ails or vexes it.

   No, you're not Sigmund Freud either.[2]

---

1 And you simply don't have the beard, tweed jacket, or sideburns for it.
2 It's a whole beard thing again—yours is simply not smart enough, not trimmed well enough, and is all, well, wrong.

3. **Bullet journaling.**

   A recent journaling fad intended to organize one's life, and in which to keep records of tasks and/or goals.

   Again, no.

   We're not looking for a planner, diary, and occasional points of meditation—however "simple" it seems, whatever colors it uses, and however well it is laid out.

4. **Scrapbook journaling.**

   A receptacle of clippings, interesting images, recipes, and the like. Memorabilia. Autographs. Postcards.
   God, no.

5. **Dream journal.**

   Kept by your bedside as an immediate record of vivid dreams used as a mechanism for further creativity during waking hours.
   Definitely not.

6. **A to-do list.**

   No.
   Just no.
   Leadership Journaling isn't a to-do list. At its heart, it's a to-be list.

7. **Daily journal.**

   There are lots of different types of journals specifically designed to record or chart a path through a particular topic of interest:

Mindfulness journal. Yoga journal. Food journal. Travel journal. Reading journal. Gratitude journal. Fitness journal. Pregnancy journal. Poetry journal...and so on. All nice, I am sure, but not what we are after.

8. **Leadership Development Journal.**

Winner, winner, chicken dinner!

This journal is about significantly better results through guided self-awareness, targeted learning, and intentional self-development over an extended period of time.

Yes, yes, yes!

SPECIFICALLY, HOW IS A LEADERSHIP JOURNAL (NUMBER 8) DIFFERENT FROM A DAILY JOURNAL (NUMBER 7)?

Great question, I'm glad you asked.[3]

Your Leadership Journal should be sure to draw specific attention to and help improve all of the five core elements of great leadership:

1. People Development
2. Company Development
3. Self-Development
4. Strategy Development
5. Leadership Development

A daily journal of things that have happened, things to do, and things that you're working on does not draw specific focus to the critical leadership competencies. Making small and con-

---

3   It was on the tip of your tongue, I am sure. ☺

sistent improvements in each of the key leadership areas of this very specific list guarantees that all of the leadership bases are covered. As you make small and consistent improvements all of these areas, you'll find that before too long, you'll only be a hop, step, and a short bus ride away from leadership greatness.

Each of the five core elements can be broken down further into four "fundamental building blocks of leadership greatness."

The list of twenty critical leadership principles are:

PEOPLE DEVELOPMENT	HELPING OUR PEOPLE REACH THEIR FULL POTENTIAL
	MASTERFUL MENTORSHIP
	UNDERSTANDING MOTIVATION
	COMMUNICATION, COORDINATION, COOPERATION, AND COLLABORATION
COMPANY DEVELOPMENT	IMPROVING THE COMPANY PROCESSES
	DEVELOPING THE COMPANY VISION / MISSION / GOALS
	SHORT, MEDIUM, AND LONG-TERM PLANNING
	INDUSTRIALIZE, SCALE, PIVOT, OR REFRESH
SELF DEVELOPMENT	MY PERSONAL LEARNING-PATH
	ELIMINATING MY LEADERSHIP BLIND SPOTS
	BUILDING MY EMOTIONAL INTELLIGENCE
	ELIMINATING MY SELF-LIMITING BELIEFS

	SOLVING PROBLEMS WITH TOOLS AND MENTAL MODELS
STRATEGY DEVELOPMENT	STRATEGIC PLANNING
	STRATEGY EXECUTION
	MEASURE, REVIEW, AND COURSE CORRECT
LEADERSHIP DEVELOPMENT	DEVELOPING TRUST
	DEVELOPING MY PERSONAL VISION / MISSION / GOALS
	LEVERAGING CORE VALUES
	COMFORT-ZONE BUSTING, AND COURAGE

Feeling brave? Visit: www.mydailyleadership.com/leader-shipassessment to run a full-diagnostic leadership ruler over yourself. If you want to get to where you need to be, it's important to know where you're starting from.

GREAT LEADERS ARE NOT BORN, THEY ARE MADE.

Great leadership: it's not nature, it's nurture.

There, I've said it.[4]

Great leaders are not those fortunate few born with the "great leadership" gene indelibly stamped on their DNA, while bad leaders are lacking in this extraordinary biological gift from God.[5]

---

4   A sixty-year-old nature/nurture argument finally settled. Again, you're welcome.
5   Or the Universe, or Buddha, or Odin, or the Big Bang, or whatever else helps keep you safe when you hear a floorboard creak in the dead of night.

We all have the leadership and greatness ability baked-in, and we can all develop these skills. BUT, those skills, no matter where we are on the spectrum—wonderful to dreadful—need to be worked and exercised in order to be improved. Your leadership muscle is developed by your Leadership Journal: it is a key component of discovering, tracking, and intentionally working on achieving just that. As mentioned earlier, our task is to reach our full leadership potential: a potential that we all possess, and Leadership Journaling is the key to unlocking and developing it.

BUT YOU CAN'T COACH TALL!

Confession time: there are some things (very few things) that cannot be improved by journaling and self-coaching alone. A basketball coach cannot, for example, coach his player to be "taller"—neither can the individual make themselves taller by simply wishing the inches upon themselves. What the coach can do (should do) is ensure that all of her team members become the best possible versions of themselves. This is as true for leadership as it is for basketball, and any other worthwhile endeavor, of course.

Remember, we can't coach someone, including yourself, to be taller; but we can be coached to jump higher.

Taller, no. Jump higher—yes.

I SKATE TO WHERE THE PUCK IS GOING TO BE.

We all want to be the Wayne Gretzky of the business world, right? We want to skate to where the puck is going to be, not where it has been, nor where it is now. A good hockey player, says Gretzky, skates to where the puck is, a great one, to where it will be.

We've already agreed that we're shooting for great, not good. This means that we must somehow predict where the business and the market that it should serve is going, its trajectory, and start moving there in advance of it. We need to predict the challenges that we are going to face—the skills and competencies that will carry us successfully through to the future state of the business and beyond. We need to become the leader of the future, not the leader for right now. When we become great for right now, sometime down the line, the *new now* will be significantly different again and you will have missed the boat (think black and white TVs). Your job as great leaders is to plan the business for the future; well, it's the same with our own personal development, too, of course. As Marshall Goldsmith argues, "What got you here will not get you there." Bravo, Marshall.

Your Leadership Journal should pay attention to the future leader that you are going to be, that you need to be. Questions that help you unravel the challenges that you will face at some future point are as critical as the issues we face now, more so.

More than half of your daily journaling schedule should be rooted in the future—in the leader that you will need to become. The added benefit, of course, is that shooting for greatness then, ensures that you're going to be significantly better now, as well as on the way to where you're going to meet that pesky puck.

Find somewhere appropriately forward-looking in your journal and complete this rather tricky thought:

> In order for me to future-proof my leadership skills and competences, I will need to pay more attention to these key issues now _____.

Lovely.

ARE YOU A MANAGER, OR A LEADER, OR BOTH?

Before you scream, "Both!" or, "They are the same thing!" or, "What's the difference?"[6] consider:

Are all great managers, great leaders?   No.
Are all great leaders, great managers?   No.

It stands to reason, therefore, that these two things, leading and managing, are entirely distinct and different entities. We oftentimes tend to confuse these two concepts believing that leading is managing, and managing is leading—but that's a very big mistake, because they are most definitely not.

I have a client who argued, quite passionately and with heartfelt conviction, that when he went on a management development course (which he paid a lot for—a lot!), the happy by-product of this training was that he also became a better leader.

When I asked him how, he struggled to define it.

Why? Most leaders think that managing is leading, and leading is managing.

Some even go on to argue that managing change is the same as leading change. It isn't.

So, for the last time, management development is not the same as leadership development.

Do all great strikers in soccer go on to make great managers? No.

Do all great pitchers naturally become great baseball coaches? No.

Do all great violinists make great conductors? No again.

Do all great actors make great script writers, or directors, or agents? You get the picture. Skill or expertise in one thing does not guarantee skill in another allied theme.

---

6   Or "Who cares?!"

Is it possible to be a great leader, or a great manager, or both? Of course. And, by daily Leadership Journaling, we are shooting for both, naturally.

Will your Leadership Journal help make you a better manager as well as a better leader? Absolutely, it will. It might be useful, though, for us to take a moment to consider the differences between management and leadership before we get too tangled up in the weeds.

LEADING IS NOT MANAGING, AND MANAGING IS NOT LEADING.

Learning to be a better leader is not the same as learning to be a better manager. As explained above, there is a world of difference between management and leadership. Management seems to come fairly easy to most people—much more easily than leadership, at any rate. We are all used to hearing orders and instructions from a very early age. We are taught and socialized how to comply, to fit in. We have all been exposed to the management model from childhood.

Management is, at its heart, "instructing"—do this, don't do that. Try this, tell her that. Email them this, ask them that. Get this done, then do that. Once you've done this, let me know. Tell him this, and then let me know what they said. Go get this. Put that there. Complete this form, then submit it over here. Make a plan for this, but change it here.

And most of our subordinates, who have been socialized to comply, comply. If they want to keep their job, most tend to comply with the directions of their authority figures—they comply with the managers' instructions—well, at least to a certain minimum extent, they do.[7]

Some well-meaning and more nurturing managers of a kinder hue and more generous disposition tend to couch their instructions more as "suggestions," or "well-intentioned advice"

---

7   A conversation for another book.

with lots of nurturing-parent tonality and slightly more fluid time frames or deadlines. However, no matter how nurturing the directives are communicated, they are still perceived as instructions. This, dear reader, is not leading, this is managing—with a smiley face, a warm piece of pie, and a friendly hat on. But, isn't it coaching if I use good tonality, smile a lot, and say "please"? No, no it isn't coaching, it's still managing—and it's still definitely not leading.[8]

SOME DEFINITIONS AND DISTINCTIONS

Consider the following list as a starting point for defining management and leadership:

- ✧ Managers delegate tasks, leaders delegate results.
- ✧ Managers give their people something to do, leaders give their people something to believe in.
- ✧ Managers tell people how to act, leaders help people learn how to think.
- ✧ Management is the use of directed authority, leadership is the process of guided discovery.
- ✧ Management is telling, leadership is understanding.
- ✧ Management is narrow focus, leadership is broad focus.
- ✧ Management is I judge you by your actions, leading is judge me by my actions.
- ✧ Management is "light a fire under them," leadership is "light a fire within them."

Without wanting to sound overtly pithy, leadership is the ability to encourage followship.

---

8   A conversation for yet another book.

Do you encourage real followship (lead), or do you encourage acquiescence (manage)? Do people follow you because of your title and position, or because of you? Would they follow you even if you didn't have the title, the corner office, and the key to the executive washroom, I wonder? I would like you to wonder this, too, for a few moments—it's a sobering thought.

Over and above the above,[9] leadership is the ability and willingness to:

> ...generate trust and collaboration in the achievement of shared goals.
> ...serve and positively influence others.
> ...set aside your own ego allowing others to shine through.
> ...define the organization mission, vision, and values.
> ...resolve conflict and allocate resources accordingly.
> ...set expectations of excellence.
> ...believe that you work for them, they don't work for you.

But you already knew all of that, right? Of course you did.

So, now that you have a clearer view of the differences, you should start thinking about what you are doing, as you are doing it. Try to third-party your interactions at work—yes, including e-mails, texts, live or virtual, synchronous and asynchronous video...in short, during every meeting and every communication, ask yourself (whilst you are in the thick of doing whatever it is that you are doing), am I managing, or am I leading? Does the answer accord with what you should be intending—managing or leading? Remember, you can't do both at the same time—you're doing one or the other: so, choose.

---

9   Couldn't resist.

START AS YOU MEAN TO GO ON.

Things that start well have a much stronger chance of ending well. Things that start badly rarely end well.

Why not make a habit of telling every new employee something that sounds like the following:

> "Instructing you or telling you what to do is the least valuable thing you'll ever get from me. My job is to help you reach your full potential, and any time we are not helping make that happen is as big a waste of your time as it is of ours. Let's get together to construct a training and development plan for you, agree on regular review dates, as well as explore ways that I can help support you. I'd love to hear about your personal goals too, and I will share mine with you."

Heck, why not tell every employee something that sounds very much like that? If you think about it, it could even somehow find its way into your vision or mission statement, right? Or even this year's goals, why not?[10]

Find a really enlightened space in your journal to complete this thought:

Instructing people (managing) is one
of the least productive things that
I as a leader can do because....

QUICK SIDEBAR, YOUR HONOR?

It's really easy to pass over any one of the leadership development exercises, like the one above, for example, imagining that

10   Delicious!

you might get back to it later: you almost certainly won't. Try not to think this way. Try hard to complete all of the quick exercises as we reach them—they all matter. Doing the exercises makes a difference. It sets you up for the next thing. It gets you thinking in the right sort of way.

If you've missed any at this point, go back. Go on, we'll wait for you. You'll feel fantastic, you'll see—and who doesn't want to feel fantastic, hmm? Off you pop, we'll be here when you get back. ☺

Going forward, if you are tempted to skip one of the exercises, it's likely that, at first flush, it seems a little long-winded or tricky. And it is for that very reason that you should not skip it. It likely looks tricky, or long-winded, or pointless, or irrelevant, or _____ (insert your own reason) because you don't want to consider the issue(s) we are suggesting. You'll complete the "easy" ones (maybe), but you'll certainly skip the tricky ones. The ones that you will want to skip look pointless because your subconscious wants to avoid the heavy lift—for reasons that will be explored in Chapter 9. The more you want to skip an exercise, the more likely it is to benefit you. Ask yourself, are you skipping due to cowardice? Ouch. You'll tell yourself it's not for that reason, it's for an entirely logical and sensible other reason, like time or convenience, or you think you have a headache coming on—but none of those will be true.

But, if you have been completing each one of them diligently so far, I want to take a quick second to say well done, you! You're a brave sausage.

Love it.

Love you.

Keep going.

We're all really proud.

SOME GOOD NEWS

Here's the really good news, while your Leadership Journal is specifically intended to grow your *leadership* skills, capabilities, and competencies, the happy byproduct is significantly increased skill and competency in *management* skills also. Hoorah! Weird, I know, but hoorah!

SOME MORE GOOD NEWS

...'cause who doesn't love another good table? I know I do.

This short list isn't definitive, nor is it even extensive, and there may well be some overlap at the edges, but you can use this table as a quick ready-reckoner whenever you need it:

MANAGING	LEADING
DIRECTING SUBORDINATES	INSPIRING FOLLOWERS
THE USE OF DIRECTED AUTHORITY	THE USE OF GUIDED DISCOVERY
TACTICAL	STRATEGIC
CONFLICT RESOLUTION	RESOURCE ALLOCATION
DELEGATED INSTRUCTION/ACTION	DELEGATED RESULT
TASK-ORIENTED	PEOPLE-ORIENTED
REACTIVE	PROACTIVE
LIGHTING FIRES UNDER PEOPLE	LIGHTING FIRES WITHIN PEOPLE
RAISING STANDARDS	RAISING BELIEFS
RESULTS AND PROCESS DRIVEN	CULTURE AND VALUES DRIVEN

QUALITY OUTPUT AND CONTROL	QUALITY PEOPLE AND THINKING
DOING THINGS RIGHT	DOING THE RIGHT THINGS
SIMPLIFY COMPLEXITY	SIMPLIFY UNCERTAINTY
PLANNING FOR THE FUTURE	VISUALIZING THE FUTURE

Of course, most business executives find themselves flipping and flopping between these two lists on a day-by-day basis (sometimes minute-by-minute) since all senior roles require a mixture of these two disciplines. But ask yourself which list you mostly resemble and how you spend *MOST* of your time.

For those who like to keep score:

We don't need more managers.

We don't necessarily need more leaders, but we do need better leaders, and that requires owning whichever lane you're swimming in at any particular moment.

As a general guide, always try to bear to the right-hand lane—the water is much more refreshing.

HOW MY OWN LEADERSHIP JOURNALING STARTED.

Another story.

Many years ago, too many to contemplate or admit to, I was appointed to my first leadership role. In truth, I wasn't quite ready for the expanded role and extra responsibility, but circumstances in the company were as they were at that time, and it made more sense for me to be bumped up, rather than for the company to look outside to fill the role. Lucky me.

However, I very soon learned by bitter experience that I was punching above my weight: I suspect that everybody knew it within a few days, but it took me a few weeks to come to the same conclusion. I had feared as much when I accepted the job, but I accepted it nonetheless because the money was better and, more importantly, the designated parking spot was much nearer the main entrance—and it rains a lot in Yorkshire.

One day, the CEO asked to see me. On entering his office and sitting in the indicated chair, he asked me whether I journaled.[11]

Never having ever given it any thought whatsoever, none, ever, "Err, no," I replied. What an odd question, I mused.

"Oh, whyever not?" he asked quizzically.

Having worked for him for a while already, I knew that he could be a mercurial sort at times and, not wanting to disappoint, I had to think fast on my feet.[12]

"Err, probably because, despite the somewhat modest appearance, I'm not actually a sixteen-year-old Victorian schoolgirl. Probably." I offered weakly.[13]

He looked rather astonished, thought for a moment, then laughed out loud.

Phew.

"Well," he said, still chortling, "I think it'll do you good. Help you get up to speed with the new role, so to speak. Why not start today, eh? If you need any help, you know where I am. I journal every day, and it hasn't done me any harm now, has it?"

"Errr, what would I write in it?" I asked.

"Oh, that's easy," he said. "First, start with a long list of things you're grateful for."

---

11 Yes, I know it sounds very similar to the earlier story, but it isn't. Different CEO. Different company. Honest.

12 I was sat down, of course, but "I had to think fast on my bottom" seemed not to scan well.

13 "Dear Diary, Mr. Darcy was frightfully boorish today, and there was an unexpected inclement chill in the air that threatens to shock the periwinkles. I wonder if Mr. Darcy will notice my new bonnet in church on Sunday." Sigh.

"OK," I said reaching for my notepad.

"Second. Write a list of all the things you want."

"Things I want. Got it."

"Then," he went on, "third: write a list of all the things you need."

"Need. Right."

"Finally, write down a list of all the areas you need to get better at. OK?"

"Err, fine. Better at. Good. Got it."

"Great, so, I'll see you at the board meeting. Mind how you go, son. My door's always open. Ta ta, now."

And with that, the uniquely bizarre meeting was over, but the suggestion (instruction) was clear: "Start journaling today, or else!"

The internet was just about spreading across the globe in those days. It was still very much in its infancy[14] though, but, since it had recently been installed in my office computer, I thought I'd give it a whirl. So, I "Asked Jeeves" about the benefits of journaling—yes, I'm actually that old. Thanks.

After a couple of hours of unexpected and absorbing research, it turned out that journaling might not be such a bonkers idea after all—after all, around three million articles and websites about the power and benefit of journaling couldn't all be wrong, right?[15] ...and so, that very day, I made a start. I asked my secretary to pop down to "stores" to grab me a brand new journal (yes, "stores". Yes, I'm really that old—thanks again). As soon as it arrived, I opened it up and made a start at the four lists my CEO had suggested earlier that day. All these years later, I still have those four lists and I still refer to them often.

...and so began my journey of transformation.

---

14 It was up and about, but still a bit unsteady on its feet. It was sleeping through the night, but its first tooth had just come in, so it was a bit crotchety now and then and sometimes needed soothing with its blanky and a nice back rub!

15 There are many, many more millions nowadays, of course.

Honestly, I have lots of things to thank that crusty old CEO for, but this was by far the single most life-altering and profound thing of all.

"Journaling," he said, "is the gateway drug to leadership greatness."

So, why not find a really good space in your journal and put those four lists together for you too? It'd be a great start. Do it now. It's not like I'm asking you to try out for your 8th Dan Kendo, now is it?

Find a few gloriously inspired blank pages and make another delicious start...

List 1: My Big Bumper List of *Things I'm Grateful For*

Once you get your juices going, you'll likely notice that this list is much longer than you expect. Get really creative, now. You're aiming for a minimum of fifty things at your first sitting—so, give yourself some space.

And, if pistachio ice cream isn't on it, I'm going to be more than a little disappointed in you. Just saying.

You will come back to this list again and again when things get tough—and they will—so leave space at the bottom too.

Make a decent start on the list, then move on to the next question.

Question: Where is happiness?

Is it to be found on a deserted beach somewhere? In the salad drawer in the fridge keeping crispy-fresh till you need it? Is it in a cocktail glass? Is it in the approval of others?

No, it's inside you right now. It's in the experiences that you choose. It's in the list that you just wrote down: take another long hard look at it and take a second to smell the roses that you have to be grateful for.

Smile, because it's a really great list and, let's face it, you're a lucky old sausage.

Another Question: When was the last time you laughed like a drain, so much that your belly hurt?

Depending on your answer, I say to you this:

Either...

"Well done, keep it up, my friend. Enjoy."

...or...

"Act accordingly!"

Remember, you simply can't have a positive life if it's filled with negativity—and this first list is a great place for all of your positivity, optimism, courage, and gratitude.
More on this topic later.

List 2: My Big Bumper List of *Things I Really Want*

This list is typically a longer list than you'd imagine too.

Again, get creative.

You can feel good about yourself by starting with the words "World Peace" of course, but, if you really put your back into it, you will likely soon get to things like: "To only wear handmade shoes," or "To only fly first class."

Again, I'd expect this list to run somewhere around fifty really cool things.

List 3: *Things I Really Need*

This list is typically much, much shorter than you might expect—maybe around twenty to twenty-five things, tops!

Most of our leaders find this list much trickier to compile than the first two.

And, what they normally discover about themselves when writing this list should go into the first list and perhaps form the start of another new list entitled *"Insights about me...."*

Much more on insights in Chapter 4.

List 4: *Where I need To Improve As a Leader*

Now then, if you have low self-awareness, this will be rather a short list. Naughty.

But, if you have good self-awareness, this will be a much longer list.

Top of the class.

We're looking for *at least* ten things, no more than fifteen—you're not that bad, I promise. You're reading this book after all, so you must be half decent, right?

Whatever your list looks like, you could probably add another line to your new *"Insights about me..."* list, right?

Good stuff. Really. Good stuff.

Once you have made a decent start on those four important lists, you can then continue to Chapter 3.
Off you pop.

Again, we'll wait while you write them down.

Now then, for your last task of the chapter, find an appropriately appreciative space in your Leadership Journal to write down and complete the following:

Managers delegate tasks, leaders delegate results.

From today, I will be more people-focused than task-focused.

From today, I will be more proactive than reactive.

I recognize that to have a positive life, I need to concentrate on the things that I am most grateful for.

My current Top 5 Gratitudes are:

1.

2.

3.

4.

5.

---

*"The world has enough beautiful mountains and
meadows, spectacular skies and serene lakes.
It has enough lush forests, flowered
fields, and sandy beaches.
It has plenty of stars and the promise of a
new sunrise and sunset every day.
What the world needs more of is people
to appreciate and enjoy it."*
—*Michael Josephson*

Congratulations! You have continued to make a great start.[16] ☺

---

16   Treat yourself to a steaming hot cup of something delicious and an extra cookie too, why not?

CHAPTER 3

Good journaling is like a good pension.

You get lots more out than you put in.

JOURNALING EARNS COMPOUND INTEREST.

Journals, just like pensions,[1] require a long-term perspective and lot of perseverance.

And the benefits of pensions, just like journals, are mostly back-end loaded.

To succeed at long-term Leadership Journaling, you need to figure out some short-term and mid-term rewards that will encourage the persistence of the new daily ritualistic behavior. In this way journaling will eventually become habitual, and eventually, a fully embedded and integral part of your life.

Those journalers who persist up to the six-month mark almost never stop: it becomes part of who they are, part of what they do, part of how they think, part of how they develop and improve.

Most humans, though, are not this extraordinarily persistent; they tend to want to take the path of least resistance—to find the quick fix, the easy wins, the magic bullet: it's called the *cognitive ease principle*. We tend to believe that the easier something is to read, to think about, and to imagine, the more "true" the idea is likely to be. If something takes some significant effort, and some strenuous mental horsepower and effort, well, it's probably not so true, we often think. We simply love shortcuts and magic bullets, right? Quick hacks? Did someone say "lazy" and feebleminded? Gasp! Heaven forefend!

Speaking as someone who more often than not stands in front of the microwave and screams "Hurry" at the top of his lungs, I'm with you. Patience has never been a virtue of mine. Nor staying power, nor persistence with discomfort, well, you get the idea, I am sure. I'm not a Navy Seal, and I'm not a concert pianist.[2]

People like me typically love that part of the Pareto Principle which, we believe, says that we can get 80 percent of the way

---

1   And 8th Dan Kendo Masters from Chapter 1, remember?
2   Things that take enormous fortitude and persistence—you get the idea, I'm sure.

there with only 20 percent of the effort. We really, really love that theory, right? I mean, it makes perfect sense...mainly because we want it to.

And, since there's not much difference between 20 percent and 18 percent—especially if we squint a bit and look at it from far enough away, maybe 18 percent will do it.

In fact, with clever rounding, 18 percent is really 15 percent, right?

And 15 percent is almost 10 percent with a bathing suit on.

And 7 percent is practically 10 percent, so that's my target: 7 percent.

But, to be fair, that's just a target;

5 percent will be close enough to call it a "win."

So that's it then, somewhere between 3 percent and 5 percent and we can call the job a good-un. Hoorah!

No!

The reality is that anything of real lasting value always (yes, always) takes a certain amount of effort, or commitment, or risk[3]. So, too, Leadership Journaling. We all know well enough that the road to hell is paved with good intentions. Lots of people begin their journaling journey only to get soon distracted by some other, more trendy, less difficult self-development initiative. We can all think of numerous examples in our own lives where the speeding car of good intentions met with the black ice of difficulty on the long and winding road to self-improvement. And, before you know it, we have crashed. And, quick as a flash, we were off to try something else to see whether that might be a little better for us, more suited to our particular temperament and unique situation.

Remember, "good intentions" butter no parsnips.

It's easy to get exhausted by the effort, or diverted by the distraction, or delayed by the unfavorable circumstances. Think about the millions and millions of lapsed gym member-

---

3   We all know it, but don't want to admit it.

ships. The billions and billions of failed diets and eating plans. The countless promises to save a minimum percentage of our salary "for a rainy day." The scores and scores of musical instruments untouched on the top of the closet in the back bedrooms. The mountains and mountains of "learn a new language" packages lying fallow. The miles and miles of bookshelves covered in never-opened self-development books gathering dust for who knows when. That pottery wheel in the garage still in its wrapping. That snazzy internet-connected treadmill or exercise bicycle in the basement that somehow became the world's most expensive clothes horse...well, you get the idea.

But, don't we all tend to judge others by their actions and ourselves by our intentions? And, if our intentions were entirely honorable and heartfelt at the time that we set them, doesn't that count for something? If we were 100 percent *going to* start something new and difficult but never quite saw it through to the end because, well, it was trickier than we thought it was going to be, and the timing was bad, anyway. And I threw my back out changing a tire. And your mother came to stay for a few days, which threw me off my groove. And who knew that Bob in accounts was going to get sick for so long—that had us all pulling overtime, which made me more tired than usual at the end of the day. Won't that go some way to ease our pricking conscience and still guarantee our eternal star in the celestial firmament on our passing?

No. No, I don't think it will.

We should own our actions, not love our intentions. Actions, not intentions, make the boat go faster. Actions, not good intentions, butter the parsnips.

WHAT MAKES THE BOAT GO FASTER?

Ben Hunt-Davis was the captain of the British Olympic eight-man rowing team—and in the late 1990s they weren't doing so well. Ben, who had his sights on Olympic gold, coined the phrase, "Yes, but will it make the boat go faster?" and drove this single overriding mantra into each of his teams of extraordinary rowers.

"Shall we go to the pub tonight?" they would ask him.

"Great question," he would reply. "Will it make the boat go faster?"

"Errr, no."

"Then no, no pub tonight."

Drat!

"Do we have to go on another training run this weekend?"

"Great question, do we need to train this weekend. Let me ask you this, will it make the boat go faster?"

"Errr, probably."

"Then yes, we train this weekend."

Grr!

"Will it make the boat go faster?" became the yardstick against which everything was measured. If the answer was "Yes," then it was, by default, approved. If the answer was "Maybe," or "No," or "I don't know," the premise was rejected.

By only doing things (everything) that made the boat go faster, from what they ate, to when they slept, to their exercise, to their clothing, to their attitudes, they would ultimately be able to say that they were going to go as fast as they possibly could—to reach their maximum potential—and who could say fairer than that?

The result? Ben and his team won gold in the 2000 Sydney Olympics. The first British coxed eight rowing team to win since 1912.

Anything that makes the boat go faster, no matter how small, compounds over time. Even Albert Einstein marveled at the power of compound interest. "It's the eighth wonder of the world," he remarked. And who could, who would, dare to argue with good ol' Berty E? Certainly not I.

But, remember, you simply HAVE to make the deposits in order for the "game" to work.

Leadership Journaling makes your boat go faster. Journaling earns compound interest at a very healthy rate. Those who can come to believe and understand a mantra that sounds something like: "I am determined to commit to this worthwhile endeavor since I recognize the power of compound marginal gains over time" will become a significantly better leader in no time at all, which brings us very nicely to the allied principle of marginal gains.

MARGINAL GAINS

The sporting world is littered with countless stories of the immense power of marginal gains—countless examples of asking the "Will it make the boat go faster?" stories. It's how tennis professional Novak Djokovic went from a lowly position of over one hundred in the professional tennis world rankings to number one.

When he hovered around 100th in the world rankings in 2004/2005, he was winning 49 percent of his points and, coincidentally, winning 49 percent of his matches. Not bad.

But then, with a little tennis hocus-pocus from a new coach and a variety of intentional slight changes to his training and development, he quickly rose to number three in the world ranking for the following four years. He achieved this by increasing his points average to only 52 percent (from 49 percent), but his winning games average suddenly soared to 79 percent. Pretty good stuff.

Then, for the following five years, he took his winning point averages from 52 percent to 55 percent, which meant that he now won around 90 percent of his games and was a firm number one in the world. Brilliant.

Marginal gains—from 49 percent points won to 55 percent points won might not seem like much progress, but it made a world of difference: from 100th in the world earning around

$200,000 a year to number one in the world earning millions upon millions.

How was this achieved? Well, if you think about it, Novak could already play tennis before he got his new coach—so it wasn't that. He was already hugely experienced—so it wasn't that. He already knew every tennis rule, move, style, surface, and play—so it wasn't any of those things either. So, what on earth could his new coach have done or said to help Novak in such staggering ways? Not much, actually. Slight edges here and there.

His new coach helped Novak improve his serve by, say, just 1 percent. Maybe he improved his backhand crosscourt volley by, say, another 1 percent. Speed and agility by maybe 0.5 percent. Belief by 3.5 percent. Hand speed by 0.5 percent. All slight edges...and, quick as a flash, he improved his points won from 49 percent to 50 percent. Now he's number twenty in the world.

Then his eye-hand coordination by 2 percent. His top spin by 0.5 percent. His volley by 0.75 percent. Belief another 0.5 percent. More slight edges.

Now he's number eight in the world...and so on.

The "solution" to Novak's challenge was not one or two or three big things. There simply wasn't one or two great big hairy things he was missing, or overlooking, or doing wrong. No, it was a series of tiny things: slight edges.

Slight edges—marginal gains—make huge differences. And it is (will be) exactly the same for you—if you do it right.

As another powerful example, a quick search of Sir David Brailsford will tell a similar tale with the staggering improvements to the British Cycling Team. A slight change here, a little improvement there, and a smattering of better attitude and belief everywhere, and the world changed considerably for Sir David's team too. I won't spoil your enjoyment of searching for the incredible story yourself; it's a real doozie and well worth fifteen minutes of your valuable time.[4]

And it's exactly the same for you, dear reader, dear leader. You will find that on your path from good leader to great leader, you will need to improve something by just 1 percent over here—turn a knob three degrees to the left over there—increase the temperature by one degree over here—slow down a thing by one meter per second over there—speed up something else up by five kilometers per hour over here—shave a bit off over there, and add a pound or two over here... and, voila! Greatness.

Your Leadership Journal will help you figure this formula out. The formula for critical marginal gains and slight edges in your world that will make your boat, bicycle, tennis racket, skis, self-development, team, and business go faster.

Ask yourself what could a series of these intentional marginal gains and slight edges each earning incredible compound interest over the next year or so do to your future leadership skill, ability, and achievements.

"A couple of years?" I hear you cry. "Will it take that long?"

Well, let's take a quick look at that, shall we, since it's often a bit of a shocker when our leaders first realize that this journaling-lark might be a slightly longer-term gig than they first suspected or hoped for? Remember Kendo?

FIND SOMETHING YOU LOVE, AND IT ISN'T WORK.

To paraphrase Mark Twain,[5] when you find something that you love, it isn't work.

Committing to any worthwhile endeavor and having a passion for it always delivers compound interest on the invest-

---

4   So, go on, do it. It's an amazing story. You'll thank me. Go on.
5   Some say it was Confucius; some say it was Marc Anthony; some say Harvey Mackay. I know that my Uncle Allan used to say it to me very often too. Whoever it was, bravo!

ment of time, effort, and energy. Positive reinforcement is a powerful motivator, and it carries us through the difficult times, challenging circumstances, or lack of immediate resources. Doing something that we love raises our dedication or level of enthusiasm for the task, and we will feel more productive and enthusiastic in doing those things. We take time to try to learn the trick of the trade, the hacks, the slight edges, the marginal gains.

Don't we all tend to avoid those tasks we find difficult, in favor of those things we find easier? When we enjoy doing something, doesn't our endurance and stamina for it expand? We tend to feel less tired doing something that we enjoy versus something that we dislike. It's amazing how I manage to find the energy for a game of 5-A-Side soccer, but can't seem to summon even an ounce of it to do the vacuuming.

And don't we also tend to relish something when we believe that we can really master it? The more we do it, the more we master it, the more we like it. The more we like it, the more we do it, the more we master it. It's a whole chicken and egg thing.

OF CHICKENS AND EGGS

Do only those leaders who love to journal, journal? Or, by journaling, do they become better at it, and therefore enjoy it more, and therefore do it more?

It's the age-old, age-old question of the chicken and egg—which came first?[6]

Some people love to listen to classical music. Were they born that way? No. They developed their love for it over time. The more they listened to it, the more expert they became, and the more nuanced and developed their thinking and apprecia-

---

6   Actually, I do know the answer to this one—or at least Aristotle did. Aristotle said (and stay with me on this, it's pure genius) that an egg is a chicken in *potentiality*, whereas a chicken is a chicken in *actuality*. Actuality should always precede potentiality; therefore, the chicken came first. Genius. In other words, the doing of it makes you eventually love it.

tion of it grew. They started to think about it more profoundly, and their enjoyment of it expanded further. They began to understand it even more deeply, and they derived pleasure from their expanded understanding and mastery of it...

...and the more they liked it, the more they were committed to listening to it.

...and the more they learned about it, the more they enjoyed learning about it.

...and, well, you get the picture.

It's exactly the same story, of course, with those people who restore classical cars over years and years in their garden sheds. They pore over manuals and painstakingly hand-craft rocker arms that haven't been mass-produced for more than fifty years.

Or those afficionados who appreciate fine wines, and somehow come to know the difference between the grapes harvested from the north end of the vineyard and those picked from the lower slopes.

Daily Leadership Journaling, like classic car restoration, or bonsai, or beekeeping, or free climbing, or extreme ironing[7] and the like is a deliberate choice. And, once you make a start, and once you get good at it, and once you start to see the fruits of your labor gather some momentum, you'll simply never tire of it.

What's the message for us here? Make a start. Make some early progress. Enjoy it more. Do it more. Get better at it. Make more progress. Revel in the glory of it. Be intentional about improving and developing. Learn even more about it. Hunt out resources for it. Dedicate more time and effort to it. Get some early wins. Find others who are as bonkers as you are about it. Share a slight edge victory or two. Enjoy it. Look forward to it.

...and before you know it, you're on your way to world-class status and feeling just as smug as a bug in a hand-knit-

---

7   Look, whatever floats your boat. No judgement here. Have at it.

ted Himalayan yak-hair rug that you "ran up over the weekend" when you learned the new knit-one, pearl-one drop stitch method.

INTRINSIC OR EXTRINSIC MOTIVATION?

What kind of person are you?

Are you the kind of person who does better at the gym specifically with the help of a personal trainer?

Do you need (a typically poorly paid) someone drumming their fingers angrily on the bench press equipment while you struggle to finish the last five reps? Do you commit to more resistance on the triceps machine only when someone threatens you with five extra burpees if you don't get your head in the game and stop complaining? Do you respond well to someone yelling in your ear while you're sweating buckets on the elliptical trainer, "Come on! Just two hundred meters more! Puuuush! Faster! You can do it! Remember, no pain, no gain. You need this if you're going to get into that dress at the reunion in only six weeks! Think about that extra cracker you ate two days ago! Come on!! One ninety-five...one ninety...one eighty-five...."?

Do you consistently need others to coax, cajole, and sometimes shame or bully you into action or extra effort?

Or, are you the kind of person who needs a hug and a pat on the back from others for having done a good job? Do you have a high need for approval and crave the praise and high esteem of others? Do you need a lollipop from the doctor for having been such a brave little soldier when he put that stitch in your knee after having fallen off your bike? Do you pine for that last stamp on the coffee shop loyalty card that lets you proudly exclaim that the last macchiato was "on the house"?

These people typically rely on external stimuli to support progress and fuel forward momentum: lollipops or attaboys; threats, growls, or reprisals; stamps on the loyalty card of life.

They require regular extrinsic motivation to achieve their more difficult milestones and goals.

If you recognize yourself in either of these two scenarios (and only you, and perhaps your counselor, know), then you are going to need to figure out a short-interval reward system to keep you on the journaling straight-and-narrow—because there are no brave-boy-lollipops for journaling three days in a row, and nobody is going to magically appear and scream in your ear till you've sat down and eaten that last piece of journaling beetroot.

Only you know what kinds of rewards will keep you sufficiently motivated in the short and medium term—depending on whether you're the kind of person who is motivated more by "gain" than by "loss", or by internal or external stimuli. Once the benefits of your new daily journaling habit are being fully realized, of course, the need for these short-interval reward/punishment events will diminish, since experience tells us that the rewards will be self-evident and sufficiently powerful to keep you going.

If this is you, and if this helps, here are some genuine early-days reward/punishment motivators that lots of our extrinsically motivated journalers use as their personal contract of consistency to get you over the "hump" of the early days:

Extrinsic Rewards

For (**insert minimum number of days**) consistent journaling:

On the day that you make the initial commitment to journal, create a voucher book of, say, twenty IOUs.

These IOUs are to be "cashed in" with a frequency consistent with the number of attaboys you need to just put your pants on in the morning.

If you need lots of small and regular rewards, they could be as simple as an extra squirt of caramel on today's macchiato, an extra fifteen minutes in bed, or a trip to the movie theater.

If, however, you're more the BHAG kinda person, well, get creative. Perhaps you'd like to pop off to Bali with the author of this book and his family for a week's sun—your treat. Just sayin'.

...or...

Extrinsic Punishments

For failing to journal (**insert maximum number of days**) in a row:

On the day that you make the commitment to journal, you must write a check for, say, $5,000 (or a sufficiently painful number—somewhere between "ouch" and "faint").

The check is to be made out to a charity that you don't necessarily support.

Keep this check as your journaling bookmark. Seeing it every day will help keep you motivated, I promise.

Failure to comply to the contract of consistency that you set for yourself will mean that you will be obliged to post the check.

...and then write another for five times the amount and start again. Clearly the punishment was not onerous enough. QED.

Rinse and repeat.

If you're a thoroughly good egg, of course, as soon as your daily Leadership Journaling practice has become fully embedded and habitual, and you are experiencing the benefits, it would be especially delicious of you if you were to send the check anyway.

Heaven will welcome you with open arms. Forever dead is such a very long time, after all. ☺

Conversely, you might be the kind of person who has a really well-developed and self-fueled internal drive to succeed, and you simply need no external stimuli to help keep you committed and on the right path. You may already have the kind of fortitude indelibly stamped on your DNA to make regular progress, despite the many obstacles in your way. In other words, are you entirely *intrinsically* motivated?

According to Daniel Pink, author of *Drive: The Surprising Truth About What Motivates Us*, intrinsic motivation comes in three delicious flavors: autonomy, mastery, and purpose.

Autonomy

This is the need to self-direct and not rely on the management or direction of others.

If this is you, once you have made the commitment to journal, you will journal: and you won't need any reminders—it's as simple as that.

Make a firm commitment to journal.

Mastery

This is the internal drive and motivation to get better at something, to really conquer and master a particular skill.

If this is you, once you decide to learn how you can get better at journaling every day, you will become an avid and active student of the process, the benefits, the different types, and you will quickly adopt and adapt to suit your own particular purposes.

Decide to learn all you can about Leadership Journaling.

Purpose

This is the ability and desire to connect to a larger cause. And, according to Pink, it's the highest form of intrinsic motivation.

If this is you, once you have decided that in order to best serve those you lead, you simply need to do all that you can to improve, your leadership journal will become your new bible.

Recognize that you journal to better serve others.

Whatever colors, sizes, and shapes of external motivators you need, and whatever types and scents and flavors of intrinsic motivation you thrive on, your Leadership Journal, if well-constructed, feeds all of these needs. All it requires of you for your contract of consistency is an investment of your single most valuable resource—so let's check that out first.

WHAT IS YOUR SINGLE MOST VALUABLE RESOURCE?

That's easy, right? Time: just ask anyone. Time, they all say, is our most valuable resource.

Nope, it's not time.

What? But everyone says it's time, so it must be. Time. It's time.

Well, it isn't time, so try again.

But I thought it was.

Well, it isn't. Get over it. Try again.

Oh, OK. Then it's money. Money is our most valuable resource, right?

Nope again.

Oh gosh. If not money, people? It must be people. Yes, it's people, right?

Again, good guess, but no.

Health?

Close, but no cigar.

Intellect?

God, no.

Devilishly stunning good looks, good teeth, and boatloads of natural charm?

Errr...no. Nice. But no.

Energy?

Yaaay! Winner, winner, chicken dinner!

It's energy. Energy is our single most valuable resource.

Physicists define energy as "the ability to do work."

Leadership Journaling, self-improvement, progress, change, all require us to do the work—these things simply won't fall out of the sky and land in our laps: would that they would, but they won't.

We mustn't think of energy as some sort of a "youth-oriented and fitness-freak-kinda-thing," because it most certainly is not. Don't think that because you're not in your early twenties and you're not doing thirty burpees every morning before breakfast, drinking gallons of hemp milk, and cycle to work you're not going to succeed.

I personally know some incredibly energetic, vibrant, and active fifty-, sixty-, and seventy-year-olds; and I know some exhausted and downright knackered thirty-year-olds.

For the purposes of our requirements here, we are going to interpret "energy" as the ability and preparedness for effort and action—we will call that little beauty, *action bias*. All successful individuals share one common trait, action bias—however old or however far down the advanced decrepitude path they may be: whatever their market, whatever their vertical, whatever their business, action bias is a sure-fire guaranteed predictor of success.

Red Bull was started by a sixty-one-year-old in the 1980s. And here we are, some years later with Red Bull a global brand with annual revenues of around $6 trillion. That's "trillion," folks. Not bad.

McDonald's, KFC, The Home Depot, Coca-Cola, and countless other global brands were all started by people ages fifty and higher, and what they all had, in spades, was action bias.

Your Leadership Journaling journey requires action bias. Action bias requires energy.

Action bias is our number one resource—to succeed at anything we need to actually "do" something.

It's fine to try to *think* yourself thin, for example, but the evidence would largely support this being a very unsuccessful and frustrating weight-loss strategy—just ask my poor, beleaguered tailor.

Again, it's perfectly OK to try to *think* your way to $1 million cash in the bank: but most bankers will suggest that you might get a headache before too long if "wishing for it to be so" is your only plan for achieving it.

It's OK to try to *think* that you're going to be a great leader, but without the required action bias (doing something intentional about becoming that great leader), it's simply not going to happen.

To paraphrase many:

A goal without action is just a daydream.

This means that great leadership requires specific and intentional activity, not just good intentions. And the hope of absorbing leadership greatness by some sort of heavenly osmosis, or wishing that it might appear as a consequence of time served? Well, neither of those strategies will do. A daily Leadership Journal, however, that will do just nicely.

To help you better understand what I'm talking about, you can interpret *action bias* as any, or all of, the following:

> Determination. Persistence. Commitment. Resolve. Grit. Doggedness. Tenacity. Purpose. Endurance. Drive. Obstinacy.

...well, you get the idea.

Does that mean that in order to succeed you have to become bloody minded and ultra-focused on the goal to the detriment and exclusion of all others?

No. No it doesn't.

Does it mean that your wish to succeed and your drive for action should be so pervasive, all-consuming, and overwhelming that it serves to overshadow all else?

No again.

Does it mean that I'm giving you a hall pass with all personal relationships, work-life balance, perspective, and proportion?

Again, no.

It simply means that in order to succeed in becoming a great leader, you have to work on it—every day—in proportion, of course, but every day. Not for hours a day, not to the exclusion of all else, but every day, twenty minutes a day.

Every day. It's called "action bias," and if you don't have it, or are not prepared to develop it, forget it, you're not going to be a great leader. What, not ever? No, not ever. Why not take up candle-making? I hear that's rather fun.

Let's put on our best Doctor Doolittle lab coat and ask the lobsters what they think.

ASK A LOBSTER.

Remember, growth comes with a requirement for a certain amount of pain: there is no growth inside your comfort zone. Growth = Pain. It's built in. Think of yourself as a lobster—run with this, it's quite brilliant:

Lobsters have extremely hard and inelastic shells for protection against their rugged environment—living, as they do, among tight rocks and razor-sharp crevices. Their shells form an efficient defense, too, against predators since they cannot easily break open the tough carapace to get at the soft flesh inside.

This hard outer shell, though lifesaving, entirely restricts the lobster's growth since it does not have the ability to grow and expand with the lobster as it grows bigger.

Unfortunately, lobsters continue to grow throughout their lives, which means that whenever they find themselves so restricted and uncomfortable and confined by their current shell, since they have become more and more tightly packed within it, they have no choice other than to molt—come what may, they must eventually cast off their current shell and form a new one, a roomier, less confining and restricted one.

Every time they molt and form a new shell, lobsters typically grow around 15 percent in size and up to 40 to 50 percent in weight: we can only imagine how uncomfortable they must have been in their old shells, poor things.[8]

Once they have begun the process of shedding their current shells and forming new ones, which can take days, the lobster is at great risk from predation and attack and therefore must remain quite still and hidden during this especially perilous time.

---

8   Zoologists, marine biologists, and arthropod pedants, please don't write to complain—no, none of us know the true inner workings of the lobster's mind. Artistic license—get over it. If you like, you can make disparaging comments in your own book when you write it, I won't mind. Let's get back to the story. ☺

This regular cycle of "'discomfort—shed—risk—growth" is an extremely regular change-event in the life of the poor lobster since younger lobsters molt five or six times a year in their first few seasons, and adult lobsters molt maybe once or twice a year.

Growth for the lobster, therefore, involves pain and risk and frequency—sound familiar? It should.[9]

What we are talking about here (although somewhat obliquely, perhaps) is personal development.

Every leader should have their own personal development plan. Formalized. Written down. Tracked. Resourced. Followed. Invested time in. Reviewed. Amended.

You know, like every single one of their people are obliged to have.[10]

More of this in Chapter 12.

SO, SHOULD I REALLY JOURNAL EVERY DAY? LIKE, EVERY DAY? INCLUDING WEEKENDS? SURELY NOT SUNDAYS, RIGHT?

A great question.

Yes, you should pay some attention to your Leadership Journal every day. Yes, every day. Yes, that includes weekends too...and birthdays...and holidays. I know!

Action bias dictates that you should journal every single day—and not just on those occasions when you are mightily gripped by siren call of the journaling muse—even on those days when you can think of a million other things you'd much rather do.

"But what if I'm tired?" you ask.   Journal.
"But what if I'm short on time?" you implore.   Journal.

---

9   Yes, in case you hadn't connected the metaphorical dots, you're the lobster in this story: yes, you.
10 Some of you might be feeling rather uncomfortable right about now. Some of you jolly well should. Naughty-step for you, methinks.

"But what if I don't feel like it?" you complain.   Journal.
"But what if it's my birthday?" you plead.   Journal.

"Every day" is what determination, persistence, commitment, resolve, grit, doggedness, tenacity, purpose, endurance, drive, and obstinacy mean.

The world does not reward intentions, it rewards action. Won't is an option, but will is a decision.

Think of it this way:

Remember when your kiddies were wee little tots and relied on you for EVERYTHING? Nourishment, shelter, warmth, protection, love.

Babies are really good, and I mean *world-class*, at eating, sleeping, and pooping.[11]

How many days did you say to yourself over the insistent cries of an angry and hungry infant, "You know what, I'm just not feeling the love for this child today. It's Sunday, and I deserve a day off! I'll feed it tomorrow. It simply has to learn that life can be tough sometimes."[12]

Some things you just have to do—like it or not. And when you decide to have a baby, you accept that you just have to do—there simply isn't a choice. And, because there isn't a choice, like none, zero, you realize that, like the Borg,[13] resistance is futile. You roll up your sleeves, and you do the very best that you can every...single...day. But take heart, my intrepid leader, the first eighteen years are the toughest—after that it gets so much easier, I promise.

Leadership Journaling requires the same kind of mindset as parenting. If you're a leader, you journal—and that's that. If you're a parent, you change diapers—and that's that.

---

11   And trying your patience. Can I get an "Amen"?

12   If you're not horrified by those dreadful thoughts, and you don't yet have children, please, don't ever have any. Or pets. Or plants. Or a mortgage. Or a job. Or a relationship.

13   One for the Trekkies. You're welcome. And if you know what this means, "Dif-tor heh smusma," then you really are a seriously dedicated Trekkie. ☺

And, like parenting, the rewards significantly outweigh the effort—though it may not appear very obvious at times—especially in the early days...well, especially the first eighteen years, anyway. ☺

At the heart of persistence is love.

That's why you change all of the diapers and clean up the goo.

Do you love being a leader? If so, persistence, grit, and determination are already at hand in more than sufficient quantity. All it requires is a decision: persistence is a choice.

SO, MAKE A CHOICE.

What are you prepared to invest?

Again, like a mortgage, or a pension, the more investment you commit to—especially in the early days—the quicker you see growth on your return at the back end, and the sooner you can get your money back out: with lots of juicy interest.

Take a moment to consider what you're prepared to invest in terms of effort, especially in the early days, to your Leadership Journal journey.

Also, think about how long you will invest this effort before you make a decision as to whether or not your journal is delivering enough significant, sustainable returns in order to justify the effort. How long will you wait before you expect to see a good return on investment? Three days? Seven days? Thirty days? One hundred days?

Before you answer that, consider this: How long does it take to develop a brand-new habit? Most people tend to think it's somewhere between three and four weeks, however, modern research shows that it's more like sixty-six days. Just over two months to change your life.

Ask yourself whether or not you can muster enough action bias for at least an initial two-month investment of twenty minutes a day. Is twenty minutes a day for two months worth the investment for a return of significant improvements in skill, effectiveness, results, happiness, insight, and so on. It's waaaay less time than you need to dedicate to a child, or a pet, or antique car restoration, or watching TV, I promise.

GOOD NEWS/BAD NEWS

Here's the good news:

Twenty minutes a day is much better than an hour.

Journaling is one of those rare pursuits where twenty minutes of intentional activity is significantly better for you than an hour of going through the motions—and who doesn't love that notion?

A few minutes every morning for your Morning Momentum, and the same again for your Evening Evaluation is all that's required—but every day. This is significantly better for your development than, say, journaling once a week for three hours straight.

Committing to your Leadership Journal a little and often makes you think like a leader a lot and often. Hurrah!

For that reason, we don't want you to write and write and write a lot, but we do want you to think, and think, and think a lot—and this is how you do that, by prompting your thinking in the right way every day and by letting your subconscious work on the issues 24/7 in the background.

We do see the "a little and often" principle everywhere.

It's significantly better for good oral health to brush your teeth twice a day for three to four minutes at a time, rather than "save it all up" and go at your choppers like a steam train for a full hour every Sunday. Your teeth will be healthier, your toothbrush will last longer...and your gums won't bleed quite so much.

Equally, we all sleep every single day, rather than electing to stay awake twenty-four hours a day for five days straight and then sleep all weekend. This is a sure-fire way to either lose our minds or fall into a catatonic coma, I imagine.[14]

It's much better to eat a little every day, rather than starve all week and then gorge ourselves stupid at the weekend, right?

It's better to drink the right amount of water every day rather than nothing all week, then go crazy on a Wednesday like some sort of demented camel—nobody wants that sad look, least of all the camels.

I don't know how to say this gently, dear reader, but, when it comes to your Leadership Journal, don't be a demented camel!

Little and often, people, little and often: it's a simple rule.

Here's the not-so-great news:

There's no quick fix.[15]

Question: How old are you today? It's OK, I won't tell.[16]

So, it has taken you exactly that many years to develop into the leader that you are right now, right? Guess what? You don't turn that rusty old oil tanker around on a dime, I'm afraid.

Course-correcting a leader is exactly like course-correcting an oil tanker: it takes some planning, some organizing, some forethought, and a rather wide turning circle.

Most every leader has quite a long and complex list of issues to resolve. Those who make the most progress normally start by accepting that their Leadership Journaling is for the long haul. Some say that, like parenting, it's for the rest of your life—maybe it is, but that's up to you. The main thing to realize, however, is that you're on a journey of self-awareness and self-improvement, and it will take a while—it just will. Years.

Since we only have one life—and this isn't the practice-run for it, this is *actually it*—it's worth getting right. Right?

The Buddhists say that in order to think clearly, you first need to make time to think. Thinking is like a glass of river

---

14   You could fact check it if you could be bothered: let me know what you learn. Thanks.

15   I know, bummer!

16   Well, you don't look it. Well done, you. ☺

water, they argue.[17] You first need to let the cloudiness settle. Journaling helps you let the cloudiness settle. It helps get your thoughts in order, and it allows your subconscious to work on the important problems and issues while you get on with the job of doing whatever it is that you do every day.

GUIDED OR FREE FORM?

We are often asked this great question: Should your daily Leadership Journal follow a set pattern, set length, and set format; or should it be more extemporaneous, unstructured, and free form?

Those leaders who are rather independent and free thinking, and who tend to lead by intuition and fly by the seats of their pants, tend not to like the answer to this question. Those leaders who pride themselves on their radical and dynamic approach to management, tend not to like the answer to this question either. Those leaders who have been around the block a few times and who like to remind people at every opportunity that they made it here by hard work and perspiration and determination tend not to like the answer to this question. Those leaders who are not used to taking advice don't usually like the answer to this question.

So, at the risk of alienating flocks of you in a single stroke,[18] the answer to the question is that we much, much, much prefer daily "guided" journaling.

---

17   Well, they tend not to "argue" per-se; it's just not the Buddhists' way, but you get the idea.

18   There is no collective noun for leaders. Some might suggest a "bark" of leaders—see the joke in Chapter 5. Perhaps a better collective might be a "consensus" of leaders, or, even better, a "collaboration" of leaders. How about a "journal" of leaders? Too much? Too self-serving? Please yourself. Shall we start a petition?

Reasons why include:

1.Blind Spots

We use our Leadership Journal to unblock some of our most restrictive leadership blind spots. Since we don't know what our own blind spots are (because if we did, they wouldn't be blind spots—QED), we don't know what issues we are subconsciously avoiding and needing to work on.

Guided journaling forces us to consider issues across the whole leadership spectrum in a way that free form allows us to goof off with the "easy" stuff that wouldn't really benefit us at all in the long run. Naughty.

2.Progress, Milestones, and Guideposts

Guided journaling allows us to develop faster by building on concepts established some weeks earlier in a more organized and intentional way. The milestones and guideposts help us keep on track. You know what you're like when you think you see a squirrel!

3.Interest and Variety

Left to our own devices we can sometimes get a bit samey, stale, and somewhat stifled. You know it's true: don't sulk—it's not very becoming.

Who wants to eat Corn Flakes every day, like every single day, like every single day for every meal?[19] That's why those clever chaps invented the variety pack, after all.

4.Writer's Block

Seriously, who has got time for writer's block? Not I.

---

19 If you're a Kellogg's lawyer, that was just a joke. Not wanting to malign or disparage your wonderful organization. Personally, I do eat Corn Flakes—but not every single day.

BUT WHERE TO START, AND WHAT TO WRITE?

Another great question.

Apart from the four lists that you've already made from Chapter 1, and the various prompts that we have met along the way so far, the very best way for new journalers to start is, like most things, with the principle: crawl, walk, run. It's an old idea, I grant you, but it works nearly everywhere in life—and journaling is no exception.

Start (crawl) where everybody starts: with your A, B, Cs and 1, 2, 3s, of course:

To Crawl: ABC, 123

1 x Afformation : 2 x Beliefs : 3 x Commitments ©

Afformation

1 x daily afformation. See Chapter 16 for more detail on afformations.

Examples could be:

❖ Why am I so good at understanding what my people need from me?

❖ How is it that I come up with so many great new ideas for the business?

❖ How is it that I invest my energy in my people so wisely?

❖ Why is it so easy for me to express myself so clearly to my team?

Beliefs

2 x rock star belief, or inspiring quotations, that I will carry with me the whole day to help me succeed and overcome whatever life might throw at me today.

Examples could be:

- ❖ Get knocked down seven times, get up eight.
- ❖ Success = Failure + Persistence.
- ❖ History will always be our best teacher.

> If you can meet with triumph and disaster,
> And treat those two impostors just the same
> "IF—" by Rudyard Kipling

Commitments

3 x things that I absolutely must accomplish today. I simply will not go to bed till these three critical things are done.

Examples could be:

- ❖ Proofread that final report for the board.
- ❖ Clear my inbox.
- ❖ Balance my checkbook.
- ❖ Finish the chapter I'm reading.[20]

Three weeks of crawling should be good enough to make a decent start. Then it will be time to start to walk.

To Walk: ABCDEF ©

2 x Afformations : 2 x Beliefs : 2 x Commitments : 3 x Develop : 1 x Explore : 1 x Fix ©

Afformations

Two daily afformations. See Chapter 16 for more detail on afformations.

---

20   I was going to say, "Complete my Morning Momentum and Evening Evaluations in my Leadership Journal," but that's already a given, right? I do hope so, mister! Don't make me come down there!

Examples could be:

✦ Why am I able to deal with every challenge that comes my way?

✦ How do I manage to stay so productive every day?

Beliefs

Two daily powerful beliefs.

Examples could be:

✦ My level of gratitude will determine my attitude.

✦ When I'm confused it's good because I am about to learn something new.

Commitments

Two daily commitments.

Examples could be:

✦ Meeting with the R&D team to discuss new initiatives.

✦ Hand write personal "thank you" cards to my team.

Develop

A short list of three things I need to develop/progress/improve over the short term.

Examples could be:

✦ The company compensation/bonus plan.

✦ Our distribution footprint in the Eastern Territory.

Explore

One thing I need take time to learn more about today. Examples could be:

✧ Social selling platforms.

✧ EBITDA reporting.

Fix

One critical thing that really need fixing. Sure, it might not get totally resolved today, but you will at least recognize the issue and begin to figure out how to move the flag further down the beach. Examples could be:

✧ The sales function needs a much better, standardized, and repeatable process.

✧ Our hiring process isn't finding us enough A-players with enough speed and frequency.

Nice. A couple of weeks of walking should set you up nicely to begin to think about some gentle running.

To Run: www.mydailyleadership.com

A fully-guided, and gorgeous "run" would be a subscription to a uniquely different daily leadership greatness prompt that starts with the leadership basics, building every day over time to reveal the exceptional leader that you were destined to be.

Just as soon as your ABCs and 123s start to feel a little samey, and your development with ABCDEF has started to plateau, hop onto www.mydailyleadership.com to see a two-year guided Leadership Journaling framework with daily prompts that develop over time, stretching you in different ways every single day. The carefully-designed prompts build over time, guiding you and your thinking and capabilities to higher and higher levels of leadership skill and competence. You'll also find tools and guided mindset suggestions, and you can connect with others just like you on exactly the same journey. Think about it.

To understand a little what a subscription might look like, a short thirty-day tasting menu is offered towards the back of this book: see Chapter 17. *Bon appetite.*

SHORTEST DISTANCE OR FASTEST ROUTE?

Most people don't realize, but modern car GPSs allow the operator to set preferences for the shortest distance, the type of road, or the shortest journey time/fastest route. They also allow you to set preferences for particular gas stations, favorite routes, or real-time traffic updates—you know, a whole host of clever GPS-type stuff.

In truth, I prefer to drive on highways, freeways, and major roads wherever possible, believing that I must be moving more quickly because the road is wider and can carry more traffic: their speed-limits are higher too. This makes me always want to favor the six-lane over the two-lane whenever I am planning a drive to, well, practically everywhere.

The trouble with my "biggest and widest road" strategy is that you can only really see the cars directly in front of you, and you don't know what's happening a mile ahead, or on the roads all around you—but guess what, thanks to the eye-in-the-sky,[21] my GPS does.

Once I realized that GPSs can be programmed this way, and that they have a much, much, much broader view than I can possibly have, I now always prefer to set my GPS to "fastest route," not "biggest/fastest road types."

This means, of course, that I sometimes have to exit my favored six-lane and pootle along at 30 mph on a smaller road or two for ten miles or so. I tend to find the concept of exiting a freeway with a much higher speed limit in order to follow a country road rather unsavory because, well, bigger and faster is always better, right? But hey, the GPS is all-knowing, right? So,

---

21   Well, a satellite or two.

I bite my tongue and do as I'm told—it's often the best way, as my wife is wont to explain...quite often...very often.[22]

What does all of this have to do with Leadership Journaling? I'm so glad you asked. Sometimes, we must accept that we have to travel further in order to get there more quickly. And sometimes we have to slow down in order to speed up. Sometimes we even have to backtrack in order to get to our destination more quickly.[23]

However, I also have to accept that sometimes the trade-off for the shortest journey time is the more difficult and winding country lane—in other words, sometimes the trade-off for higher speed is increased frustration and difficulty in the short term.[24]

Another Story to Illustrate This Point

Mark Twain[25] in a letter[26] to a friend[27] began with these words, "I'm sorry this letter is such a long one, I simply didn't have time to write a short one."

The point that he was trying to make is that the "perfect" letter—fully edited, carefully considered, painstakingly crafted, and beautifully expressed—takes a good deal of thought, intentionality, and time.

---

22 All the time. **sigh**

23 A QUICK WORD OF CAUTION: We can sometimes become too reliant on technology. There was a guy who put the "fastest route" in his train app—it came up with a journey involving two stops and two train switches—but he searched for the quickest time, and that's what it came up with—two stops and two train switches. What he didn't realize, though, was that there was another option with no changes, BUT it was ninety-seconds longer than the route his app had suggested. I wonder which was the "right" trip, the first or the second?

24 Word!

25 Or maybe someone else—it's not very clear.

26 Or some say, a postcard. Really, it's not very clear.

27 Possibly. Again, we're not entirely sure. It may have been a friend—who knows? Sorry. But stick with it, it's still a genius journaling lesson.

A long and rambling piece of slightly disconnected and imprecise prose is relatively easy and therefore much quicker to get down on paper. However, even a shorter but much more carefully considered and well-edited piece with each word a study in eloquence and every phrase a masterpiece takes much more time. Such a clever chap was old Mr. Twain.[28]

We don't want you to take the shortest route (fewest words to write every day), but we do want you to take the fastest route—that's why we give you a guided framework. Sometimes, as mentioned, the fastest route in the longer term takes a little more effort in the shorter term.

So, think about this for a second—how big should an umbrella be?

ERGONOMICS

Ergonomics is defined as the science of fitting things to the user's needs—it aims to increase efficiency, productivity, ease of use, safety, and comfort.

So, did you decide yet how big should that umbrella be?

Big enough, right? Ha. Well, yes, but to be a trifle more precise:

The average male is five feet nine, and the average female is five feet four. The average male shoulder width is one foot six, and the female is one foot four.

An umbrella should be big enough to shelter a human body from the rain and small and light enough to carry.

Umbrellas are typically twenty-one to twenty-five inches wide, and they weigh around 0.64 lbs. To quote Goldilocks, "Juuuuust right."

How big should stairs be?

Around six to eight inches in height (risers) and double that in depth (treads). Why? Because of the length of human legs and the size of human feet. Goldilocks again.

---

28   Or someone. ☺

Rakes or ramps should rise one unit vertically for every eight units horizontally. Goldilocks.

Internal doors are two feet six inches wide and six feet six inches high. Goldilocks.

Bricks are about the size and weight that allows a person to grab and maneuver them when building walls.

Mattresses are almost never narrower than three feet—any less would make sleep impossible for the regular person.

The average length of a movie is eighty to 120 minutes—any longer would be beyond the length of time that a normal person can sit still, concentrate, and not need a toilet break.

Rooms should sit around 70°F.

Air should be about 78 percent nitrogen, 21 percent oxygen, and 1 percent other "stuff."

You get the idea.

Things that "work" are built around the human frame (scale) and requirements, and they need to bear in mind comfort and limitations in materials regarding stresses and compressive strengths, for example.

So, how much should I write in my journal?

You should write enough to make a significant difference but not so much as to demotivate you. Goldilocks-zone again.

Somewhere from ten to fifteen minutes in the morning (Morning Momentum), and ten to fifteen minutes in the evening (Evening Evaluation) is the Goldilocks zone: no more, but no less.

Consumer Tip #1:

Most people tend to happily complete their Morning Momentum, but then they tend to want to skip the Evening Evaluation. Why? Well, they've probably got beddie-byes, wooly slip-slops, and fleecy jimmy-jams on their mind, and almost nothing else seems quite so important at the end of a long and challenging day.

However, your Evening Evaluation should *never* be skipped—it's at least as important as your Morning Momentum: both serve to bookend the day.

Your Evening Evaluation has two key components: it serves to review the day and measure it against the intentions that you had set for it in your Morning Momentum, as well as giving your subconscious something important and juicy to chew on and resolve while you sleep. Your Evening Evaluation is peanut butter to your jelly—it's mac to your cheese—it's pancakes to your syrup—it's beans to your rice—it's thinly sliced quail breast and Jerusalem artichoke slowly cooked in a lemon and monk fish broth and pomegranate oil to your grated truffle in a light red wine and balsamic reduction...well, you get the idea.

Remember (at the risk of overstating it), wisdom comes from evaluated experience, not time served. The clue to why the Evening Evaluation is so critical is in the word "evaluation," that means reflect, consider, weigh, gauge. It has the added benefit of asking your subconscious to get creative—it's the key to it all.

But you don't have to just take my word for it; let's see what the inimitable Mr. Thomas A. Edison Esq. had to say on the matter of Evening Evaluations, shall we?

He said, "Never go to sleep without a request to your subconscious."

Nice one, Tommy Ed. ☺

Back to our earlier question: What is the minimum length of time I should journal before I see a positive return? A week? A month? Surely not more than a month, right? A week or two will do, won't it?

Well, the answer is ergonomics, stairs, and umbrellas again—it should fit the users' needs and, like a well-set-up GPS, it should give us the fastest route, not necessarily the shortest distance.

So, can you live with twenty to thirty minutes a day, every day, for at least a year, possibly two?

Too much? Too long a commitment? Too much like hard work? Is it over?[29]

MORE JUICE—FEWER LEMONS

What we've just been talking about, of course, is the trade-off between efficiency versus effectiveness.

I'm quite sure that you already know the difference between the two, but just for completeness, let's jot them down quickly:

Efficiency is doing things right.
Effectiveness is doing the right things.

We see so many managers and leaders spend so much of their effort looking for more and more efficiency improvements—shave a second off here, reduce a pound of weight there, ask him to do both roles, use technology to speed that up, multitask, stretch goals, reduce cost, but increase output—more, more, more.

Basically, "More juice out of the same lemons."

In fact, "More juice out of fewer lemons."

In fact, "More juice out of significantly fewer lemons."

In fact, "More juice than last year, from significantly fewer lemons this year!"

In fact, "All the juice out of all the lemons, or else we'll get someone else to squeeze them!"

And, sure, efficiency has some merit, of course. Nobody likes "waste"—we all want a streamlined set of workflows and

29   See "lifelong learners" in Chapter 6.

processes ensuring that all assets are utilized to their maximum effect.

Plant Utilization to the high 90s.

On Time in Full to the high 90s.

Net Promoter Score to the high 90s.

Customer Retention to the high 90s.

Employee Satisfaction to the high 90s.

Return on Assets to the high 90s.

World-class engagement and click-through rates.

You get the idea—optimal efficiency and stretch targets in ALL things.

BUT, our addiction to efficiency and "more" is, in the end, a fool's errand.

MORE, even in journaling, is not always better.

Medicine is good. More medicine does not get patients cured more quickly—it often kills them. Too much medicine is often poisonous. More medicine is bad.

Food, great. Overeating and obesity, bad.

Handwashing, great. OCD handwashing all day? Bad.

Internal decorations at holiday time are good. Nice. Pretty. To be encouraged. But the whole outside of the house with a forty-foot Santa, reindeer on the roof, and five hundred thousand bulbs sucking up half of the power from the local power grid practically blinding your neighborhood for a quarter of a mile radius in the middle of the night? Behave.

You get the idea...everything to excess is bad! Yes, everything. Including the tireless pursuit for efficiency.

Busy is not always better.

Efficiency is better, but it will only get you so far.

Efficiency is believing that sweating the assets even harder will allow you to out-work the competition thereby gain market share and increased Earnings Before Interest Tax Depreciation and Amortization and, ultimately, we hope, profitability.

I've even heard leaders say, "Folks, we might get outsmarted by our competitors, but as God is my witness, we will never be outworked."

Forgive my French, but what a load of old leadership bull-shit! Short sighted. Leading by fear. Killing creativity. Stifling risk. Awful.

I'd MUCH rather hear a leader say, "We might get outworked by our competitors here and there, and that's OK, but as God is my witness, we will never be outsmarted by them!" YES! This is a leader I would back—a leader much more interested in effectiveness than efficiency.

The first leader is an efficiency freak, and efficiency ALWAYS leads to quality spills, increased turnover, lower profits, more stress, and dissatisfied and underserved customers.

Effectiveness will get you (and the business) much further, much faster, with much less stress. Effectiveness (doing the right things) is, at its heart, "strategy." And intelligent strategy ALWAYS eats hard work for breakfast.

You, the leaders, should always look to work smarter, not harder, and you should be leading by example, always, right? This way your people, your business, your culture should *all* be working smarter, not harder.

Working smarter eats working harder for lunch. Journaling smarter eats journaling harder for lunch.

Your smart daily Leadership Journaling is your leadership development microwave, your fast-forward button, because it forces you to think and develop strategically as well as tactically. Just look at how bees get things done by working smarter than harder.

DO BEES BUILD THE BEST BUSINESSES?

When we think of the humble honey bee, we think of enterprise, frenzied activity, the ceaseless pursuit of a single goal.

We think of tireless industry and single-minded efficiency, sacrifice of the individual for the greater good of the hive.

We wish our business was as well organized as the hive. Everyone taking orders from the queen. Everyone serving to the best of their ability, unquestioning, and without complaint. Marvelous—or so we think.

We've all heard the expression "as busy as a bee" and wish our people were so oriented.

But, as mentioned above, we'd be wrong trying to have our business emulate the bee and the industry of the beehive if it were only for the appreciation of those ideals.

The reasons that I really like the way the bees do business and the real reason that bees do so well is not down to work ethic and their enterprising and selfless approach to efficient industry, it's down to the opposite. The single best thing about bees is that they are wonderfully and gloriously inefficient, not that they are supremely well organized.

Bees are hardwired to be meaningfully and efficiently inefficient.

The queen bee does not tell all the bees to work harder, plunder faster, increase efficiency, and get more juice out of the lemons because she knows that that is the sure-fire way to certain death for the hive. The leader knows that if her bees only plundered the nectar from the flowers which the hive is currently aware of, it wouldn't take too long before there would be no more flowers, no more lemons, and no more bees.[30]

Bees spend a good proportion of their time farming but an even bigger portion of their time hunting for new fields to farm. They are encouraged to wander around hunting for pastures new, uncharted lands, unmined riches—sometimes up to eight miles from the hive! Think about that for a second. How is your new product development process set up right now to skate to where the puck will be? How much of your resources are

---

30   And what would I put on my morning toast then? Exactly.

allocated to new markets and new products? How does your marketing and sales team go about its business? How much time do you spend being intentionally inefficient?

Once the bees find new and rich seams to mine (mixing my metaphors again—sorry), they return to the hive and explain by a process of (happy) dances where the new, new thing is to be found, and off they all go.

The future success of the hive was ensured specifically because the hive was encouraged to set off:

On a mission to explore strange new worlds,
To seek out new life,
And new civilizations,
To boldly go where no bee has gone before.[31]

Now then, to extend the analogy even further...

Sometimes, despite all their best foraging efforts, there are simply no new opportunities to be found—despite how amazingly efficient they have all been in their inefficiency—and despite all of the hollering and cajoling the leader might have attempted—and despite whatever incentives and encouragements were promised.

Sometimes it's time to stop making black and white TVs, or renting DVDs in boxes, or making photography paper, and it's time to step off the efficiency merry-go-round, and step on to the carousel of effectiveness, and find new markets to operate in, or new products to sell.

Once this happens, the queen, the leader, tells the team to get ready for a big change—and off they trot[32] as a single-minded unit, without complaint, without hesitation, without anyone left behind, without any fuss, and without any trepidation. Efficient effectiveness. Marvelous!

---

31   Shatner! Yes! What a great leader Kirk was. Picard? Don't make me laugh. If you know, you know.
32   Yes, yes, Captain Pedantic—I do know, I know, bees don't trot—mixing metaphors again for artistic effect. Chill.

Businesses (leaders) should learn how to be intentionally and effectively inefficient—it leads to efficient effectiveness.[33]

Busy is not better. Smart is better. Your Leadership Journal should be designed to make you more effective, not just more efficient—bee-like, but in the good, less sting-like way.

PRACTICE DOES NOT MAKE PERFECT.

Despite what you may have heard, practice does not make perfect. Practice makes permanent. Only perfect practice makes perfect. Crappy practice makes, well, permanent crappiness.

The world's best athletes, musicians, professionals all share one common trait: they practice every day despite already being among the best of the best of the best. Intentional, purposeful practice, not half-hearted, tick-a-box-and-get-a-pat-on-the-back practice. Remember Novak and Sir David from earlier?

Another Story

I remember when my son, Alexander, first started taking piano lessons; he was around eight or nine years old. There were days when he was really enthusiastic and eager to practice; and there were days, of course, when he'd rather have been doing almost anything else than trying to perfect a difficult passage of music, or preparing for a concert, or an upcoming proficiency exam.

When he had asked for piano lessons, and we bought him the piano that he had requested, he had assured us that he would practice every day (yes, every day—sound familiar?). And then, at the agreed time, we would call up to his room reminding him that it was time to practice.

On good days he would come thundering down the stairs with a big grin on his face and would often stay at his piano

---

33   Yes, you do have to read that one a few times, unfortunately. Write it down, why not? In your journal? Good question. Yes, in your journal. See, you're getting the idea nicely.

thirty to forty minutes beyond the established thirty-minute minimum. Those were good and developmental and intention-ally-perfect practice days.

However, on other days he would trudge down to the music room with a face like thunder and would set the timer making sure to not go one second beyond the absolute minimum agreement...and, on those days, the very second that the thirty-minute beeper sounded, he would slam down the lid of the piano and be off again, tearing up the stairs like a shot to play on his PlayStation before the last bleep was able to get out.

Sometimes, I would come home from work halfway through Alex's practice, and within ten seconds or less I could hear whether or not this was an intentional, effort-based, mindful practice session, or whether or not he was going through the motions in order to tick a box and get back to his room on the very first "b" of the very first bleep.

Intentional practice sounded like unhurried determination. Repeating the same phrase or short passage again and again till it was just right—sounding just as the composer had intended. Then, he would try to link these passages, trying them together and together again. Building on a theme. Trying a difficult few bars, very slowly, and then a little quicker, and then quicker still.

"Intentionality" sounded like someone was developing deeper understanding and embedding long-term muscle memory. Intentionality sounded important and worthwhile.

Tick-a-box practice sounded like deep breath—head down—start at the beginning—count the seconds—make mistakes—push through unabated—keep going till the end—rinse and repeat till the alarm goes off. It sounded like a snow plough thundering through the icy drifts: snow plough piano-playing. Tick-a-box-practice sounded almost worthless: doing more long term damage than good.

This is exactly the same for Leadership Journaling. Intentionality looks like thoughtful, meaningful reflection.

Purposeful. Focused. A few well-chosen but emotional-ly-charged sentences that really get the juices going.[34]

Tick-a-box journaling looks like a few scribbled sentences. No real depth of thought. No intentionality. No real reflec-tion. Nothing that requires sorting out in one's mind. Hurried. Meaningless, vapid platitudes. Count the seconds till the alarm goes off. Snow plough journaling.

Remember, Lionel Messi, or any other world-class (insert profession) practices with intentionality every single day—this despite already being among the very best in the world. If Lionel Messi has the fortitude and enough professional humil-ity to show up to training and intentionally getting better every day, so, too, should you, dearest reader.

QUICK QUESTION:

Did Messi become the best in the world as a consequence of his willingness to intentionally try to get better every day, or is it that he was already the best in the world, and he is very intentional about staying there? Oooh, it's that pesky chicken and egg again. Cause and effect. Tricky.

Whether you're the kind of person who is intrinsically or extrinsically motivated, your Leadership Journaling success is entirely correlated to the amount of effort and energy you invest in your commitment to your journaling practice. Just like Alex learning to play the piano better, and Messi perfecting his soccer genius, right?

The amount of effort and energy you invest in your journal-ing is entirely correlated to your level of conviction and belief in the value of the ultimate payoff/reward.

Let's take a look at belief in payoff/reward.

---

34 For "juices" read "subconscious." ☺

JUST KEEP SWIMMING, JUST KEEP SWIMMING...

In the 1950s, Dr. Curt Richter, a research professor at Harvard, conducted a series of rather grizzly experiments with rats. He wanted to discover differences between how long wild and lab-bred rats could tread water.[35]

He found that the average adult rat could tread water for around fifteen minutes—much less time than was expected. At around the fifteen minute-mark almost all the rats would give up treading water and they would, well, simply drown.

But then Dr. Richter made a truly startling discovery. If he took the rats out of water mere second before drowning, dried them off, let them rest for a minute or two, and then put them right back in the water, guess how long they would now swim for. Seriously, have a guess.

Another minute or two?

Another five minutes?

Another ten minutes?

Another fifteen minutes?

Another thirty minutes by some sort of rat magic?

No!

Another sixty hours!

What? You read that right, dear reader, another sixty hours! Days and days of continual swimming.[36]

But that simply doesn't make any logical sense, right? From fifteen minutes, to sixty hours, how is that even possible? It seems way too counterintuitive to be true—but it *is* true.

Astonishing.

The question then is, why? Why can the rats who have been reintroduced to the water hold out for such an incredible and astonishing length of time?

---

35 Who knows why? Probably important. Just go with it.

36 No, for real! Honestly. Here's the peer-review evidence: https://www.psychologyib.com/ib-psychology-blog/you-look-like-a-drowned-rat

Conviction.

Belief in the eventual payoff and reward.

According to the research team, the only thing that changed between their first submersion and the second was these particular rats have a clear vision of a better future—a rescued future. They had the conviction that all their effort would ultimately pay off—and so they persisted...and persisted...and persisted.

Don't misunderstand me, I'm not advocating that you journal for sixty hours straight, like Dr. Richter's rats, but what I am saying is that if you BELIEVE in the value of persistence, your level of commitment to the process will significantly improve. And, according to Peter Pan (yes, that Peter Pan—of Lost Boys and Tinkerbell, and Captain Hook fame), "The moment you doubt whether you can fly, you cease forever to be able to do it."

We close the chapter with this thought: if exhausted lab rats can endure and persist beyond their natural limits, fueled only by the power of belief and conviction, what could you achieve in the persistence of your Leadership Journaling even through whatever hardship may lie ahead? The question is: Do you believe, really believe?

Let's find out.

Find a convincing space in your Leadership Journal to write and complete these words:

I am committed to my daily Leadership Journaling practice because I believe in the immense power of marginal gains. I know, too, that my ability to succeed is directly related to my belief in my own determination and conviction in the value of my daily Leadership Journaling practice.

And then, find an inspiring way to finish off this sentence:

Whenever I feel my determination to Leadership Journaling success wane, I will do/remember these three things in order to renew my commitment and conviction...

1.

2.

3.

Marvelous. ☺

"Constant repetition carries conviction.
Success is the sum of small efforts—
repeated day in and day out."
—Robert Collier

CHAPTER 4

Thomas Jefferson was wrong.

Information is not power.

BEWARE WHAT YOU PAY ATTENTION TO.

Most CEOs and senior executives take enormous pride in the way they can interpret the numbers in a complex spreadsheet, monthly report, or the latest set of management accounts: for all I know, you may feel the same way too.

They believe that the answer to better business performance lies deeply hidden somewhere in the monthly key performance indicators, profit and loss statement, balance sheet, cash flow projections, revenue forecasts, and so on. And their job, they believe, is to use their vast experience, extraordinary training, and wily foxlike cunning to pore over the data in some sort of unique way in order to divine what the company should do next, and where its resources should best be allocated in order to most increase business performance and shareholder value.

They applaud themselves for being able to "see beyond the numbers" with much more perspicacity and alacrity than anyone else in the boardroom. They have, they believe, a borderline savant's gift for number and pattern recognition. They can, they believe, somehow cut through all the noise and get right to the heart of the matter—often within mere seconds.[1]

And sometimes, I suppose, by dint of probability if nothing else, their interpretations/predictions will sometimes be broadly correct—in the same way that soothsayers of old used chicken entrails (hieromancy), or studied the behavior of birds (ornithomancy), or watched how melted wax built up (ceromancy)[2] to advise the king whether or not the crops this year might do well, whether the queen might bear a successor, or whether the faltering battle might turn in their favor. If you guess enough times, the little ball will eventually end up in 17 black—but it says nothing about your powers of foresight when

---

1   Oooh, what clever old sausages they are.

2   Basically, any old "...*mancy*" will do, it seems.

it eventually does—despite you telling yourself how clever you were for having put your last ten dollars in the world on it.

Good leaders, I grant you, do seem to have a knack for spotting patterns in the clouds. When we take data, filter out all of the background extraneous noise, we are left with information. Data is extremely broad, information is more narrow and specific. Information is, therefore, a subset of data.

Good leaders make decisions based on information. Good information leads to good decisions, they believe. See Chapter 11 for much more on this.

Poor interpretation of good (accurate) information, however, sometimes leads to very bad decision-making. And, since the decision was based on "factual data sets," the person making the decision typically has a very hard time moving away from their initial decision—but that's a conversation for another time.

Take the example of the UK ambulance service:

In 2013, the University of Sheffield undertook the largest ever study of the response times and service levels of this critical, life-saving service.

It was reported that the general public complained that ambulances seemed to be taking longer and longer to arrive at patients' homes—especially during very busy times of the month. They noted, too, that the demand for ambulances had been rising steadily for some years.

The researchers assessed a long list of key performance indicators so they could help the service become more efficient. They started to measure "time": on average how long each operator took to deal with the incoming emergency telephone calls. The time it then took to dispatch a vehicle to the required address. How long it took the paramedics to get to the address. How long it then took to deal with the patient at the address, and then how much time it took to get back to the hospital with the patient aboard.

Lots and lots and lots of gorgeous time-based data was gathered and processed.

After having analyzed the reams and reams of data, it was decided that each call operator should be given a time target—an average of sixty seconds to receive a call, assess a call, and have an ambulance enroute to the patient.

How gorgeously efficient.

It was also decided that the optimal target response time from a received call to the driver arriving at the patients' location should be only eight minutes—and call operators and drivers were given this key information—targets were given and measured. Operators, drivers, and paramedics were now being assessed based on "time" (speed).

What a tremendously forward-thinking decision, right? This eight minute target was bound to drive up customer satisfaction and net promoter scores: to say nothing of onslaught of the inevitable 5-star glowing Google reviews for the improved service.

Imagine then that an operator received two calls at almost the exact same time. One call was to an address fifteen minutes away. The other call was to an address five minutes away. Remembering the target KPI "time," which of these two calls would *you* likely prioritize if your only target was "time"? The closest address around the corner, right? Then you'd have extra wiggle room to get to the second patient, right?

This way the data could report that most calls have an ambulance on site within eight minutes. Gorgeous.

The trouble is that more people were suddenly now dying before the ambulance even arrived at the hospital.

Oh, not gorgeous. But why?

Well, what if the call from the address fifteen minutes away was because of a suspected heart attack—and the closer address was for something much more benign—a minor burn from touching a hot pan on the stove, perhaps? If the target KPI is exclusively "time-based," terrible consequences unfolded. In other words, a good and reasonable and sensible and "obvious" time-based KPI was leading to very bad outcomes. Unintended consequences. Belay those 5-star reviews, after all!

It was eventually agreed that the real overriding objective should be "life," not "time." Operators should be given all the time they need to properly assess an incoming call in terms of its severity and not merely in pursuit of its location and handling-efficiency.

Ambulances are now targeted with an average seven minutes to get on-scene (yes, less than before) for a life-threatening issue—a Category 1 event, but longer if it's a Category 2 event (eighteen minutes). Category 3 issues were given KPIs of up to 120 minutes. Category 4 issues were targeted up to 180 minutes, which is, of course, a looooong way off the original target of eight minutes for everyone and everything, no matter the severity or location.

Data, you see, if misinterpreted and mismanaged can be very tricky and dangerously misleading.

MISLEADING DATA

Sometimes (often) data misleads us all.

In 2007, the Colgate toothpaste company ran a series of advertising campaigns stating quite clearly that 80 percent of dentists recommend their product—you probably saw the advert yourself. Quite convincing stuff, right? Based on this contention, most consumers would assume that Colgate toothpaste was the best choice for their dental health, right? Well, maybe, but maybe not.

The data was "accurate," of course, otherwise the advertising standards agency would have vetoed the advert. But the information as presented was somewhat misleading. The adverts suggested that 80 percent of dentists preferred Colgate over all other toothpaste brands. However, the survey had only asked the dentists to list as many brands of toothpaste that they would recommend—the word "Colgate" was on 80 percent of the lists that dentists liked or knew—it did not measure what position Colgate was on the lists at all. There may well have been another brand that was every dentist's number one choice. Hmmmm, Colgate's original claim is not quite the same 'convincing' claim at all now, is it?

Leaders use data and information all the time to make decisions; but oftentimes the data can be misleading, or worse, just plain wrong. Average leaders make decisions based on data. Better leaders make decisions based on information. But, if we're aspiring to greatness, remember, we need to keep going, we need to dig a little deeper into those business numbers.

As we have seen, information is a subset of data: it is data with all the extraneous background noise removed. But, as mentioned, we shouldn't be making decisions based on information alone.

The linking of all the separate bits of information is what "knowledge" looks like. More often than not this knowledge comes from training and experience, and is often also a function of time served. And lots of leaders, as we have seen, stop there, relying on their experience and knowledge—they've been around the block a few times, and they think that if it was good enough to get me here, it will be good enough forever more. Tsk, tsk.

But not you, dear reader, not you. Knowledge is long way away from where the best leaders make their decisions.

Great leaders have developed a deeper and rarer skill—a skill that looks far, far, far beyond the numbers that anyone else on the board or team sees. A skill that is in woefully short supply: insight. Great leaders focus on developing insight— good leaders do not—they don't seem to have the stamina or the wit for it.[3]

---

3   How do they develop this insight muscle? Go on, take a guess. Yes! By daily guided Leadership Journaling. www.mydailyleadership.com

Insight is knowing which pieces of knowledge to engage and link together—often in new and unexpected ways. Marketing teams, the great ones, at any rate, try very hard to uncover new elements of consumer insight in order to weave new and interesting pieces of magic into their campaigns and communications. They do this in an effort to differentiate their products/services/brand from their competitors in the minds of their targeted market segments.

Insight is in very short supply right across the leadership world.

Insightful leaders don't just explore the things that make sense—they try the things that don't make sense. "Obvious" and "sensible" and "rational" things are normally too obvious, and sensible, and rational to work—and everyone else does them.

If I had a bus, or a fleet of them, I'd much rather charge, say, thirty dollars a mile, than the usual fifty cents that all other bus companies charge, wouldn't you? Impossible, right? Can't be done, right? Market forces, right? Supply and demand, right?

I don't know, let's ask The Big Red Bus Company what they think.

Your daily Leadership Journal builds insight like nobody's business. But what does insight look like, and where does it come from?

INSIGHT IS LIKE AN OPTICAL ILLUSION.

Have you ever looked hard at an optical illusion that purports to show both a horse drinking as well as a cockerel on a wooden fence? Or an image that claims to show either an old man talking or a young woman asleep? It's always extremely simple to see one of the reported images, but the second image often eludes us...that is until, quite suddenly, it doesn't. There comes a time when you squint your eyes a certain way, or you orient the paper at the right angle, or you allow your gaze to relax just enough—when suddenly, there it is—as clear as day—the horse, the woman, the talking faces, and not the vase.

And, once you see it for the first time, you can't unsee it. And every time you see the image again, you can easily switch between the two images.

Insight is like this—blindingly obvious when you do see it, but really difficult to see, well, until you do. And then, once you see it, you can't unsee it.

Three Random Examples:

What is the most widely printed book in history?

The Bible? The Quran? Harry Potter?
Nope.
It's the IKEA catalogue—more than two hundred million printed every year.
Now that you know it, it's rather obvious, isn't it?[4]

How does bottled water in the supermarket, naturally filtered for ten thousand years through Icelandic volcanic rock, have an expiration date on it? How has the water taken ten millennia to reach us—and now that it's on the supermarket shelf, it has a sell-by date of April 18th?

The expiration date on bottled water is for the bottle, not the water. After so many months, plasticides from the bottle leach into the water, tainting it.
Now that you know why, it's rather obvious.

---

4   Although December 2021 saw the last ever printed catalogue. In 2016 IKEA catalogue circulation reached its peak of two hundred million copies printed. More than double the number of bibles in the same year.

Blood banks in Sweden notify the blood donors by sending them a text whenever their blood is used by the hospital to help save someone's life.

What does that do to the rates of blood donation do you think?
Retention rates soar. Recruitment soars. Exactly.
Now that you see the insight, it's blindingly obvious.
Why doesn't every country do the same? You tell me.

You can't see insight till you see it, and then you can't unsee it, and you wonder why everyone else doesn't see it also.

The thing is, you can't go to college to get a PhD in insight.

You can't go to a business coach and demand to be taught it.

You can't expect insight to magically arrive as a consequence of time served, because it never does.

Insight is the stuff you can't learn from others; and you can't see it till you see it.

Insight is blindingly obvious once it has been revealed, but the revealing of it is the real genius. To see what others can't see, to divine where the well should be dug, or to predict where the lightning will strike, or to skate to where the puck will be—not because you can predict the future, but because you've learned that lightning will hit the tallest spot that gives it the path of least resistance, so you fix a lightning rod to the side of the house, and you sleep soundly in your bed at night.

Experience, age, and a raft of university degrees doesn't lead to increases in insight—in fact, they often squash it.

Some favorite examples from the business world to illustrate the rarity and (obvious, not obvious) power of commercial insights:

Bata Shoes

In the world of footwear manufacturing, they tell the story of Bata Shoes even today.

Towards the end of the nineteenth century, colonial Africa was starting to open up to the West. Representatives of British shoe manufacturers flocked to Africa in order to investigate the size of the potential opportunity for their wares.

Having examined all of the data and information, all of the representatives reported back to their respective headquarters that there was simply no market for shoes in Africa, since almost nobody in the country wears them.

All, that is, except for the Bata Shoe Company representative. He reported back something else—something that required looking beyond the data, beyond the statistics. He reported back something that required insight. "There's a huge and untapped opportunity here!" he reported. "Almost nobody in Africa wears shoes."

As a consequence of this single piece of insight, to this very day Bata Shoes appear all over Africa, even in the remotest corners. Bata's shoes are known as the shoes of Africa.

Walmart

Very early on, Sam Walton declared that he was going to build his biggest stores "in the middle of nowhere."

But that sounds crazy, right? Who builds stores in the middle of nowhere? All other retailers were building stores in the middle of the most densely populated areas—not our Sammy.

He reasoned that the "middle of nowhere" (the empty spaces between two or three towns) would make much more sense: larger shopper radius—easier and quicker to drive fifteen miles on "out of town" roads than to drive five miles inner city. Middle of nowhere has lower rates, fewer competitors, cheaper land costs, and the like.

"In the middle of nowhere" was the foundation of Walmart. Good insight, Sam.

Apple

As you might imagine, Apple's journey is literally littered with countless examples of leadership insight.[5] One of my Steve Jobs' favorites is the iMac story.

In 1998, just as Steve Jobs had returned to the troubled Apple, the iMac was about ready to roll: fully designed, tested, and industrialized. They were just about to launch when Steve Jobs called a meeting of the engineers to announce that they weren't launching it in the beige color that had become the standard for all computer consoles—the iMac, he declared, would be available in four radical and different colors!

The engineers went bonkers—more inventory, more components, more complexity, launch delay, increased cost, lower sales forecast accuracy, and so on. The "crazy" decision would delay the launch and seriously threaten the existence of the brand. Nightmare.

Jobs said, "We are going to do four colors, because color is a critical way that people express themselves. This will make the computer a way that people express themselves."

Did Jobs ask its customers by carrying out expensive and protracted surveys before he made this momentous decision? No. This kind of insight does not come from a spreadsheet, data, or the findings of a market research program—it comes from intentional practice.

Put simply, the new iMac saved Apple...and the color palette guaranteed the success of the iMac.

As a consequence of them being so vibrant and colorful, you simply couldn't walk into a room with a new iMac in it and not see it.

---

5   The size and success of Apple alone serves to illustrates my argument, I feel.

Their advert declared:

> *SORRY, no beige.*
> *Apple.*
> *Think different.*

"Think different" is what insight is about.

OUTSIDE OF THE WORLD OF WORK...

Of high buses, and low bridges.

There was once a double-decker bus in the UK. It was, like all double-deckers, a standard fourteen feet six inches high. A new driver who was unfamiliar with the route for this particular bus took a wrong turn and ended up going down a lane that had an ancient Roman stone-built bridge over it. The under-side of the bridge was, unfortunately, only fourteen feet four inches from the ground. The Romans simply hadn't predicted double-decker busses, it seems. The driver assumed the bus was shorter than the bridge, or that the bridge was taller than the bus: neither of these things were true.

Of course the top of the bus crashed into the underside of the stone bridge at around 20 mph.

Fortunately, there was nobody on the upper deck when this calamitous event occurred else there would have been even more problems.

Builders, welders, fire trucks, police, structural and civil engineers were quickly called to survey the mayhem to work out how best to free the bus while protecting the integrity of the ancient and valuable monument.

Measurements were taken. Plans were drawn up. Cherry-pickers were ordered. Steel struts, sandbags,[6] and shiny new hard hats were requisitioned.

---

6   Because, well, what disaster is free of sandbags, after all?

The inevitable local news crews arrived.

A six-year-old local lad was wandering past the scene on his way home from school. He asked a policeman what all the ruckus was about. The friendly police officer explained that they were trying to free the bus from the ancient bridge without having to dismantle and rebuild the bridge since the bus was well and truly stuck and couldn't easily or safely be separated from the bridge without dangerous torches or cutting equipment. Most of all they were trying to minimize further damage to the historically-important bridge.

The boy, looking at the chaotic scene, asked why they didn't just let the air out of the tires and reverse the bus out![7]

Of fighters and flack.

Abraham Wald was a Jewish statistician who had been chased out of Hungary in the second World War. He made his way to America and eventually took up a position in New York with the Statistical Research Group (SRG).

Wald was given the task of figuring out how to best armor plate the underside of bombers such that their chances of returning from their perilous bombing missions significantly increased—a little over half of the Allied aircraft were being shot down never to return.

The obvious answer seemed to be "install lots more armor—everywhere." But armor makes planes heavy and shortens their range. It made them much slower and less agile—and therefore much easier to shoot down. Tricky.

The SRG team was tasked with optimizing armor plating to ensure that more planes returned safely from their dangerous missions.

Wald and his team started to review the bullet hole patterns from returning aircraft. They noticed, of course, that the

---

7   Mike drop! Insight! Genius.

bullet holes were not uniformly distributed—there were more holes in the fuselage and fewer in the engines. The obvious answer, of course, was to protect the areas where the planes were sustaining most hits—represented by most holes, right?

Wrong!

The armor, Wald declared in the teeth of popular opinion, must go where the bullet holes aren't, not where they are.

Think about it this way—the holes in the planes that returned weren't that much of a threat. Why? Well, because they returned home. Wald's eureka moment was when he tried to figure out where the holes must have been in the planes that didn't return home since they must have been more deadly—otherwise these planes would have returned also.

A great leadership lesson in insight for us all—remember it; it will be useful one day, I promise—the armor goes where the bullet holes aren't.

Of the freshest of fish.

The Japanese palate highly prizes good quality, fresh fish.

As population grew in the 1970s, demand for fresh fish increased. But, due to the lack of sufficient regulation or the policing of it, the shores around Japan were heavily plundered: the catches were thinning out, with smaller and smaller fish and lower quality produce. This was becoming a problem of national importance.

As a consequence of this, the Japanese fishermen had to build bigger boats, fund larger crews, and go further afield for longer in order to find the bigger, higher quality fish.

The problem however was twofold: the price of fish in the markets went up; and, more importantly, since they had to fish much further out, by the time the fish were brought to shore three or four days later, the fish were not quite so fresh.

The sophisticated Japanese palate was still not happy.

In order to keep the fish "fresh-tasting," the fishermen had to build even bigger boats with ice factories in them so that once the fish was caught, it could be immediately frozen.

Prices went up again, of course, to accommodate costs.

But the sophisticated Japanese palate could tell fresh from frozen.

The consumer was increasingly unhappy—prices further up, quality further down.

The solution, they thought, was to build even bigger boats and install enormous sea-water tanks where the caught fish could swim till it could be brought ashore and then killed "fresh."

Prices went even further up to accommodate increased costs.

But unfortunately the sophisticated Japanese palate could tell fresh fish from "fresh but got a bit flabby and lazy swimming in a tank for a few days" fish.

The consumer was grumpier still.

Fishing companies were at a loss to know what to do next.

The solution was inspired, or should I say, "insightful"? A local zooologist[8] suggested that they try a shark in the sea-water tanks.

A small shark would be sure to keep the fish on their toes, so to speak.

The fish were caught fresh and then held in the seawater tanks on board the fishing vessels—along, of course, with an eagerly-awaiting peckish shark or two. Sure, the sharks ate a few of the fish, but the remaining fish were like Olympic athletes by the time they were brought ashore a few days later.

The Japanese palate was finally satisfied once again.

Shark.

Genius.

Insight.

---

8   Three Os? Crazy.

Of the great fake off.

In the 1950s, food technicians developed a pre-made cake mixture that only required the baker to add a little water, mix with a fork, and pop in the oven. Et voila—instant (well, almost) cake. Super simple, super convenient, super smart. I bet you imagine that people were forming a line that stretched out the shop and round the corner to buy the stuff, right? Nope—it was an overnight disaster!

The developers simply couldn't understand it—all of their research indicated that their new super-mixture was the perfect solution for the time-restricted housewife who still wanted to give her husband a nice piece of home-cooked cake right after dinner.[9] Their forecasts all predicted that the packets of new powdered wizardry would practically fly off the shelves. Fly off the shelves, it did not: it was an unmitigated proverbial flop.

They parachuted the behavioral psychologists in to figure out what was amiss.

Their moment of insight appeared when they realized that simplicity did not trump authenticity when it came to wives baking cakes for their husbands.

They looked beyond the data and realized that they needed to change the recipe. The new Betty Crocker mixture from General Mills required that the baker now crack an egg into the cake mix (rather than simply adding a little water) before putting it into the oven, and sales went through the roof! Why? Well, now it was cooking! Simply adding water wasn't cooking, but adding an egg now felt like genuine baking.

Some things taste a little better and feel a little more authentic when we put a little effort into them. Things that seem too free, too easy, too simple are not as highly prized or valued.

Insight.

Gorgeous.

---

9   Please, no letters: it was a different world where social protocols ran on much clearer (not better) gender-based norms. Just watch any *I Dream of Jeanie* reruns.

Of loyalty to the bean.

We've all seen the kinds of loyalty cards that coffee shops hand out.

Every cup of coffee entitles the owner to receive a stamp on their card. Once the card is full, the owner can redeem a "free" cup of coffee. The intention of these handy little gizmos is to build brand loyalty, of course. OK, so where's the insight? Good question, read on.

Consider: Which loyalty card fills up quicker, the card with eight spaces for stamps or the one with ten? The one with eight spaces, right? Stands to reason, eight is fewer than ten. Nope again: the one with ten fills up more quickly...*IF* you manage it in a particular way.

Let me explain.

The consumer who receives the blank eight-stamp loyalty card with their freshly brewed cup of coffee feels all warm and toasty because their particular brand of coffee loves and cherishes them and wants to see them come back—and they are prepared to "pay" for their loyalty. At the cash till, the server stamps their freshly-minted card and hands it over with pride. Only seven cups to go. Smashing.

Now imagine how *this* customer feels—the one in a different coffee house that receives a ten-stamper; but when the server gives them their coffee and stamps their card (leaving nine blanks), they then say, "Hey, know what? I'm in a good mood today, and you seem really nice, so let me go ahead and get you started even quicker"...and they give them a *double-stamp*, leaving eight blanks, not nine as the customer expected.

How does this second person feel compared to the first person? Extra cherished and loved, right? When in fact they are further away from the finish line than the first guy, but their feelings of goodwill to the brand are much, much higher—therefore they tend to return more quickly and more often. They tend to burn through the eight remaining stamps more quickly and more assiduously than the person in the first coffee shop with the seven remaining un-stamped spots.

Whoever dreamed up that piece of marketing (behavioral/psychological) genius—bravo!

Insight.

INSIGHT = IMPACT

The reason we are trying to encourage insight is that it leads to wisdom, which leads to impact—and that's the leader's purpose: to make a positive impact. All leaders need to make a positive impact on their people and on the trajectory of the business. Daily Leadership Journaling is the tool to achieve this impact since it helps us understand ourselves, others, the business, and the future state of the business.

To make an impact, we have to understand ourselves.

To make an impact, we have to understand others.

To make an impact, we have to understand business.

To make an impact, we need to understand the market.

To make an impact, we have to be able to predict where the puck will be.

HEALTH WARNING: INSIGHT DOES NOT NECESSARILY HAVE TO MEAN REVOLUTION!

Some of our more bullish leaders hear the word "insight" and excitedly think big, new, fast, expensive, risky, far-reaching change! Revolution! Take up arms! Man the barricades, there's an angry mob flocking down the Rue de Lyon to storm the Bastille! Chaaaaarge![10]

---

10   Some think "legacy." Some think "promotion." Some think "chairmanship." Beware: more often than not, it's an ego-play. Don't let the thing that you are remembered for be building that monstrous folly in the middle of the beautifully manicured lawn. Be glad that you're not the executive in the '80s who suggested the brand-new flavor for Coca-Cola might be rather fun and just what the brand needed—look how well that went down. NOT!

But insight does not necessarily mean angry mobs and pitchforks and flaming torches; it can, of course, but that's not what we are encouraging. We are encouraging regularly targeted evolution: step-change, yes, but in small and controllable steps. In other words, not revolution, evolution...but speeded up.

Charles Darwin in *On the Origin of Species* described evolution as a countless series of small steps that enable the species to survive and thrive, to adapt to its environment. Those that adapt over time survive; those that do not, do not.

Evolution, then, is a series of small changes—some of the changes worked, some did not. Those that worked got repeated and developed, and those that did not work were abandoned.

Progress was slow and inexorable, but always forward.

SURVIVAL OF THE FITTEST

In the business world, we often hear the phrase, "Survival of the fittest," and it's often misused and misunderstood.

People tend to think that Mr. Darwin meant that the 800 lb silverback gorilla wins the fight, and therefore wins the right to pass on its genes. That is not what survival of the fittest means—it means the species most adaptable to change wins—it's the same for business, and it's the same for leaders. You don't have to be the 800 lb gorilla to win (in business or leadership), but you do have to be able to adapt and adopt: insight. "Survival of the fittest" in a business sense means being nimble and using insight to skate the leaders and the business to where the puck will be.

The best leaders seem to have developed the skill to consistently tie together a string of really insightful evolutionary ideas—really good ones—ones derived from really clear and perhaps not-so-obvious thinking. Sure, some ideas or initiatives or plans will miss, but so long as seven or eight out of ten "hit," just like the process of evolution, there will inevitably be progress and inexorable forward momentum.

Sometimes, some problems or challenges need revolutionary ideas, sure, but insight normally fuels smart planning and execution too—think laser-targeted sniper fire, not atom bomb. Both approaches can change the course of a war, but we're after the solution that offers the least unnecessary collateral damage with the maximum impact and the least difficult delivery mechanism.

Remember, don't dismantle the bridge or cut the bus in half if you don't absolutely have to: try letting the air out of the tires first. In business, as in life, if the solution is simple and elegant, it's probably right: if it's complex and cumbersome, it's probably wrong.

Leadership Journaling isn't intended to promote risky revolution and all-out war, it is intended to inspire insightful and elegant evolution.

Well, that might not be such good news, especially if you're a Type A leader just itching for a revolutionary bust-up every month or so. Revolution is sometimes the answer, of course, but not every single time a quarterly number isn't reached—just ask the folk who stormed the Bastille during the French Revolution—Madame Guillotine had something to say about those guys, after all. Or Che Guevara—he didn't die in his sleep of old age. Or Emmeline Pankhurst—she didn't expire in a freak skating accident on the River Thames. Or Benito Mussolini—he didn't choke on a chicken nugget. Revolution can be risky, very risky—especially for the leader that instigated it.

Don't get me wrong, sometimes revolution is 100 percent necessary, but this time right now likely isn't it: what we're after here is evolution. Sure, evolution takes longer, but fewer people are likely to die a gruesome death in the process—and that's always to be preferred.

DOES SIZE MATTER?

Insightful evolution doesn't necessarily mean "big" either—we don't always have to throw the baby out with the bathwater. Think of the tiny mosquito carrying the malaria virus—they're not so big, but they can make massive change to the organism that they infect. Look at the way the whole world flipped on its head as a consequence of the coronavirus—and look how tiny that little blighter is.

Creative solutions do not necessarily have to be big and expensive and risky and job-threatening.

CREATIVITY

The most creative leaders are, at their core, playful—playing with ideas and scenarios and messages. Great leaders have creativity sessions actually scheduled on their weekly calendar. Forty-five minutes peppered here and there for blue-sky thinking, or ideation, or "thinking on paper," or thought showers.[11]

Sometimes these sessions are intended to explore possible answers to the questions, "What is currently broken? What needs to be improved? What systems or processes need a redesign or a refresh?" These types of questions encourage the leadership team to identify problem statements and to start to better describe them—remember, a problem really well defined is half solved.

Identifying what needs to be changed is critical. The anthropologist Gregory Bateson once said, "You can't have a new idea 'til you've got rid of an old one." Nice one, Gregory.

"Great," you might be thinking, "I'll just do some market research—that will tell us what our customer really wants and needs."

The problem is that creativity rarely comes from market research or customer surveys.

---

11   I know. It used to be called "brainstorming," but that's no longer de rigueur, I'm afraid. Woke. Sigh.

Einstein claimed that all research is fundamentally flawed because whenever someone undertook some research, they already knew the kinds of things they were looking (hoping) for.

Henry Ford went further. He said that customer research typically sends you scurrying in the wrong direction. He simply didn't believe in customer surveys because, he said, if he were to ask people what they would want, all they would say is a faster horse!

This all means, of course, that on top of everything else, as a leader, you're also in charge of creativity.

Most leaders tell us that this is a rather sobering and disappointing exercise:

> Take a look in your calendar right now. Go to next week. How many scheduled, blocked-off slots are there for "thinking" or "creative time," or "idea generation"?
> How many?
> Count again.
> None?
> Not even one?
> Exactly.

Creativity and imagination and insight are muscles that need developing.

Guess what—the great news is that when you commit to Leadership Journaling, you immediately get at least twenty minutes a day to do just that.

Some leaders abdicate their responsibility for creative evolution by outsourcing the problem. Let's give the problem to someone who's a real expert in the field of...new product development—or marketing—or software implementation—or IT management—or security—or...(insert practically any business function). And that is all OK, of course, but the responsibility for organizational evolution and figuring out where the puck is going to be, and how to get there, rests firmly with you and the senior team. Gulp.

BE STILL

According to John Cleese of Monty Python fame—and of all the things you might hold against that bunch of comedy mavericks—a dearth of imagination and creativity are not on that list. Cleese says that great ideas are like new babies, they are easily strangled.

A truly awful expression, I know, but he's arguing that all new ideas are very easily discounted or rubbished—especially by a team.

Like babies, new ideas need to be nurtured and nourished. Kept warm. Watered. Fed. Given a warm hug or two. Read a nice story before bedtime. Allowed to grow and develop. Critically, they need protecting.

How often does a new idea go into a committee looking like a Ferrari J50 convertible[12] and comes out three weeks later looking like a Suzuki Samurai?[13]

It's very easy (too easy) to be critical of brand new ideas. There is no such things as a creative mistake—all ideas likely have some kernel of usefulness in them. Critics, according to the Irish poet and playwright Brendan Behan, are like eunuchs in a harem; they watch it every night, and know what needs to be done, but can't quite come up with it themselves.

If you're wondering where the "critics" of the new ideas usually live, they are easy to spot since they are very well signposted. They normally have a shiny plaque on the door that reads "Accounts Department."

Question:

How many accountants does it take to kill a new idea?

---

12   Gorgeous.

13   If you have one, three words: Uber. Lyft. Walk.

"None," they say. "If the market really wanted a new idea, it would have already come up with it."

A quick joke:

A traveler wandering on an island inhabited entirely by cannibals comes upon a butcher shop. The shop specializes in human brains.

The sign in the shop read:

Artists' Brains	$9/lb
Philosophers' Brains	$12/lb
Scientists' Brains	$15/lb
Accountants' Brains	$19/lb

Upon reading the sign, the traveler noted, "My, those accountants' brains must be rather popular!"

To which the butcher replied, "Not really! But do you have any idea how many accountants we have to kill to get one pound of brains?!"[14]

Creativity needs to be born, developed, and marinated in the subconscious.

Thomas Edison, knowing that the best (most creative) ideas came while asleep, would define a problem, gather a handful of ball bearings—and then intentionally doze off. When he fell asleep, the ball bearings would fall out of his hand and drop to the floor, and the noise would immediately wake him. He'd grab a pen and start to write what his subconscious was working on just before the moment he was awakened. Thomas Edison still

---

14 If you're an accountant, you likely wouldn't have found that joke funny in the least. In fact, you could probably identify at least three areas where it's factually inaccurate. It's a banal and pointless joke, right? If it helps, change the word "accountant," to "salesperson." See? Hysterical. Let's move on. ☺

holds the record for the most granted patents to any individual: 1,093 of them. Coincidence? You decide.

Setting your subconscious on to the problems is what great leaders do. That's why you journal in the evening as well as in the morning: creativity.

CAN YOU DEVELOP YOUR CREATIVITY AND INSIGHT MUSCLES?

Thankfully, yes.

Other than children, who are happily unencumbered by the practicalities of the real world and who often come up with the best insight gems of all, the best examples of insight can be found in comedy clubs across the land.

Comedians, when writing new material, work on developing their insight muscles—looking at the world from oblique and unexpected angles.

Often, like Edison, they sleep with a journal next to their beds too.

Comedy is a study in insight. How often does a comedian say, "Have you ever noticed that..." and the second the punchline drops, we suddenly see things that we have seen a thousand times, but now, quite suddenly, we have made new and unexpected connections and linkages?

> Why does SeaWorld have a seafood restaurant? It's a bit cruel, isn't it?. I'm halfway through my meal when I suddenly think, "Oh no...I could be eating a slow learner!"

> Why doesn't glue stick to the inside of the bottle?

> How do they stick the non-stick to the inside of the frying pan?

If a book about failures doesn't sell, is it considered a huge success?

Have you noticed those TV ads for detergents that promise to take out even the most stubborn bloodstains? I think if you've got such a heavily bloodstained t-shirt, maybe laundry isn't you biggest problem.

Why did kamikaze pilots wear helmets?

I got a German Shepherd for security. This dog has been bred to be rough and tough and ruthless...and I'll probably be OK, so long as the burglar doesn't come into the house pushing a vacuum cleaner.

Most comedians would make great business consultants, I'm sure of it. And, if not, at least everyone would be laughing like drains while the ship was sinking beneath the waves.[15]

Gerard Huerta said, "When you are stuck, walk away from the computer and draw. It will teach you how to see."

Get up—take a walk. Get some fresh air. Get a new perspective. Take a nap.

Best of all, "draw" the problem...in your journal.

Find an inspired place in your journal: think about and try to answer at least one or two or possibly three of the following insightful questions—you can come back to the others later—like comedians, sometimes insight takes a bit of a run-up:

---

15   Please, no letters of complaint. I was just joshing. Lighten up.

How can your business, like Bata Shoes, explore and exploit new, possibly completely untapped and undervalued, areas or markets?

Do you, like Walmart, need to think of a better distribution footprint or a different channel to market strategy?

Is there, like Apple, a project in development that you need to pump the brakes on a little in order to make it significantly better?

Where, like the plucky lad considering the bus that appeared inexorably stuck under the bridge, do you need to have a step back to consider the bigger picture?

Where, like Abraham Ward, do you need to give some extra support, and where can things be streamlined and made more agile?

Where in your business do you need to add a shark or two in order to make a step-change improvement in quality?

How, like Betty Crocker cakes, can you make a change in processes that will dramatically improves the customer experience?

How, like the inspired customer ten-stamp loyalty card, can you significantly increase customer usage and satisfaction at the same time?

Where else in your own development, or in that of your business, do you need to focus your insight muscle(s)?

If I could wish for you only one thing, dear leader, that your daily Leadership Journaling will deliver to you, it is the gift of increased insight.

...oh, and self-awareness, obviously.

...and emotional intelligence, of course.

...and, yes, increased empathy—but that goes without saying.

...and...oh, never mind.

Many companies now urge their recruiters to specifically look for this rare gift of creativity and insight, and they ask their candidates for specific examples of the eureka moments that they have had, and how they developed and delivered on them

The future belongs to those leaders with the greatest gift of insight—data crunchers, we got plenty of. AI? Yes, we got that covered too. Accountants? Again, we have those in spades. Ops guys? We got tons of 'em.

To learn more about insight at play, you could do a lot worse than pick up a copy of *Freakonomics*, or *SuperFreakonomics* by Steven Levitt and Stephen Dubner. Their extraordinary books are simply littered with dozens of examples of the differences between causation and correlation (insight).

If their tagline, "Why suicide bombers should buy life insurance" doesn't grab you and inspire you to look deeper, then likely nothing will.

Insight, as standup comedians will tell you, like any other muscle, strengthens with use.

Also, check out the amazing guys at Nudgestock; all they do is barrage you with tremendous insight based on behavioral science—if you don't think that the musings of Rory Sutherland, Joint Chair of Ogilvy Consulting, concerning why having two dishwashers makes much more sense than just having one, well, I don't know what will.

People had taken lots of baths—Archimedes's insight was the birth of obesity.[16]

People had seen lots of apples fall off lots of trees—Newton's insight was gravity.

People had seen lots of similar birds—Darwin's insight was natural selection and evolution.[17]

People knew what the chemical elements were—Mendeleev's insight was to arrange the Periodic Table with the gaps for all the undiscovered ones.

People had seen bombs dropped from planes before—Barnes Wallis wondered what if bombs could perhaps bounce across water before hitting their target.

At its heart, insight is the leadership ability to perceive things that are objectively similar, but are subjectively different, or vice versa.

Give that one some thought, if you dare.

POOR LEADERSHIP TO GREAT LEADERSHIP:

The following image is perhaps best at explaining the relationship between data and impact. It is a development of the DIKW Hierarchy model: also known as the DIKW pyramid. Data, information, knowledge, wisdom. Many believe that the original idea was developed following the two lines in the poem: *Choruses*, by T. S. Eliot, that appears in the pageant play: *The Rock*, in 1934:

> *Where is the wisdom we have lost in knowledge?*
> *Where is the knowledge we have lost in information?*

Whether it originated in *The Rock* or not, well played, Mr. Eliot. Well played.

---

16   No, not obesity, sorry. Density—though on second thought....

17   More on this in a couple of pages.

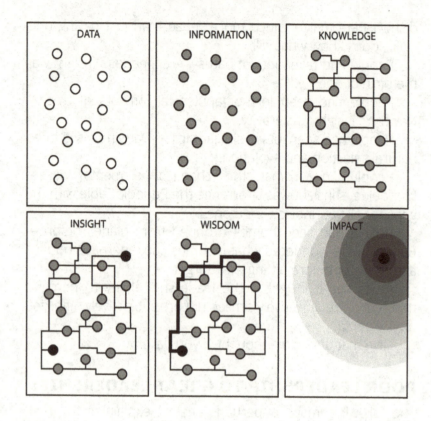

Data	Very broad, untargeted, non-specific.
Information	A subset of data—cutting out all the extraneous and unnecessary noise.
Knowledge	Linking all the uniquely salient information points in order to address a specific problem statement.
Insight	Recognizing which specific pieces of knowledge to engage, and which to ignore. The objective is to reveal power-

ful but previously unseen, unnoticed, or overlooked connections.

Wisdom   By using evaluated experience, knowing which path to take in order to connect the points of insight and create the uniquely powerful plan from Point A to Point B.

Impact   The result of the successful implementation and execution of the plan.

We mustn't, as Jefferson contended, simply rely on good information to make impactful decisions. Information, which is only a subset of data (and there's usually no shortage of data-gathering and dissemination in a business) is in no way basis for impactful decision-making: it simply doesn't go deep enough. When you hear accountants (or consultants) argue that "information is power," or "information is knowledge," don't believe them. Anyone with good Excel skills can work pivot-tables—ask them for insight and wisdom, not information, however and it's a case of, three blind mice, see how they run.

The role of leaders is to make decisions that deliver positive impacts on the business, its customers, and on the people the brand impinges. Impact is born of wisdom.

Data, information, and knowledge come from the business.

> ...and live mainly in spreadsheets in the accounts department.
>
> ...and have very little differentiated value.

Insight, wisdom, and impact come from great leaders.

> ...and live mainly in their Leadership Journals.
>
> ...and have enormous differentiated value.

In short, great leaders consistently employ insight to promote progress, change, and creativity.

"You can't use up creativity. The more you use it, the more you have."
—*Maya Angelou*

CHAPTER 5

The truth, the whole truth, and nothing but the truth.

The truth is in short supply.

THE TRUTH WILL SET YOU FREE.

What do leaders need more than anything from their people?

Hard work? Yes, of course, but no.

Dedication? Again, yes, but, no.

Enthusiasm? No.

Loyalty? Grow up.

The truth.[1]

OK, good—so, take a second to consider this: What percentage of the time do your people tell you the truth, the whole truth, and nothing but the truth?

Hint:

It's almost definitely NOT 0 percent,[2] but neither is it 100 percent.[3]

A sad and sobering thought, perhaps?

People almost always tell us a version of the truth that they think it's in their best interest to have us believe. They do this for lots of reasons including fear of reprisal, lack of trust, fear of blame, or for fear of your critical response—remember, you likely sign their monthly paycheck, after all.

President George H. W. Bush once bemoaned how many games of golf he lost since *leaving* the White House.

Something to think about, *n'est-ce pas*?

The single most important currency of leadership is truth: no matter what industry, size of organization, or market. So, all leaders need to trade in truth. The trouble is, of course, the truth is often in short supply—especially so for leaders.

Why? Well, they are the boss, with the power to hire, fire, promote, and so on. It's really difficult to challenge the boss. When was the last time an employee came into your office and said, "Hey, boss, do you have a minute? I'd like to talk about the really crappy job you're doing around here."

---

1   The clue was in the chapter title—keep up. Honestly!

2   I should jolly well hope not!

3   Poo.

It doesn't happen very often, right? Is it because they think you're wonderful and marvelous in every single possible regard? I'm guessing not.

Bad leaders largely want to be left alone: they're doing just fine they tell themselves. These kinds of leaders definitely don't want to hear the truth—but you're not that kind of leader, right?

Poor leaders don't want to trade in truth at all. The truth can be tricky. But that's not you either.

Average leaders want to be given a little guidance every now and again, because, well, largely they know that they're really rather smart and can figure stuff out with the occasional bit of advice or steer. They occasionally want to hear the truth—only the convenient truth, however. But you're not that kind of leader either, are you?

Good leaders want to be coached and held accountable by others. Sometimes they want to be mentored. They want to hear the truth, but not to the extent that they always have to act on it, not if it makes them feel too uncomfortable, you understand? But, thankfully, this isn't you either. Phew.

Great leaders proactively coach themselves, and they hold themselves to a very high standard of personal growth and self-development. They mentor themselves and others, and they work hard to make more leaders. They demand the truth of themselves and others, and they act on it—they make decisions that will change the trajectory of the business based on it.

As Brené Brown often says, "It's important to have people who speak truth to our bullshit."

Well said, Brené, well said. The problem is these truth-speaking folk are few and far between...and that's probably our fault too.

Napoléon Bonaparte had a brilliant plan to deal with the noise of convenient truths.

THE IDIOT GENERAL

Napoléon Bonaparte (August 15, 1769–May 5, 1821) was a French military and political leader. He rose to power during the French Revolution and, due to his extraordinary military savvy, he led countless successful campaigns. He dominated European and global affairs for more than a decade, winning the vast majority of his battles, building an empire that spanned over continental Europe.

Bonaparte was acutely aware of the importance of "speaking truth to the leaders' bullshit." So much so that he developed a battle strategy that won him half the world.

He would meet with his generals in his forward tent outside the walls of the city he intended to besiege. Napoléon, while poring over the maps and reading reports from the advanced scouting parties, sent one of his most trusted generals out of the tent. This general (the "idiot general") was not allowed to take part in any of the battle-planning process, nor take part in any of the ensuing conversations between the senior group.

However, once the battle plans were laid, the idiot general was invited back into the tent to learn of the proposed plan. This general had no idea what conversations took place, no idea who offered what suggestions, no idea who proposed any of the parts of the plan, nor any idea of who supported which parts of it.

The "idiot general," knowing nothing (hence the unfortunate moniker), was then asked to explain why the battle plan that had been suggested would not work—he was invited to pick holes and find fault in the strategy and tactics. The reason that this unorthodox strategy was so effective is that he had no idea which ideas were Napoléon's and which came from others. It's the perfect strategy to deal with "yes-men"—and, being the Emperor of France, yes-men were in no short supply.

Are you, like Napoléon, surrounded by yes-men?

Ask them, they'll almost definitely say "no," right? ☺

Does Leadership Journaling help you get closer to the truth from your people? Yes. Yes, it most certainly does.

How? It helps you to become the kind of leader where people are not afraid to challenge the boss: the kind of leader who really encourages open and frank communication; the kind of leader who does not overreact to situations; the kind of leader who does not play favorites; the kind of leader who actively seeks "low-diplomacy" feedback; the kind of leader who has a strategy for truth.

SO, WHAT'S YOUR STRATEGY FOR TRUTH?

This is a tricky question, right? But it's worth some thought before reading on. **Do give it a moment or two...tell me, what's your strategy for truth? Write it down in your journal, and here:**

My strategy for truth is...

What? You don't really have a specific strategy for truth?

Hmmmmm, what does that say about you as a leader, I wonder?

Remember earlier when I asked what percentage of the time do your people tell you the truth, the whole truth, and nothing but the truth?

Ask yourself what percentage of the time you tell *them* the truth, the whole truth, and nothing but the truth?

How about resolving to adopt a gold-standard leadership principle—always, always, always tell your people the truth. Easy, right?

The number one secret to start getting the truth from others is to always tell them the truth first.

And, when others are brave enough to tell you the unvarnished, uncensored, unabridged, uncomfortable truth, no matter how unsavory it might be, you simply must thank them for their candor and honesty.

Remember, what gets rewarded, gets repeated—that's the second secret.

For secret number three, we have a tricky wrinkle: always tell the truth to others, *and to yourself*.

Ouch.

What? Self-awareness?

Fiddly.

Telling *yourself* the truth is much more difficult than telling it to *others*.

How good are you at dealing in the truth that you tell to yourself?

Doesn't it always seem to be the case that the worse we are at something, the better we believe we are; and the better we are at something, the worse we know we are?[4]

Let's figure out why.

GREAT LEADERS NEVER START WITH "WHY?"

Despite what we are repeatedly told, great leaders don't start with "why" because that's not where self-awareness lies; that's where self-delusion lies.

As we mentioned earlier, the subconscious is a powerful and creative force.

Most of the time we do what we do because, well, our subconscious instructs us to do it.

This means that whenever we then try to fathom the reasons for having acted a certain way by asking ourselves, "Why

---

4   Deep. Think about that too much and you'll need to fan yourself with a piece of toast and have a little lie down clutching blanky!

did I do that?" the answers that we give ourselves are almost always not true: they are convenient, or expedient unconscious fabrications.

Similarly, when we ask others, "Why did you do that?" all manner of justifications, intellectualizations, and rationalizations reveal themselves—trouble is, they are almost always 100 percent unconscious fabrications also!

These unconscious stories that we tell ourselves to justify why we think we might have done something this way and not that are called confabulations.

Confabulations are not truths.

We invent these confabulations, these (vaguely theoretically reasonable) "reasons" for having done a particular thing this way and not that way because otherwise, well, we wouldn't appear to know what we are doing and/or we wouldn't be in control otherwise, would we? And that's too horrifying a thought to admit to.

If you're a parent, you're likely to recognize this frustrating chattypoo:

Grumpy parent:

"Sebby, why on earth did you do that? What could possibly have possessed you to kick a ball in the house? Look, you've gone and broken mommy's favorite vase."

Forlorn Sebby:

"I don't know. I'm sorry."

Even grumpier parent:

"Never mind, sorry, and what do you mean you don't know? Think, boy! Just tell me why anyone would be dumb enough to kick a soccer ball in the house!"

Upset Sebby:

"But I don't know!"

Really angry parent:

"Well, young man, you're going to sit there till you can tell me. No supper for you, I can tell you that! In fact, on second thought, get out of my sight—I can't even look at you right now! Go to you room this instant!"

Here's the sad news: poor Sebby genuinely had no idea why he did it...and neither do you know why you do almost everything you do as an adult either. Think about that next time you're sending someone off to the naughty step.

I tell you what, though, the next time you ask Sebby *why* he did something, he will, sure as eggs is eggs, at least give you a reason—however spurious—for fear of not knowing why again. Sebby has learned that confabulations are better than "don't knows."

Didn't we, as a glorious example of parenthood, just teach Sebby something wonderfully devilish—how to lie to himself as well as us? My, what truly marvelous parents we sometimes are.

Even as fully formed and well-adjusted adults, whenever when we try to analyze why we did something, unless we have developed enormous self-awareness, we have genuinely no idea why we did it that way at all.

...and if we don't know why we did it that way, then neither do others—so, stop asking them "why?"—they'll just continue to learn to confabulate to themselves and you.[5]

The organizational psychologist Tasha Eurich discovered that when her research team asked people how self-aware

---

5 Debates are raging like wild-fires in the hallowed halls of academia this very moment concerning the principle of free will: whether we really have it or not. And, if not, what that might mean for the philosophical tenets of justice and truth. Meaty topics for another leadership book, methinks.

they thought they were, around 95 percent of people believed that they had good self-awareness.

When these very same people were subsequently tested for their real levels of self-awareness, only around 10 percent of them actually were self-aware to any extent at all.

This means, according to Eurich, "...that on a good day, a very good day, at least 80 percent of us lie to ourselves about how well we lie to ourselves!"

"Why" doesn't get us any closer to self-awareness—in fact, it pushes us further away from it because when all else fails we invent a "rational" reason, and that's a bad thing, of course.

The better question we should ask ourselves is, "What?" No, no, that's the question, "What?" Oh, never mind....

Instead of asking ourselves, "Why did I do that?" we should simply ask, "What can I do now to fix this?"

Instead of, "Why am I so unhappy with that person's results?" try, "What can I do to help that person succeed better?"

Instead of, "Why did that customer leave us?" ask, "What can we do to keep customers longer?"

Instead of, "Why did that person lie to me?" try, "What can I do to ensure more people tell me the truth?"

Ownership.

Nice.

Asking yourself "what?" leads to self-awareness much more quickly than asking yourself "why?"

Next time Sebby runs through the house kicking a ball, and he breaks a vase, ask, "OK, Sebby, now that you have broken that vase, what can you do to make amends?"

Making him think about the consequences of things starts to develop Sebby's self-awareness muscles. Then guess what—before too long, he'll come to tell himself that if he runs through the house with a ball, there may be unpleasant consequences; so, ixne onye ethay ousehay occer ballsay.

People with high levels of self-awareness are constantly asking for feedback—they actively seek ways to improve. They review their performance and look for ways to make it better next time. They record their thinking and revisit it against initial expectations. They learn to analyze their own strengths and weaknesses, and spend time figuring out how best use their strengths and how to mitigate their own weaknesses (a self-SWOT, if you like). They make efforts to understand how their own self-limiting beliefs impact their performance as well as the quality of their interactions with others. They frequently ask themselves, "How can I get better at this...?" and they pay attention to the answers.

Find a well-reasoned space in your journal to copy and complete the following gorgeous thought:

Here's what can I do right now to begin to improve my self-awareness skill and ability:

1.

2.

3.

As a quick aside, here's what low self-awareness and lying to ourselves also looks like: the apocryphal story of Winston Churchill and the perils of drink. Reportedly when Churchill read about the many dangers of alcohol, he immediately resolved to give up...wait for it...reading! Nice one, Winston, good self-awareness. Not! Still, priorities. Am I right?

What part of your business or your own leadership skills are you similarly shutting your eyes with your fingers firmly in your ears calling out, like the good Mr. Churchill, "Nope, not listening! La, la, la!"?

DO YOU TELL YOURSELF THE TRUTH, THE WHOLE TRUTH, AND NOTHING BUT THE TRUTH?

About what? Everything. Almost definitely not!

Shocker, I know. So, what's getting in your way?

That's easy: confirmation bias. Sometimes called "myside bias."

Put simply, confirmation bias really gets in our way when we are trying to learn how to improve our leadership skills. Confirmation bias is the tendency for people to favor information that jives with what they already believe and to discount information which does not: people are not nearly as open-minded and flexible and accommodating as they like to think they are.

Humans tend to give much more weight and credence to ideas and concepts that confirm their own preexisting beliefs, and they work hard to devalue and minimize evidence that contradicts them.

It goes beyond that, unfortunately: we actively look for evidence that supports what we already believe, and we tend to reject evidence to the contrary.[6]

Kallum is the divisional team leader for a manufacturing company. He fervently believes that hard work is at the root of business success.

While the business has historically beaten its sales targets, it has seen a recent slump in sales.

Because of his belief that effort and commitment are at the heart of every successful enterprise, he naturally infers that his people are not as motivated as they have been, and they are now not working hard enough.

He remembers how one or two of his employees took a couple of "sick days" recently.

---

6   Did someone say COVID Vaccine?

He concludes that he must have been too soft on them recently and that they must be looking for other jobs.

He starts micromanaging the whole team, and he comes down hard whenever he sees any evidence of slacking or "lack of earnestness." He threatens to dismiss anyone he sees goofing off.

Before too long morale drops further, quickly followed by even lower sales numbers.

A couple of the team leave—meaning more work for the remaining team members. Kallum knew they weren't committed all along.

Morale drops further.

Kallum gets even grumpier and begins to crack the whip even harder.

Down and down and down we go.

We all suffer from confirmation bias—yes, even you. Where might you come to understand and explore them, I wonder?[7]

Biases, like leadership blind spots, are difficult to see—especially in ourselves.

I once asked a room of around four hundred executives whether any of them believed that they did not have any leadership blind spots. If they thought they were perfect, they were to raise their hands. Thankfully, none of them raised a hand, of course, recognizing that they, too, must have at least a few. You probably recognize the same is true for you as you read this principle right now.

Great.

Next question: What are your blind spots? List them down here:

...errr.

That's right, we don't know what our blind spots are, because we can't see them. Tricky.

Where might we explore this thorny issue, do you think?

Confirmation bias and leadership blind spots lead to poor judgement and ineffective decision-making. Which is a shame, because that's what leaders do more of than anything else—make value judgments and make decisions.

ARE YOU MAKING GOOD DECISIONS?

How are you to know whether or not you are making good decisions? All decisions seem like the right decisions at the time of making them, of course.

In *Noise: A Flaw in Human Judgment* by Daniel Kahneman, Oliver Sibony, and Cass R. Sunstein we learn that in order to understand errors in judgment, we must understand cognitive biases as well as random noise.

The book illustrates how medicine is noisy and prey to confirmation bias—how else would a range of doctors faced with the same patient arrive at different diagnoses and prognoses? It's the same set of inconsistencies when we study child custody decisions, insurance underwriting, sales forecasts, personnel decisions, bail decisions, granting or rejecting patents, even sentences given by experienced judges: all "noisy" and all prey to biases. Is leading similarly "noisy", similarly prey to biases? You betcha.

Intelligence, experience, precedents, guidelines, research, and so on do not seem to serve to eliminate bad decisions. Wherever there is judgment and a decision to be made, confirmation bias and system noise are always at play to some extent—and more of it than you think, according to the authors of the book.

The book goes on the explain that the goal of judgment is accuracy, of course, not individual expression. The authors call this "the first principle of decision hygiene."

"But what of 'intuition'?" I hear you cry, "Is there no place for that?" Yes, of course there is, but the best way to address (minimize) noise and bias is to first recognize the noise at play in the system, as well as your own biases. Whom do you consult with? Whose council do you seek? How much research do you do? Are you making intuitive or informed decisions?

IS RESEARCH THE ANSWER?

Yes...and no. Sorry.

As mentioned earlier, research can be good because it can give us a broader view of the issue. The trouble is that our inbuilt "search engine" (just like all search engines) are prone to confirmation bias too. Let me share some examples.

If you were to search something like: "Is Manchester City the best soccer team in the world?"[8] you would easily find countless websites and articles arguing that Manchester City is indeed the best team in the world. You will find reams and reams of facts and figures to support the argument that they are—which they are, by the way.

But consider, if you were a Manchester United fan and were to search, "Is Manchester United the best team in the world?"[9] you would find countless pages of facts and figures to support the argument that they are—which they are not, because Manchester City is, of course!

The lesson is this: phrasing questions in a one-sided way will significantly assist you in finding data that supports your predetermined world view. We are all victims of our own self-fulfilling prophesies.

Guess what, this confirmation bias also comes into play in many other ways: it biases our search for information; it biases our interpretation of "facts"; it biases our memory of events

---

8   They most definitely are, by the way. Why? Because I'm an ardent Man City fan, of course. Come on you Blues!

9   Which they most certainly are not—just ask any Manchester City fan worth their salt.

or facts; it biases our feelings of high or low self-esteem—you get the idea.

Just for sport, watch how a fervently religious person can explain why their interpretation of a particular passage of scripture supports their own religious beliefs, while it rubbishes those of other, less "sensible" religions. If you were to show that very same passage to a person of another religious belief and ask them to explain how the same passage of text reinforces *their* beliefs, you would hear a very similar argument. But they can't both be right, right?

It's exactly the same with politics; how recruiters select candidates; how we all interpret and manipulate data; how we choose a new marketing agency; why we fall in love with one person rather than another—again, you get the idea.

If a leader tells her CFO that she is worried that a particular sales manager seems to be a little "off their game" lately, and could she have "a look at the numbers" to figure out whether or not there was any truth in her supposition...and the CFO felt the same way, guess what "the numbers" are very likely to show? Right.

Magicians play on confirmation bias and exploit our predilection for them too. How? Well, think of confirmation bias this way—we typically see what we expect to see. The magician knows this and uses it to deflect your attention, set expectations, and manipulate our beliefs and understanding of a particular set of circumstances, methodology, or apparatus.

Same, too, advertising executives.

Same, too, politicians.

Same, too, preachers.

To be read without any trace of irony:

The "Cognitive Bias Codex" designed by John Manoogian III, based on the original categorization by Buster Benson, is really worth studying since it groups and details all of the most common biases and their roots. You really must check it out. Why? Because it's brilliant—because I say so.

How do we combat "research bias"?

"THE TRUTH," THEY SAY, "WILL SET YOU FREE!"

Well, the "real" truth, the empirical truth, will surely set you free; a "convenient truth," however, will do just the opposite.

There are lots of convenient truths that leaders tell themselves in order to make themselves feel better about their leadership skill and prowess and/or the lackluster performance of the business:

> *"The person I just fired was never going to work out anyway."*

> No, not the way you were treating and developing him, no he wasn't.

> *"My door is always open."*

> It might well be, but you're almost never in the office; and if you are in the office, you're normally too busy to talk; and nobody wants to come talk to you anyway for fear of being barked at or given extra tasks.

> *"I'm 100 percent transparent—an open book, really."*

> No, no you're not. Your employees found out about the last merger the day that it had been announced to the press—but you must have been planning it for at least six months.

> *"Being vulnerable is a sign of weakness, and what people need from their leaders, now more than ever, is strength."*

Well, true leadership strength is the ability to show vulnerability. Yes, you were going 180 degrees in the wrong direction with that one, I'm afraid. Ouch.

"Look, I know that I scream and shout sometimes, but it's only because I want the best for the company and the families it supports—and they all know that too."

For the purposes of time, we'll leave that one well alone!

"I only ever hire A-players."

Again, we'll let that one slide for now because if that was actually the case, why do you complain about so many of them and consistently bemoan the fact that no one other than you does all the work around here, or understand the seriousness of the situation?

"I encourage feedback, and I really welcome push-back."

Taxi!

It's significantly easier, of course, for leaders to tell themselves a series of convenient truths rather than face the fact that their convenient truths are usually just comfortable lies in a nice pair of pants and a well-tailored blazer, with a good PR agent. Squirrels are just rats with good PR, after all.

Where do these unfortunate convenient truths come from? Pride. Fear. Ego. Jealousy. Take your pick. Basically, they stem from low self-awareness, low self-regulation—in short, low Emotional Intelligence (EQ).

As far as convenient truths are concerned (for "convenient truth" read: self-delusion), *The Emperor's New Clothes* by Hans Christian Andersen will tell you all you need to know.

Maybe the trick to better decision-making lies in only dealing with facts. Facts are always true, right? The numbers don't lie, right? Remember the Colgate advert earlier? Let's dig a little deeper.

FACTS AND FAKE NEWS

Are facts likely to save us? Well, as ever, that depends.

> Fact: China emits more greenhouse gasses than any other nation.

One might suppose this means that China is more culpable than any other country for climate change, right?
Perhaps.
But when you divide each country's greenhouse gas emissions per capita, the USA fares *significantly* worse.
I can't imagine the president of the USA volunteering the second fact too readily, but I can certainly imagine them mentioning the first one whenever they have a certain point to prove.

Source: United States Environmental Protection Agency: Boden, T.A., Marland, G., and Andres, R.J. (2017). National CO2 Emissions from Fossil-Fuel Burning, Cement Manufacture, and Gas Flaring: 1751-2014, Carbon Dioxide Information Analysis Center, Oak Ridge National Laboratory, U.S. Department of Energy, doi 10.3334/CDIAC/00001_V2017.

> Fact: Some (most) hand sanitizers kill 99.99 percent of germs, they say.

Yes, under "laboratory" (entirely controlled) conditions. In the real world? You're lucky if they kill 46 percent of them.
Funny how that isn't mentioned on the bottle, right? Not even in small print. Odd.

Source: Microbiologist Jason Tetro in *The Germ Files*

Fact: In 2012 the Centers for Disease Control reported a surge in the incidents of autism in children.

What caused this spike? Vaccines? Food colorants? GMO foods? Pollution?

How about significant increases in the ability to identify autism and a national campaign to identify at-risk children earlier?

Yes, but sometimes it's more expedient to draw attention to the lobbyists that don't fund my campaign, right?[10]

Source: Hansen SN, Schendel DE, Parner ET. Explaining the Increase in the Prevalence of Autism Spectrum Disorders: The Proportion Attributable to Changes in Reporting Practices. *JAMA Pediatr.* 2015;169(1):56–62. doi:10.1001/jamapediatrics.2014.1893

Look, everybody knows that 76.32 percent of all statistics are made up on the spot.[11]

See how statistics or data or facts can mislead even the most exacting and data-based minds:

Imagine you were asked this question:

Do you believe that you should be taxed more so that other people don't have to work?

I'm going to guess that most people would say "no" to this question.

Let's imagine that 80 percent of people who were asked said "no."

What about this question:

---

10   Allegedly.
11   Not really, I just made that up. QED.

Do you believe that the government should help those people who try, but can't find work?

I'm going to guess that most people would say "yes" to this one.

Let's imagine that 80 percent of people who were asked said "yes."

Both of these questions essentially deal with the same topic: government assistance. The way the question is framed makes a significant difference to the tenor of the answers.

Be careful how you make decisions based on facts, data, figures, pie charts, and spreadsheets. Be mindful too of who is asking, and why-which lobbyist they work for. It often helps to ask yourself questions in two ways: one assuming a positive disposition, and one assuming a negative disposition. Does your thinking change with each style of asking—it normally does; and might your decision change with each set of answers—they normally do.

What's the best way for leaders to make the best decisions if relying on cold, hard facts isn't the answer? Well, facts are part of the answer; they are important, so too experience, so too intelligence...but best of all to help with good decision making: Emotional intelligence.

EQ, IS IT REALLY ALL THAT?

Yes it is.

But most leaders don't really understand EQ. They don't really know why it's important in terms of leadership performance and decision-making. They don't know how to measure it. And they don't know how to improve it.

If any of that sounds like you, today's your lucky day.

Due to the mountains of research papers and the weight of evidence in its support, most managers and leaders these days accept that EQ (emotional intelligence) is somehow increasingly important and an accurate predictor of success.

The term EQ was first coined in 1990 by researchers John Mayer and Peter Salovey, but it was later popularized by psychologist Daniel Goleman.

Goleman highlighted the importance of emotional intelligence in leaders. "The most effective leaders are all alike in one crucial way: they all have a high degree of what has come to be known as emotional intelligence. It's not that IQ and technical skills are irrelevant. They do matter, but...they are the entry-level requirements for executive positions."

Over the years, emotional intelligence—also known as EQ—has evolved into a must-have leadership skill. There is now a mountain of evidence that shows that emotional intelligence is the strongest single predictor of leadership performance. And hiring managers have taken notice: 71 percent of employers surveyed by CareerBuilder said they value EQ over IQ. They argue that individuals who demonstrated high-scoring EQ abilities are more likely to stay calm under pressure, resolve conflict effectively, and respond to co-workers with more empathy.

Ask most leaders to define EQ with any sort of precision, however, and they start looking down, shuffling their feet a lot, and they start talking about the weather. EQ, though valuable, seems to be a real head-scratcher, and no mistake. But the really great news is that your Leadership Journal is your key to EQ progress and development.

To complicate matters somewhat, there are lots of different definitions of EQ—some say this particular attribute is more important than another. Others say that their particular definition supersedes any other—tricky. BUT and let me be super-clear on this, just because there are a variety of definitions of EQ and different "recipes" of it does not mean that EQ isn't critical for leadership success: it most definitely is!

Travis Bradberry and Jean Greaves, authors of *Emotional Intelligence 2.0*, contend that 83 percent of people with high self-awareness are top performers, while only 2 percent of bottom performers display this trait. Also, those with high emotional intelligence earn significantly more money that those without—so that's a bonus.

Research from Harvard Business School demonstrated that EQ counts for twice as much as IQ and technical skills in determining who will be successful!

EQ, it seems, is a bit like my wife's recipe for Yorkshire Puddings. Think of it this way, there are LOTS of recipes for Yorkshire Puddings—some say only use sunflower oil. Ha!

Some say let the batter rest for a minimum of thirty minutes. Madness!

Some say never open the oven door—not even to check on them. What?

Heck, some even say that the ingredients must all be chilled before starting...I know, crazy, right?!

The fact of the matter is my wife's recipe for Yorkshire Puds (handed down from great-grandmother to grandmother to mother to daughter—in Yorkshire, no less) is, hands down, the best that there is.[12] Simple.

If I were to even come close to suggesting to my wife that her puddings might be improved by adding a little butter to the mixture...well, let's just say that another night sleeping in the garden shed is not exactly my idea of fun. Sometimes the best thing to do is to find a recipe that you like; and if it works, and if everyone else thinks it's as yummy as you do, and if everyone else asks you for your recipe, then stick to it, I say.

There are, it seems, as many recipes for EQ as there are recipes for Yorkshire Puddings. Does that mean that Yorkshire Puddings are somehow diminished and not the very yummiest accompaniment to a Sunday roast? No, it does not.

It's the same for carrot cake, of course...and sherry trifle... and...well, you get the idea.

---

12 She makes them "laugh." If you know, you know.

WHAT EQ ISN'T.

It's often useful, when attempting to understand what something is, to consider what it definitely isn't. See if you know anyone who looks like this (hint: the mirror *might* help).

People with low EQ:

Always have to be right.
It's very important for these kinds of people to "win" at all costs. They could argue with a tree stump. Active listening? What's that?

Are oblivious to the feelings of others.
They're completely unaware that someone might be upset with them—even those as close to them as their family.

Are insensitive.
They crack a joke at a funeral. Nobody laughs. "Too soon?" he asks with a weak smile. Yes, Teddy, too soon. Empathy? What's that?

Externalize their problems.
When things go wrong it's the economy, the weather, the virus, other people. If it is ever their fault (and it almost never is), it's because circumstances made them do it, and there simply was no other choice to make. Circumstances, you see?

Don't cope with stress well.
Emotionally charged situations and emotions are difficult to understand. It's easier to duck difficult issues rather than face them head on.

Have poor self-regulation skills.
Controlling emotions and moderating behavior is tricky for these people.

Make themselves the subject of every conversation.

Oh, you just got back from India? I went there in 2012—did you visit the Taj Mahal? Isn't it wonderful? Did you know that it was originally built as a mausoleum, a tomb? I saw it right at sunset. Did you see it at sunset? No? Shame: it's the very best time to see it. Have you visited New Zealand? No? You really must go. Middle Earth, I call it. I went there once in '87 and again in '92. You'd love it. You simply must do what I did and go see the North Island. There's a small café there right by the beach that sells simply the best ever....

Have superficial relationships.

They typically have few friends—they're not so much into give and take, and sharing. Compassion? Emotional support? No thanks.

THE FORMULA FOR EMOTIONAL INTELLIGENCE

There are many different definitions and formulas for EQ, but my all-time favorite is the one constructed by Daniel Goleman in his seminal 1995 book *Emotional Intelligence: Why It Can Matter More Than IQ* and it is the one that *My Daily Leadership* aims to specifically improve:

Emotional Intelligence =

Self-Awareness + Self-Regulation + Motivation + Empathy + Social Skill

Self-Awareness

Understanding yourself and the effect you have on others. Understanding your own strengths and weaknesses. Self-aware leaders are consistently asking for feedback and improvement notes. Put simply, those leaders who can see themselves clearly, can see their people and their company clearly. Those who can't, don't!

Self-Regulation
These leaders measure twice, cut once. They think before acting. These individuals have a high degree of control over their emotions and impulses. They are comfortable with ambiguity. They are thoughtful and have high integrity even at times when tempted to take an easier/quicker/less-difficult path. These leaders are highly principled and controlled. They are good with change, and they create atmospheres of trust and fairness.

Motivation
These leaders have an unquenchable thirst for improvement: always looking to raise the bar in all areas. They are committed and naturally buoyant. Their optimism is self-evident, and they spread a passion for the goals and doing the work. These individuals love to learn, and they want to stretch and be stretched. They exude a drive to excel. Someone who sets the bar high for themselves does so for others and the company.

Empathy
Leaders with a well-developed empathy skill serve to build companies where people want to work—employee satisfaction goes up, staff turnover goes down. They give great feedback and know when to do so with sensitivity and a light touch. These people build teamwork and manage corporate talent well. They can read between the lines, and they have a good sense for what's important but is not being said.

Social Skill

This is not just being a jolly chappie, it's being a jolly chappie with intentionality and purpose. It's not just idle schmoozing when they pass someone in the corridor; it's setting up a culture of team building and collaboration. These people are solutions-oriented and always have at heart the best interests of the majority. These people are relationship-builders and connectors. The best leaders realize that they simply cannot achieve what needs to be done on their own: everything that gets done in the business happens only through the efforts of other people.

JOURNALING AND EMOTIONAL INTELLIGENCE (EQ)

Your Leadership Journal is your portable EQ gym—it's where you work out and develop your EQ muscles.

Let's take a few minutes to try to unpick your current levels of EQ.

Construct a quick league table of the EQ ingredients. Self-awareness. Self-regulation. Motivation. Empathy. Social skill.

Which do you think you're best at and worst at? Rank them top to bottom.
1.
2.
3.
4.
5.

Great. Now give each of them a score from 1 to 10.

1 = Aaaargh! Help! Police!

...to...

10 = I think I'll write a book.

If you've written 10s across the board—do it again.

If you've written 1s across the board—visit www.psychologist-near-me.com.

Now then, let's play a quick game. Let's assume, just for fun, that you're not quite as good as you think you are in any of the EQ areas—take two off each score. I mean, you're good, but you're not an EQ-god, right? This new (probably more accurate) adjusted score means that you've got some work to do.

Here's the tricky part (stay with me now, I'd hate to lose you after all of the good work that we've done so far)—each of these areas and scores mean that you're not admitting something to yourself right now. Hold on to your hat, it's "truth time"!

Find an honest-to-goodness really, really self-aware space in your journal:

What two or three things are you not admitting to yourself in each of these areas?

Self-Awareness:

1.

2.

3.

1.

2.

3.

Motivation:

1.

2.

3.

Empathy:

1.

2.

3.

Social Skill:

1.

2.

3.

Make a solemn pledge to *always* tell the truth—especially to yourself.

*"To be aware of a single shortcoming within
oneself is more useful than to be aware
of a thousand in somebody else."*
—Dalai Lama

A QUICK SELF-AWARENESS JOKE. BECAUSE, WHY NOT, AFTER ALL THAT HARD WORK?

To lighten the mood a little:

It's August 12th, the Glorious Twelfth, the first day of the grouse hunting season.

Two friends in the Scottish Highlands decide to meet at the shooting lodge to buy cartridges, arrange their shooting permit, and hire a gundog for the day.

Once they arrive, they organize everything as planned. But when it came to securing the gundog, they discover that all the dogs had already been rented out. It was, after all, a very busy day.

They were devastated, knowing as they did, how much more enjoyable it is to shoot with a fully trained gundog.

"Look, we do have one brand new dog," said the lodge manager. "He's a puppy, only part way through training, and has never even been tried on the job. I can let you have him for only five pounds for the day."

Since five pounds represented such a bargain, the friends decide to give the puppy a chance. After all, they thought, how bad could he be?

"What's his name?" they asked as they took the dog's lead.

"Chief Operations Officer," the man replied. "But we just call him the COO around here."

"Right you are," said the friends. "COO it is."

COO, it turned out, was absolutely fabulous. Alert. Attentive. Quick to hunt out the downed foul, returning them gently, diligently, and without single error or complaint. A real find—adding enormously to the pleasure of the day.

A couple of weeks later, the friends returned to the shooting lodge to arrange more cartridges, permits, and hopefully COO: he was, they had both agreed, the very best dog they had ever rented—and so inexpensive too.

"Is COO available?" They asked the very moment they entered the lodge.

"He is," said the manager. "And I can let you have him for only twenty pounds for the day."

"Twenty pounds?" They replied, amazed. "But last time he was only five?"

"Oh, yes," said the lodge manager, "But COO is very in demand these days. He's a real find, a real superstar. Everyone wants our new COO," he said. "The best there has ever been, they tell me. Twenty pounds, take it or leave it. What'll it be?"

"Fine!" they said after a short consultation with one another. After all, COO was truly amazing.

And that day's shooting was the best ever, made even more exceptional by COO's extraordinary performance! He was even better than before. Quicker, stronger, even more attentive and hard-working. Every grouse rooted out and returned in a flash—undamaged and right to their feet. Spectacular. The friends made sure to reserve COO for next week's shoot. "We wouldn't want him getting away," they said to the manager with a smile and a knowing wink.

On returning the following week, the friends discover that COO's rates were now one hundred and twenty-five pounds for the day—a new gundog record!

"But why?" The friends implored. "He's only a few months old. Nobody pays that kind of money for a new dog...or any dog, for that matter!"

"I know", said the manager. "But COO is our number one requested dog. People come from miles around to work with him. He's a real draw. The best dog we ever had!"

"Fine," they said as they gladly paid, expecting that they would have the best day-shoot ever. And they did! And COO was, as expected, a revelation! Simply the best gundog in the Northern Hemisphere by far.

Of course, the friends reserved COO for Wednesday, since they had both decided to take a day off work to get in an extra day's shooting with COO before the weekend.

Wednesday morning could not come quickly enough for the guys. They were beaming as they entered the lodge and asked, "Is our dog raring to go?"

"He is," said the manager. "And I can let you have him for only two pounds for the whole day!"

"What?! Two pounds for our COO?! But he's probably the best gundog that has ever lived!"

"Well, he was," said the crestfallen manager. "But he was so good that unfortunately we promoted COO to CEO...

...And now all he does is sit on his arse all day and bark!"

Ba Dum Dum Tssss

WHAT'S YOUR STRATEGY FOR TRUST?

Before we leave this very introspective and chewy chapter, we must give some thought to trust.

According to Stephen Covey, author of *The Speed of Trust*, 57 percent of employees do not trust their leaders. This explains why many change messages do not land because of the trust deficit with leaders. Since we've sorted out your strategy for truth earlier (from yourself and others), let's turn our attention to now to your strategy for dealing with the trust deficit that is there—even if you can't see (or feel) it. Take a second and write down your strategy for trust or your leadership trust statement if you prefer. Again, not an easy concept to get your head around, but give it a go.

Trust, like truth, is tricky, right?

Have you ever played the trust game where someone is blindfolded and then encouraged to stand straight and fall back hoping their partner will catch them—and, if they lose faith in their partner and take a step back, they lose? It's scary, right?

In leadership, your trust statement will need to be a little more complex than, "I will be sure to always try to catch them when they fall."

Great leaders work tirelessly to build trust between themselves and their teams, between departments and divisions, between people and processes, between the business and its customers, between the business and its suppliers, between the business and its stakeholders.

Businesses, like brands, are run on trust—trust is the fuel for them all. What is the stock market, money, partnerships, contracts, the law, cryptocurrency, marriages, brands, even governments built on, if not trust?

Trust, however, does not flow easily: it can take years to build—and, unfortunately, it can be lost in an instant. Remember the words of Kevin Plank, founder of Under Armour, "Trust is won in drops and lost in buckets."

As you might imagine, winning trust from others, like truth, is reciprocal: it relies on the level of trust that you show to them and that you share with them.

Truth is the number one leadership currency; trust is number two.

A trust question to get your trust-juices flowing:

How trusting and how trustworthy are you?

Your answer likely looks like "I'm 100 percent trustworthy, and around 80 percent trusting," I'd wager.

Do you think it's better for leaders to be more reserved or more open? More cynical or more optimistic? More guarded or more demonstrative? More untrusting or more entrusting?

When we ask leaders the questions above, they often struggle to answer them—sometimes because they don't like the answers they are forced to give—they think that it doesn't portray them in a very favorable light. Perhaps they're once bitten, twice shy about the whole trust issue.

Some leaders find refuge in the famous Russian rhyming proverb, *"Doveryai, no proveryai"*—a firm favorite of Ronald Reagan when in meetings with his Russian counterpart, President Gorbachev: "Trust, but verify."

"Trust but verify" might be great for political soundbites, but at its heart it is really a synonym for "don't trust." At worst it's duplicitous, and at best it's passive aggressive. It's not pithy, it's not clever, and, as a leader, it's beneath you. Trust or don't trust, it's up to you—make a decision: are you untrusting or entrusting? It's a binary question, and it deserves a binary answer.

Now blind trust, well, that's a different thing and can be abused, of course. Nobody wants anybody to be naïve and unquestioning, but the amount of trust that you offer is directly proportionate and correlated to the amount of trust that you receive.

> *"People will forget what you said, people will forget what you did, but people will never forget how you made them feel."*
> —Maya Angelou

To help you think about the level of trust you foster, maybe think about it this way: Are you happiest when playing councilor, policeman, or judge?

GUIDELINES, RULES, LAWS

All companies have guidelines, rules, and laws.

> Guidelines are: whenever possible, try to do this; try not to do that. Councilor.
> Rules are: whenever possible, don't do this; do that. Policeman.
> Laws are: never do this; always do that! Judge.

Take a look at all of your policies, rule books, staff handbooks, procedural documents, SOPs, and systems. If there is a mountain of them, and they are all "law-based" (where non-compliance ends up in a conversation with a manager and/or HR), then unfortunately, you're "law-based"—low on the trust continuum.

Policy-overload is not good business management, it's poor people management. Rules stifle creativity, make people feel undervalued, constrained, and mistrusted.

Law-based businesses are high in doubt and low in trust.

If there is a room in your business (even if it's virtual) that looks like the Library of Congress piled high with laws and rulings and policies and procedures, it's simple: you don't trust your people (what does that say about your company's hiring policies and people management skills?), and, in return, your people don't trust you.

...and whose fault is that?

...hint: it's yours.

What do you do when someone puts an unusual claim on their expense report? Do you send an email to the whole of the business highlighting what will henceforth be an allowable claim and what will not?

If so, watch out.

If someone's grandmother dies, and they ask for a day's leave on compassionate grounds, do you send out a chart detailing the amount of leave permissible dependent upon the genetic closeness of the recently deceased?

If so, watch out.

If one manager approves an expense claim for staples, and another rejects one for Post-it Notes, is it time for a jazzy new twenty-page stationary-policy?

If so, watch out.

Where do you draw the line with mobile phone use at work? What about which internet sites are permissible and which ones aren't? What about your working from home policy? Sick days?

I once worked at a company that told an employee to remove tinsel from her desk lamp at Christmas because "the canteen is the place for frivolity." The tinsel was very tasteful and restrained (to the extent that tinsel can be, of course). No customers ever ventured as far as her desk. Guess what I did over the Christmas holiday other than eat and drink too much—I brushed up my CV, that's what! And so did she.

Policies, rules, laws, processes all serve to design compliance and acquiescence in and squeeze trust out of the system. In fact, they largely achieve the opposite of their intention—they positively encourage untrustworthy behavior if you think about it for long enough. Unintended consequences again. Ouch.

DESIGN TRUST IN, NOT OUT.

Submarine hatches need to be extremely well designed and installed—they need to potentially withstand enormous pressures with a high degree of reliability and precision—lives are at stake. They must not, for example, ever be installed upside down.

Because of this, submarine hatches are specifically designed to be manufactured slightly wider at the bottom than the top—this way they cannot possibly be installed the wrong way up—they simply wouldn't fit the hole,[13] and it would be blindingly obvious that an error was made.

The Japanese call this kind of thinking *"Poka-yoke"*—it means "inadvertent error prevention." It was developed in the Toyota quality-management processes in the 1970s, and the principle quickly spread to aircraft manufacture, as well as submarine design and assembly, and countless other disciplines.

Are all of your processes and guiderails, and procedures, and approvals, and levels of authority and oversight inadvertently designing mistrust into the system?

Poka-yoke serves to design trust into a system (business) recognizing that sometimes people make mistakes—and that doesn't mean that everyone made a mistake, nor does it mean that a new policy has to be written on the back of every infraction.

Write polices as shields, not swords—to protect, not to harm—with honey in your heart, not larceny. People are NOT out to screw you, steal from you, swindle you. Maybe a particular person is, here and there, but *people* aren't.

Until someone (a person—not a team, not a department, not a division, not a group, not a shift) gives you a concrete reason not to trust them, you should, of course, always trust them. And always give them the benefit of the doubt; because if you don't give them the benefit of the doubt, why should they extend to you the courtesy that you don't willingly extend to them?

"Judge me by my intentions, but I will judge you by your actions" are not the words of a trusting (or trusted) leader.

Want to know who trusts least? Those people who are most untrustworthy trust the least. So, let me ask you again, do you trust your people, and do they trust you?

Prison inmates tend to not trust one another—and, considering where they all live and what brought them there, that's

---

13   There's probably a much better word for this. Access port? Substructure? Opening? Flanged-aperture? Naval architects—answers on a postcard, please. Anyway, "hole" it is for now.

probably smart thinking. But you're not a prison warden having to keep an ever vigilant and suspicious eye on the inmates and the high wall with the razor-wire.

Your default position should be to trust—trust the potential of your people, your business, yourself. Sure, prudent verification is maybe important—but your default should be trust. Mistrust is easy—it takes no imagination and wit: batten down the hatches, grab, hide. Trust takes courage and vulnerability and benefit of the doubt.

We often struggle to trust because, well, "discretion is the better part of valor," right? No. No it isn't. Stop it. Use your journal to help you see that almost everyone who comes into work in the morning does not do so in order to make things worse and to screw things up for the company. They do good work almost all the time. They try hard...right up to the very point that they no longer trust the company: and then things change. The leader's job is to build trust EVERYWHERE.

Which policies and procedures and instructions and SOPs need to be scrapped, and which need to be written with the watchwords of "chill the f*ck out" in the mind of the author?

FREEWRITING ABOUT TRUST.

Find a free page in your journal. Set a timer for five minutes. Perform a quick freewriting exercise about how you feel about trust. Just let your thoughts meander and flow without restriction or evaluation. Write fast. How do you feel about trusting others? What things build your trust? What things reduce your trust? How easy is it to trust someone you meet for the first time? What things do you think about before deciding whether or not you trust someone? How trustworthy do you think people find you? How scared are you of trusting others? Do you find yourself trusting anyone and everyone who seems nice? Do you find yourself trusting people who tell you their sob stories? Consider your relationship with trust issues. Have you been influenced by people close to you and their trust issues? Are some businesses more trustworthy than others? If so, why? Are some leaders more trustworthy than others? If so, why? Are your current levels of trust mainly influenced by good experiences or bad? If you trusted more, what good things and what bad things are most likely to happen?

Just write as much as you can, as fast as you can. No restrictions. Chaotic ramblings are perfectly fine. No thinking, no evaluation, no restrictions.

Wait a couple of hours then come back to your entry. Read it slowly. A self-awareness sandwich. Nice. Does someone need to try on a different pair of trusting pants? It's time to decide what your approach to leadership and trust should be.

Trust drives out fear, and at the heart of mistrust is fear.

Find a safe and trustworthy place in your journal to write down your "Leadership Trust Statement." It starts with these words:

From today, my "Leadership Statement of Trust" is to...

Will you share that with anyone, I wonder?

"Let your hopes, not your hurts, shape your future."
—Robert H. Schuller

"They say that seeing is believing...but it's more true to say believing is seeing!"
—Seth Godin

CHAPTER 6

Be the CEO of you.

Building a leader is just like building a business.

YOU CAN'T MANAGE EVERYTHING.

You can't manage anything that you can't control. Can you manage (control) the weather? No, of course not; but you can control your response to it and what you wear. "There is no such thing as the wrong weather, just inappropriate clothing." Ranulph Fiennes—British explorer. Nice one, Ranulph.

Can you manage (control) the mortgage interest rate? Again, no. But you can manage how you manage your own money.

Can you manage (control) the speed limit on the nation's roads? Nope. But you can manage how fast you elect to drive.

Can you manage (control) time? No. But you can manage what you do in the time that we are all given.

Quite simply, there are some things that you can manage (control) and some things that you cannot. For those things that are outside your control, what's the best way to manage and respond to them, I wonder? And, for those things that are inside your sphere of influence and control, what's the best way to manage and respond to those things? You can only control (manage) the things that are controllable (manageable).

CONTROLLING THE CONTROLLABLES

Viktor Frankl, the author of *Man's Search for Meaning*, argues that we can all decide/choose our attitude despite whatever difficult circumstances we find ourselves in...and this from an inmate of a concentration camp who underwent all manner of dreadful humiliations and hardships that you can possibly imagine.

> "Those who have a '*why*' to live can
> accomplish almost any '*how*.'"
> —Viktor Frankl

We should concentrate all of our efforts only on the inter-section between "things that matter" and "things we can control." All other things should be ignored since they will only serve to confuse, frustrate, and confound us.

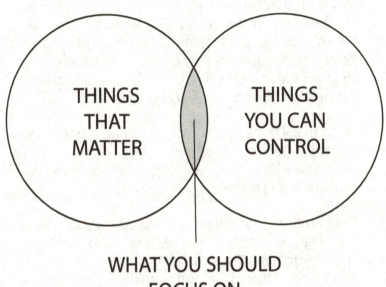

Consider for a moment an Olympic downhill skier. We've seen them at the top of the mountain looking very steely-eyed and determined in the little hut-starting-contraption[1] waiting for the clock to count down to zero before they charge down the hill at breakneck speed trying to, well, not break their necks as they plunge to the finish line a mile below.

As they wait for the bleepy-machine[2] to send them careening down the mountainside, take a moment to think about the sorts of things that are 100 percent outside of their control—there are more than you might imagine:

---

1   It's probably got a rather technical and clever name, but I don't know it, and I don't know any Olympic downhill skiers to ask. Google doesn't seem to want to share this information either. Naughty Google.

2   Again, it has probably got a name. Not a skier.

The weather. The race order of the skiers. How well the other skiers ski. Who their competitors are. The condition of the snow. The layout of the course. Which mountain they ski on. Their competitors' equipment. The behavior of the crowd. The amount of ice on the course. The placement of the slalom gates. The determination and skill of the other competitors. The length of the course. When they ski. The gradient and difficulty of the slope...well, you get the idea.

With so many things outside of their control one wonders why they even bother.

Now consider what they can 100 percent control—thankfully there are lots of these too:

Their attitude. Their optimism and confidence. Their planning and preparation. Their sleep and nutrition. Their hydration. Their breathing. Their choice of equipment. Their drive and ambition. Their belief-sets. Their support team. Their attitude toward defeat. Their history. Their expectations. Their effort... well, you get the idea.

Building a successful business and being a successful leader relies on them controlling the correct controllables and dealing with all of those that they cannot. Journaling helps the journaler identify, focus on, and control the controllables, as well as guide them on what things, circumstances, impediments, and challenges to entirely ignore.

As a general rule of thumb, whenever things are worrying you, the "1,2,3 Worry Model" should be your guide 99 percent of the time.

1. Write down all of the things that are worrying you.
2. Delete from the list all of the things that are out-side of your control.
3. Deal with whatever is left.

Let's have a bash at it now.

Find an enlightened spot in your journal and complete the following:

Write down the Top 10 things that are currently worrying you:

1.

2.

3.

4.

5.

6.

7.

8.

9.

10.

Now cross out all of the things that are outside of your *complete* control from the list above. Since these are not yours to manage, they are not yours to fix.

STOP DRIVING WITH YOUR FOOT ON THE BRAKE.

Consider how much more useful it would be to channel *all* of your energy on the things that you can help fix, rather than some of your energy (entirely wasted energy) on those things outside your control.

When we look at the long list of things that are worrying us, so many of them are not worth the wasted energy worrying about them—much better to use that unproductive energy in a productive way. Stop driving down the freeway with your foot on the brakes: it's a waste of energy, it's unhelpful, it slows you down, it frustrates you, it creates heat and noise, it places unnecessary strain on the engine (and the brakes), and it is entirely dangerous in the medium to long term. Heck it's even dangerous and stupid and counterproductive in the short term. It probably adds to global warming too—so stop it.

There is a wonderful sketch by the genius comedian Bob Newhart, "Stop it!"

In the sketch the psychiatrist played by Bob Newhart learns that his client is worried about being buried alive in a box. She explains that whenever she starts to think about it, she starts to panic.

The psychiatrist asks her whether anyone has ever tried to bury her alive in a box. She reports that no, nobody has ever attempted to do that.

His solution? He simply tells her to stop it.

Take a moment to think about cause and effect.

If you're the kind of leader who is worried about the possibility of a heart attack, for example, there are some elements which are 100 percent outside of your control, genetics, for example, your childhood environment, and so on. What you 100 percent *can* control now, however, is your diet, your exercise, how much you smoke, how much you drink, how you respond to stress, your work/life balance, whether or not you meditate, whether or not you have an annual health check, your sleep, your ability to recognize trigger events, and so on.

Wouldn't it be better for everyone if all the energy you spent worrying about the possibility of a heart attack were re-invested in heart attack prevention and the better enjoyment of life today? Wouldn't the quality of your life improve? And wouldn't your chances of having a heart attack reduce, and wouldn't your chances of surviving the heart attack, if it were to ever transpire, be significantly increased?

If you're worried about the possibility of having a heart attack, either do whatever you can to prevent it, or, in the words of Bob Newhart, "Stop it!"

Fix it, or stop driving with your foot on the brake.

Find a particularly sanguine spot in your journal to write down the following:

> When all else fails, the three things that I can 100 percent control:
>
> My Attitude—My Gratitude—My Effort

YOUR JOURNAL IS YOUR MENTOR.

While some leaders are content to remain in their current role for the foreseeable future, there are others who elect to be on a more structured and developmental career path.

The journey of leadership can look something like the following, with each discrete role requiring different skills, capabilities, and focus:

Lead Self
Lead Others
Lead Managers
Lead a Function

Lead Leaders
Lead a Business
Lead a Group or Enterprise

This means, of course, that before leaders can properly lead others, they need to be able to fully lead themselves. Before they can lead managers, they need to be able to lead others...and so on.

As leaders transition up the corporate ladder from one of these leadership rungs to the next, they sometimes discover that the increase in complexity and demand is, perhaps, beyond them. Others, recognizing that they have perhaps reached a plateau of development and predicting this potential leadership development pinch-point, elect to work with a mentor who helps prepare them for their next role up the ladder. The mentor offers guidance, motivation, emotional support, and a model of leadership that the mentee aspires to master. Your Leadership Journal can help you prepare and transition from one role to the next up the ladder—it can be your mentor. How? Lifelong leadership learning and development with intentionality.

LIFELONG LEADERSHIP LEARNING

Those who believe in lifelong leadership learning have a few groovy things going on:

Self-awareness

Professional humility

A drive for excellence

A willingness to help people reach their full potential

A collaborative spirit

A passion for self-improvement and professional development

Let's take a quick peek at professional development, shall we?

If you're an architect, a doctor, a lawyer, a pilot, an accountant, an engineer, a psychologist, and the like, you will almost certainly be obliged by your certification body to undertake a minimum number of hours of Continuous Professional Development (CPD) for every year that you intend to continue practicing.[3] And you will accept this condition of lifelong learning and accreditation when you elect to pursue that particular career path.

Why it is that leaders are not similarly obliged to continue their learning and development is beyond me, but that's probably the topic of another book.

In order to maintain their chartered status, architects in Britain, for example, need to complete A MINIMUM of thirty-five hours a year (every single year) of structured learning and development from ten topics in the Royal Institute of British Architects (RIBA) core curriculum—a minimum of two hours per year per topic. It's how they, the RIBA and those who carry its chartered status, guarantee a minimum standard of competence in the profession and retain a minimum level of confidence in its proponents.

These minimum development/improvement hours invested in CPD are recorded and sent for approval/accreditation. And, if the hours are not completed, nor the subjects authorized, the individual will lose their professional standing/qualification. Harsh? I don't think so.

Architects and doctors are lifelong learners—otherwise they would have chosen different careers. Lawyers and accountants are lifelong learners—otherwise they would not be allowed to continue to practice. Pilots and psychologists are lifelong learners—otherwise they would not be able to demonstrate competence in their role.

---

3   Interesting word, right?

Why then are leaders let off so lightly? Why are leaders not obliged to undertake a minimum number of CPD hours? It's a scandal—it really is.[4]

YOUR LEADERSHIP JOURNAL IS YOUR RECORD OF CPD PROFESSIONAL ACCREDITATION.

Let's break it down:

Continuing — Ongoing. Lifelong. Progression.
Professional — High level of education, skill, training, and minimum standard.
Development — Processes that create growth, progress, and positive change.

A typical CPD cycle includes the following phases:

- ❖ Analyze your professional role and priorities
- ❖ Define your professional goals and expectations
- ❖ Assess your professional development needs
- ❖ Create a professional development plan
- ❖ Carry out your planned development activities
- ❖ Formally record your evidence
- ❖ Reflect and evaluate your learning
- ❖ Submit evidence for accreditation review

CPD is a commitment to lifelong reflective learning development—sound familiar? It's exactly like your journaling path, isn't it? In my opinion, every year *all* leaders should be obliged

---

4   The topic of another book?

submit a copy of their Leadership Journal in order to receive their CPD accreditation which allows them to continue to lead.[5]

Your daily Leadership Journaling practice is your own personal commitment to maintaining and improving your professional skills, knowledge, and leadership competencies. It should be relevant to your own development goals, aims, activities, and interests—it should form a record of learning over time, and it should require a minimum standard of application.

YOUR LEADERSHIP JOURNAL IS YOUR PREFLIGHT CHECKLIST.

Imagine that you're a commercial airline pilot—yes, with the posh hat and everything, if you like.

Before each and every flight, you would be required to perform all of your preflight checks in order to satisfy yourself that the aircraft was entirely air worthy. You would check all of the control surfaces, the fuel, the radio, the equipment, the instruments and dials in the cockpit, the paperwork and flight-plan, and so forth.

It is a minimum standard that your airline and passengers would expect.

You would never consider taking the aircraft to the skies unless and until you had fully completed these critical processes. You would not call, "Chocks-away!"[6] unless you knew exactly where your destination was, where you were starting from, the weight and balance and range of the aircraft, the full cargo manifest, and so on.

What's more, you would complete these critical steps not on some flights, not on most flights, not on those flights that you fancied it—but on *every single flight*—even if you didn't somehow quite feel like doing it one day...or you didn't have

---

5 Where should they send them, and who would review them? No idea, but it's worth thinking about.

6 Yes, I do know that they don't really do this these days, but I'm an incurable romantic at heart, and I like to think that they still do.

time and were running a little late...or you had had a rough night...or you had a headache...or you just forgot.

It's as fundamental and non-negotiable as this: if you're a pilot, you simply 100 percent have to do these things, 100 percent correctly, 100 percent of the time. Preflight checklists as well as CPD hours is what you sign up for when you take on the piloting gig—and they are 100 percent non-negotiable.

Your Morning Momentum in your journal is your preflight checklist for the day.

Every day you should take at least a few moments to consider what route you are planning on flying today—what's on the schedule for the day. Basically, where you are, where you want to be by the end of the day, and whether or not the tools and resources at your disposal are ready for the trip...and if not, you fix them—otherwise you can't fly.

YOUR LEADERSHIP JOURNAL IS ALSO YOUR FLIGHT SIMULATOR.

Sticking with our commercial airline pilot analogy for a moment.[7]

Imagine that you were a commercial airline pilot and that the airline you flew for had sent you a request to attend your annual CPD session in the company flight simulator. What do you imagine the airline would say if you wrote back arguing that you've been a professional pilot for over fifteen years without incident, and you didn't think that a person with your skill and experience needed to attend these pointless flight simulator development sessions?[8]

What do you imagine that professional pilots do in their flight simulator time: take off from JFK and fly an uninterrupted, uneventful nine hours in beautiful weather conditions till they

7   Yes, I know we do this a lot—but there are a lot of similarities and parallels between leadership and flying—there just are.
8   Clue: the second word would likely be "off."

land in London, Heathrow? No, not a bit of it. They are given a series of unexpected and extremely taxing scenarios: the engine catches fire on takeoff; the plane gets hit by lightning; they have to land in fog, and their instrument cluster is on the fritz; the hydraulics have failed, and landing gear doesn't lock when winding manually; systems start to shut down randomly in a critical cascade of electrical shortages, and so on.[9]

Why does the airline do this? It's the single best, cheapest, safest, fastest way for airlines to guarantee a minimum standard of pilot competence as well as the best, cheapest, safest, fastest way for commercial pilots to improve their skill sets and abilities.

Now then, what do you imagine the airline would say if the pilot in charge of the simulator crashes and burns time and time again when presented with any of these tricky scenarios in the simulator? Do you imagine they say, "Oh well, Frank, never mind. Not to worry—at least you tried. Here are the keys to one of our newest $420 million 747s[10]—you're off to Dubai tomorrow with three hundred and sixty-five passengers. Fingers crossed, old boy! Off you trot. All the very best!"?[11] No, no they wouldn't.

So, flight simulator training is designed to explore the tricky and challenging situations that pilots may face, as well as offer a way to record lessons learned and improve skill sets. Hmmmm, does that ring a bell?

Leaders need to complete their daily preflight checks and flight simulator training just as much as do pilots: and surgeons, and architects, and accountants, and engineers, and so on—it's just non-negotiable. At least you can take some comfort from the fact that you're in esteemed and august com-

---

9   A pilot friend of mine, when she read that paragraph, said, "Oh, you mean a busy Saturday night over New York?" Wait, what?

10 I checked.

11 Clue: the second word would definitely be "off".

pany. You should think of your daily Leadership Journal as your preflight checklist as well as your desktop flight simulator.

Let's consider some of the preflight checks of other professions we have already mentioned:

Architects.

Yes, I do realize that architects don't perform preflight checks in quite the same way as pilots; but they never, ever, ever, build without first surveying the land and ensuring the foundations and superstructure are appropriate for the loading. Whether they feel like it or not, they simply must submit plans for approval to the town planners—otherwise the building just doesn't happen—it's that simple: it's that binary.

Surgeons.

I recognize, too, that surgeons don't perform preflight checks in the same way that pilots do either; but they never, ever, ever operate without first ensuring that they have all of the equipment they might need in case the surgery goes south. They check and re-check that the person they are about to slice open is the same person as on the roster. They check and re-check the medication that they have on hand is appropriate for the procedure that they are planning. They count and recount swabs and scalpels and retractors and so forth. They check MRIs and x-rays—otherwise they aren't permitted to cut—it's that simple: it's that binary.

Accountants.

It's simply not good enough for an accountant to wing it. They have to be completely familiar with all of the ever-changing rules, laws, and regulations. If they want to retain their professional status, they are obliged to keep up to date with the current best practices and secure their ongoing professional development credits. It's that simple: it's that binary.

Your Leadership Journal is your CPD log, as well as your preflight checklist at the start of every day: it's also your essential flight simulator, as well as your captain's log.

CAPTAIN'S LOG[12]

All commercial and navy captains are required to keep a ship's log.

Logbooks (also referred to as captain's logs or deck logs) record a series of chronological entries documenting the daily activities of the ship and its crew.

The level of information ranges from simple entries documenting mundane daily routines all the way to detailed meteorological and operational accounts. Information can include:

✧ Documentation of disciplinary hearings

✧ Sick lists

✧ Occasional injuries

✧ Important conversations with senior teams

✧ Use of daily rations and the like

The primary reason for maintaining these logs is for navigation and safe passage. It is here that the captain records fixes, courses steered, weather forecasts, wind speed and direction, including periodic readings of the ship's heading and speed, and its regular barometer readings. Why do you imagine that captains are required to take such detailed daily notes?

---

12   If you just said "Stardate 43945.7" in your head, I think I might be in love with you. If you don't know what I'm talking about, I still love you...just not as much. Sorry.

Similarly, pilots are obliged to keep logbooks that record every flight the pilot has flown—flight time—miles flown—registration and configuration details of the aircraft—types of instrument approaches—weather conditions, and so on. They are also required by their country's aviation authority to keep records of their hours in flight simulators. These are legal documents, and completing all of these details is mandatory. Why do you think pilots are also all required to take such regular, accurate, and detailed notes?

How do you imagine that the navy, for example, uses these logs to help with more accurate scenario planning? How might they be used in training? What about drill preparation, how might they be utilized here? Chapter 12 will explain how navigators would use these daily logs (journals) in order to help ship captains and pilots get to where they ultimately need to be.

On April 22, 1850, the Prussian Minister of War, August von Stockhausen, ordered that all commanders of major units should keep daily war diaries. Since 1907, British commanders have similarly been obliged to keep daily war diaries. Why do you imagine this is?

WHAT WOULD JULIUS CESAR SAY?

We all know that Julius Cesar famously declared following his Pontic triumph, "*Veni, vidi, vici.*"

I came, I saw, I conquered.

He could almost just as easily said, "*Veni, didici, vici.*" We would have known at that point that he, too, journaled.[13]

I came, I learned, I conquered.

---

13 Which he certainly did, by the way. OK, he had somebody else do the actual writing for him, but he did it diligently. Coincidence? You decide.

Seek out a captain-type space in your journal, and complete your captain's log for yesterday. Your vessel is your company, of course.

CAPTAIN'S LOG

Your Surname _____

Your Vessel _____

Date: _____

Yesterday I...

Yesterday we...

I learned that...

I must remember to...

---

*"All leaders are learners. The moment you
stop learning, you stop leading."*
—*Rick Warren*

CHAPTER 7

Who coaches the boss?

Your journal is your executive coach.

COACH YOURSELF BEFORE COACHING OTHERS.

Can I be super-honest with you for a quick moment? I'd sit down for this one if I were you, it might sting a little. Ready? OK, here we go...you're not perfect!

No, not even nearly.

There, I've said it.

Deep, slow breaths; you'll be OK in a few minutes once you're over the shock and disappointment.[1]

Look, I'm not saying that your mom lied to you as she bounced you on her knee as a toddler assuring you that you were simply the cleverest, most beautiful, and talented special little soldier ever in the history of the world, yes, yes you are. Yes, you are. Yes. Who's mommy's clever helper? You are, that's who. Mwah!

...No, she didn't lie exactly. She meant those things, of course, but I'm going to argue that she was a tad biased, wouldn't you say?

In fact, you're far, far, far from perfect. Ouch![2]

But take heart, my young journaling warrior, help is at hand in the very beautiful shape of a specialized ceramic Japanese art form, *kintsugi*.

KINTSUGI

This is the Japanese art of taking something broken, something like a ceramic bowl, for example, and by repairing it in a very specific way, it becomes stronger and even more beautiful and valuable than it was before.

Proponents of *kintsugi* take the broken ceramic pieces and glue them back together with lacquer that has been mixed with powdered gold (typically) or other powdered precious metal, silver or platinum, for example.

---

1   Maybe go have a nice cup of tea and break out one of those fancy biscuits that you were saving up for when someone special pops around unexpectedly.

2   Maybe two of those biscuits after all.

The practice is intended to actually highlight or draw attention to the breaks/cracks/imperfections, not to try to hide or mask them. In other words, the beauty of the restored piece is to be found in the fact that the flaws are specifically celebrated, not ignored or camouflaged.

The wisdom of *kintsugi* is that you, just like the bowl, are a much better leader because of your flaws, not in spite of them.

You, like all leaders before and after you, will, at times, fail and flounder—you will make missteps and mistakes—you will mess up and screw up BUT, if you celebrate and, critically, take time to learn the lessons from them, you will be made stronger and all the more glorious because of them. If you try to hide, deny, ignore, or mask your flaws and imperfections, you will be left all the weaker and significantly less valuable.

This is not a case of "what doesn't kill you makes you stronger," this is a case of "where we have messed up, and recognized it, and made a commitment to 'fix' it makes us stronger."

Remember how we said in Chapter 5 that all leaders trade in the currency of truth? This principle extends to your own personal development—it requires trading in truth. Truth is the cryptocurrency of all leaders.

You should make a solid commitment to always tell your journal the truth. In this way, you can recognize the cracks, however gruesome, and start to figure out how to draw attention to them, just like the *kintsugi* bowl: it, like you, will be made more glorious because of it.

Find somewhere really honest in your journal and make a commitment to truth and a commitment to celebrating mistakes just as much as victories—remember, we learn more from our failures and challenges than our victories, after all.

Do it now—twenty to thirty words making a commitment to always tell your journal the truth, the whole truth, and nothing but the truth. Brutal truths, not convenient truths.

Start with these words:

> I swear by Almighty (insert something appropriately significant to you and your life), that I will always tell myself via my Leadership Journal the truth, the whole truth, and nothing but the truth to the very best of my ability to do so, because...

Nice.

THE 12 LS OF PERSONAL LEADERSHIP

Let's take a few moments to pressure test the truth commitment you just made to yourself and your journal by considering the 12 Ls of leadership.

> NOTE: This list of 12 is not a definitive leadership list, it's just to get you started—but it's enough of a starting point that covers at least 80 percent of things we need to think about with some consistent regularity.

Maybe give yourself a quick temperature check against each of the elements of this list. Maybe return to it again in, say, three months. Compare the answers. Act accordingly.

Where you have to give yourself a score: 1 = OMG, dreadful. 10 = OMG, outstanding. Then, write down a few honest words (ten to twenty words, max) about how you're *really* doing.

Be super-honest—otherwise, who are you fooling—only you. Remember the solemn commitment you made just three short paragraphs above.

1. How have you *lived* your life so far? 1–10

2. What have you *loved* the most about your life so far?

3. How good are you at *listening*? 1–10

4. How good are you at *looking* ahead? 1–10

   Looking ahead. Visualizing. Planning. Imagining.

5. What are the most important things have you *learned*?

6. What makes you *laugh*?

7. How good is your *ladder*? 1–10

   Who's on your team ahead of you? Above you? Below you?

8. What do you want to be your *legacy*?

9. How should you *lead*?

10. How good are you at getting you *legal* house in order? 1–10

    Tax, money reporting, wills and trusts?

11. How good are you at measuring your own *landmarks* and *guideposts*? 1–10

12. What do you need to *leave* behind? Let go of?

ANOTHER DIRTY DOZEN...

If you enjoyed that list of 12 questions that were mainly focused on you, why not have a run at these 12? These ones are more focused on the business.

Again, as you answer these questions, let "truth" be your watchword.

Again, in order to track progress, this list will also need revisiting pretty soon.

This list below and the list above are the starting points for self-awareness, self-development, and, more importantly, self-coaching.

So, deep breath again...let's dive in:

In my business...

1. Here's what's currently right, or working well...

2. Here's what's wrong, or currently broken...

3. Here's what's missing, or lacking...

4. Here's what am I confused about right now...

5. Here's what needs simplifying right now...

6. Here's what's most important to the business right now...

7. Here's what makes me happiest about the business...

8. Here's what I am most proud of in the business...

9. Here's the single most important skill that I need to develop...

10. Here are the Top 3 goals for the next ninety days...

    I.
    II.
    III.

11. Here's what I am refusing to accept or admit...

12. Here's the single best thing for me to do right now...

Before we put a bow and a lovely handwritten tag on this gift of a chapter, take a moment to consider these final three questions:

1. How valuable do you think this exercise has been? 1–10?

2. How often should great leaders have these kinds of conversations (reflections) with themselves? Once a lifetime? Once a decade? Once a year? Once a quarter? Once a month? Once a week? What say you?

3. Which questions reveal the most: the really easy questions, or the really difficult ones?

Find a suitably gorgeous and self-aware space in your journal to consider the couple of dozen answers you gave in the two exercises above.

Based on my answers to the questions above,
I now realize...

   1.

   2.

   3.

Terrific! Good stuff.

This has been a short but powerfully important chapter, because you just learned the basis of self-coaching. The questions above, when asked of yourself with some regularity and answered with bucket-loads of honesty, will tell you all you need to know about developing the *critical* leadership skill of self-awareness.

> *"What is necessary to change a person is*
> *to change his awareness of himself."*
> —Abraham Maslow

CHAPTER 8

Self-coaching— session one.

First, let's define the scale of the issue.

A PROBLEM WELL DEFINED IS HALF SOLVED.

You can't solve a problem that you cannot first see, recognize, or define. That's why doctors take x-rays, MRIs, blood tests, and a full history before writing out a prescription, after all.

Charles Kettering wisely espoused: "A problem well defined is a problem half solved."

And Albert Einstein said: "If I were given only one hour to save the planet, I would spend fifty-nine minutes understanding the problem, and one minute resolving it."

While Bertie E.'s position might seem a little extreme and far-fetched, the point is well made: your success as a leader will be directly correlated to, and determined by, your ability to predict, identify, and corral resources in order to help resolve problems. And your ability to resolve problems will be directly determined by your ability to first accurately define them.

Remember, poor leaders often go charging off half-cocked in their eagerness to go fix things without first having a crystal-clear view of the real problem—right down to its very root, its very core.

It is, of course, reassuring that they want to go charging headlong in, tilting at dragons like the noble old Don Quixote but, if you're familiar with the tale, sometimes those dragons are actually windmills, not dragons at all; and in the long run that doesn't help anyone, least of all the fair Dulcinea.

The moral of the story is that you should not attempt to fix problems that aren't well understood. For that, first recognize the power and usefulness of accurate Problem Statements.

THE POWER OF WELL-DEFINED PROBLEM STATEMENTS

A Problem Statement is a well-considered and well-crafted description of the issue(s) that need(s) addressing, or the condition(s) that need(s) prioritizing and improving.

Constructing a well-defined Problem Statement allows the considered leader to accurately and specifically identify the gap between the current state and the desired future state or goal. It also helps everyone understand in detail exactly what needs to be improved, what success looks like, and how it will be measured.

Without encouraging anyone to wax lyrical till their heart's content, a good Problem Statement usually runs to around a decent-sized paragraph—four or five sentences at a bare minimum.

> "We need to find another two million dollars in profit by year end, or else," just doesn't cut it, I'm afraid.

Try...

> "In order to deliver to our shareholders the fifteen percent EBITDA detailed in the business plan, we likely need to make some immediate top line, as well as bottom line, changes in trajectory.
>
> Due mainly to the unexpected increase in the costs of raw materials over the last three quarters, which have risen from twelve percent cost of finished goods to around nineteen percent cost of finished goods, we forecast a deficit of two million dollars EBITDA over the next three quarters. It might be sensible to want to tackle this issue on three fronts—taking a share of the burden between them: purchasing, overheads, and sales.

Purchasing
Especially short-term gains (spot pricing, perhaps), ensuring no loss of manufacturing quality or detriment to our ninety-three percent OTIF targets.

Overheads
What projects can be mothballed that would not impact next year's performance? What CAPEX projects need to be revisited with perhaps a more realistic (deferred) commencement date?

Ideally there would be no reduction in marketing spend, nor R & D projects—since these two might seem like easy wins—but they mortgage our future and take no real wit or skill to execute.

Sales
A normal spread of business may not, in time, deliver the increases that we need, therefore projects over three hundred thousand dollars seem our most sensible target.

Our typical sales cycle for projects of three hundred thousand dollars plus in value is six months, and our typical conversion rates for these types of projects is around eighteen percent. Perhaps switch sales efforts to larger account sales."

...you know, something like that. It certainly makes clear what you want to establish, and how it might be measured and managed.

A real plan can be born of that kind of problem statement without too much effort.

CAB-SAV LANGUAGE

When the best leaders define their problems, they don't use euphemisms.

They don't pretty-up the problems by positioning them as "challenges," or "tasks," or "trials," or "difficulties," or "concerns."

Instead, they use "Cabernet Sauvignon language" to define them.

> For "Cabernet Sauvignon" read: full-bodied, robust, fruity, and emotional language.
>
> I'm not advocating that you should exaggerate or overstate the issue, of course, but do pepper your Problem Statements with visceral and highly charged and emotional language. They are not "challenges," but they are "threats," "risks," "suffering," "troubles," "hazards," "menaces," "perils," "scourges," "blights," and so on.

We don't want gentle and polite and politically-correct euphemisms. Gentle euphemisms round-off the sharp edges and child-proof the kitchen. We don't want that. We want danger, and peril, and threat wherever you look.

Use full-bodied language that gets you really grumpy with the situation. Grumpy enough to really lose patience with it. Grumpy enough to start to move the furniture around. Grumpy enough to care. Grumpy enough to measure. Grumpy enough to persist. Grumpy enough to fight. Grumpy enough not to settle. Grumpy enough to move the needle.

If you were to write the Problem Statement above and add a few really juicy expletives (poetically and judiciously inserted, of course; we're not barbarians, after all), you will note how the tenor of the issues becomes soooooo much more immediate, visceral, and compelling.

Go on, give it a go: it's fun, really.

Also, it helps the people who will have to deliver the solution to the problem(s) to be under no misapprehension or misunderstanding as to the severity of the situation, nor the level of commitment that will be applied to solving it.[1]

LOOSE/TIGHT SOLUTIONS

Behind every problem to be solved, there is a human problem and a resource-allocation problem to also be solved. This means that whatever your solution looks like, it has to include full consideration of people as well as time, cash, competitor response models, and so on.

> For "people" also think: effort, attention, resources, change, comfort-zones, habits, culture, values, risk, and the like.

If your solution statement to your problem statement does not consider these issues, it will fail. Do I mean it "might" fail, or it will "perhaps" fail, or it will "possibly" fail? No, I mean it will definitely fail. Why? Because NOTHING happens in any business other than through the efforts of its people. More on this in Chapter 12.

The Problem Statement should be loose enough that people can get creative in the delivery of it, but tight enough that people don't misunderstand what needs to be achieved.

"Ah, but Antonio," I hear you cry. "People are important, yes, but do we really need them all that much? What about 'emerging technology'? What about cryptocurrency or blockchain? What about 'plug and play'? Is artificial intelligence the answer to 'people' problems? Is 5G the solution we have been hoping for? Quantum computing? Virtual reality, robotics, web3, or

---

1 Judicious expletives are always to be entirely encouraged. When writing Problem Statements, when giving good news, and for town halls. Give them a try—you'll see. If anyone is offended by them, perhaps the commercial world is not for them. I wonder what these people *really* say when they hit their thumb with a hammer. Sugar? Not a chance!

biometric computing? Can emerging technology and computing help us?"

Well, maybe...but, not really, no. For the moment,[2] you will always likely find that humans, not technology, are at the core of your most immediate solutions.

If you were to reread the problem statement above, you'll see that it's loose-tight: loose enough for the management teams to figure out the nuts and bolts, but tight enough to see where you are looking for solutions. With the statement shown above, nobody should be zooming off looking for companies to purchase, looking to reduce workforce by 20 percent, and so on.

With the right type of Problem Statement the source of the solution should not be like looking for the source of the Amazon.

THE SOURCE OF THE NILE AND THE AMAZON

In August 1858, Captains John Hanning Speke and Richard Burton discovered the source of the Nile—Lake Victoria Nyanza.

In the future, whenever you go in search for the source of any solution devised in response to a business issue you have faced, it will likely be a much easier search for you than that of Hanning and Burton, who both nearly died in their pursuits.

All you will have to do is go check it out in your Leadership Journal because, if you're doing it right, that's likely where the issue was first identified and where the Problem Statement was first explored—remember the Captain's Log, the Pilot's Logbook? And countless CPD record-books? Explorers, too, were methodical at keeping journals.

---

2   In some post-apocalyptic, dystopian future things might well be different, of course. But for now, the answer will likely be found in people (managers and leaders) who can design and implement processes, products, services, and systems to cure the company of its ills. Ask me again in ten years, and I am sure the answer might well be a different one. But, for now, it's Charlie and Emily and Mark who will fix things.

If leaders don't journal, the original identification of their challenges and the source of their solutions will be as difficult to pin down as the source of the Amazon.[3] If you have five minutes, Google it—it's worth the search—"Where is the source of the Amazon?"—to see why, you'll have to go take a look, but even today it's still a topic of heated debate.

Remember, too, that the source of some problems are extrinsic (outside your personal motivations), and the source of others are intrinsic (take a look in the mirror).

GO BACK A CHAPTER.

Remember the two lists of questions that we considered at the end of Chapter 7? Go take another look at your answers.

> NOTE: If you didn't fully complete them, now's the perfect time to do so. You'll need the answers to those questions to form the source of the answers we will be looking for next. Go on, off you pop.

The answers to some of the questions explored in Chapter 7 will, as sure as eggs are eggs, give you some new ammunition to start to think about a problem or two that need addressing. This is the perfect time to flex those new Problem Statement muscles.

Find a solutions-oriented space in your journal and construct a beautifully written and expletive-laden loose-tight Problem Statement—you'll feel all the better for it, I promise.

And, if you think about it, hasn't your journal just become your leadership coach? Lovely.

---

3   And, no, the answer is not Jeff Bezos. Naughty!

SPEAKING OF COACHING

Whenever a leader (or a manager, or a coach, or a parent, or the like) is coaching someone, the best way for them to develop as quickly and as effortlessly as possible is to have the coachee define what "great" might look like, and, conversely, what "dreadful" might look like for the particular attribute, or belief, or skill at hand.

Let me demonstrate what that means for, say, a leader.

Let's construct two lists: one for very well-developed leadership attributes, and one for very underdeveloped leadership attributes.

Before you read on, you might want to have a go at this one—it's a doozie of an exercise for developing leaders.

I leave some spaces at the bottom of this table where you can insert your own ideas:

CHARACTERISTICS OF VERY UNDERDEVELOPED LEADERSHIP EXCELLENCE	CHARACTERISTICS OF VERY WELL DEVELOPED LEADERSHIP EXCELLENCE
Does not "think outside the box" and is restricted by current methodologies and systems.	Is an effective coach and regularly commits to the coaching process with their team(s).
Is inconsistent and does not stick to agreed goals. Priorities change too often. Is inconsistent, unreliable, and unpredictable.	Views areas of personal weakness as a challenge to overcome—actively thinks of better ways to compensate for weaknesses.
Does not stay calm and organized in the face of adversity. Is negatively affected by high-pressure situations.	Looks at problems as stimulating challenges and encourages good problem statements. Prioritizes all of the "open" issues well.

Is largely reactive and does not properly plan ahead. Is inconsistent with how they utilize resources.	Has realistic expectations of their own capabilities and readily admits those areas where they are not proficient and might need help.
Is poor at delegating preferring to try to fix everything themselves. Does not have time to develop their people.	Will call on others for assistance instead of allowing their own weakness to negatively impact the business.
Plays favorites and does not manage their broader relationships well.	Accepts full responsibility for what's happening.
Poor at communicating short-term, medium-term, and long-term goals. Prioritizes poorly.	Has high degree of self-awareness and is aware of the power of their behavior and responses. Consistently seeks critique and feedback.
Is unclear and inconsistent in management style.	Is high in EQ and collaborative in their approach to all things.
Externalizes issues. Builds walls and a culture of fear and reprisal.	Maintains appropriate emotional composure during times of stress/crisis.
Is not good at encouraging a culture of full accountability and self-responsibility.	Listens to actively understand, not simply to respond. Elegantly clarifies the others' point of view.

Ooof, what a heavy-duty list.

WHERE DO YOU CURRENTLY SIT?

Imagine the table above represented a continuum from left to right.

1 = all the way over on the left (dreadful) to 10 = all the way on the right (godlike and delicious in every single conceivable leadership way).

Where would you grade your own current skill sets and competencies from 1 to 10? Are you a 6? A solid 7? It's not a 10, I promise.

Let's pretend you just self-graded as a solid 7. Great. I thought so too.

Now think about the things that you'd have to do more of over the next 30-60-90 days in order to move the needle from a 7 to an 8.

Obviously, you'd have to do more of the things in the right-hand column and fewer of the things in the left-hand column—so let those things shape your thinking.

Well, haven't you just started to draft the bones of a gorgeous leadership self-development plan? Yes, yes you have. Clever old you.

Remember the list from Chapter 1—the list of what a dreadful leader looks like? All of that stuff goes into the left-hand column, of course.

If you were so inclined, couldn't you also draft all of the stuff that you've just identified into a gorgeous Problem Statement with lots of Cab-Sav language? Couldn't you also then have it sit front and center in your Leadership Journal while you work on the problem with some regularity and intentionality? I think you could.

For now, though, let's put together a quick 30-60-90-day action plan so that we can gallop off to Chapter 9 with a clear head and all due dispatch.

Find a suitably solutions-oriented space in your journal: copy and complete this important thought:

In order for me to continue on my development path to truly world-class leader status (or at least the very best leader that I can be), I need to find out how to develop these attributes and skills over the next 30-60-90 days...

1.

2.

3.

4.

5.

OK, sounds like a good plan. Go do that then. Quickly. Today.

"The secret of getting ahead is getting started. The secret to getting started is breaking your complex, overwhelming tasks into small manageable tasks, and then starting on the first one."
—*Mark Twain*

CHAPTER 9

Gratitude changes your attitude.

Attitude changes everything.

TRAINING OUR REPTILE BRAIN

Our brains are a very busy and complex system. They have lots to do: control thought, regulate emotion, lay down memory, process vision, understand touch, organize motor skills, manage speech and communication, regulate temperature, ensure breathing...and nearly every other single biological and conceptual process that controls and maintains us as we pass through life. It's a clever old sausage, our brain, and no mistake. But it is not infallible, it's not perfect—not by a loooooong stretch...and that means neither are you.

Let's take a quick Big Red Bus Tour of what's rockin' in our noggin'. In truth, humans really have three main brain structures, not one. I know, shocker.

The oldest part of our brain is to be found at the basal ganglia and the brain stem. This basic circuitry began to form around 560 million years ago, and it became what we now commonly refer to as the primal brain, or lizard brain.

This part of the brain is mainly concerned with our most primitive drives related to thirst, hunger, sexuality, and territoriality, as well as balance, habits, and procedural memory. Basically, this part of the brain tries really hard to keep us safe as well as produce more lizard brains, given half the chance. It makes sure that we care for our young, and it manages all of our primal basic urges such as pleasure and fear. It's where our fight/flight/freeze impulses live large, even today.

The next part of the brain to emerge/evolve was the paleo-mammalian or emotional brain, which developed around 250 million years ago. This part of our circuitry is primarily concerned with more sophisticated processing: more complex emotions and more advanced aspects of laying down memories and more sophisticated learning and recall.

The new kid on the evolutionary block, so to speak, is the neocortex, or rational brain, and it is where we hold our higher brain functions such as perception, decision-making, social skills, language, complex learning, and conscious thought. This first appeared around 200 million years ago, and it is found in mammals, but in no other animals.[1] It is this remarkable and uniquely complex wiring that allowed human culture to uniquely develop and evolve so quickly.

All three parts of the brain, though entirely separate evolutionary components, work in close conjunction with one another—they are very well interconnected, and each part influences the other parts in countless ways, of course.

Depending on the circumstances, certain parts of the brain take charge. When, for example, we place our hands on something hot, the reptilian brain does not send a memo to the other parts of the brain asking them to think about bringing up at the "any other business" segment of the next brain board meeting the fact that our absent-minded human has put their hand on something hot, and if we could spare the time, might we advise it that it would be better to consider removing its hand for fear of damage to the skin, nerves, and other systems. No, it *immediately* takes over full control of almost every part of our anatomy, without question, hesitation, or permission, and it has our motor system rapidly move the hand without thought, without discussion, and without question. It makes us blink when something approaches our face at speed. It makes us violently cough when we swallow a fly. It keeps our blood constantly flowing, and it maintains our digestion and breathing without any thoughtful intervention from us whatsoever. The part that controls all of this self-preservation stuff is the reptilian brain.

This same part of the brain is hard-wired to look for danger—it's how our species managed to survive and persist to this stage of development, after all.

It firmly resists the unknown and tells us to stick to what we are familiar with, and it warns us against taking risks: it constantly scans the environment, on the lookout for anything that

---

1   It's the gray, slimy, walnut-looking bit that we all think of when we think "brain."

might threaten us. "The red berries are OK," it says. "We have eaten the red berries before. Eat the red berries, sure, enjoy yourself...but beware the blue berries. Stay well away from the blue ones; we don't know what they do. Blue berries might be dangerous—they look dangerous." The reptilian brain (and we all have one) is extremely adept at keeping us alive, but it is, at the same time, extremely rigid; it can be very persistent, overly insistent, and it's somewhat of an overzealous and compulsive worrywart.

FIGHT, FLIGHT, OR FREEZE?

As mentioned, our lizard brain is the seat of our fight, flight, or freeze response as well as the root of all our most primal emotions.

You've probably already guessed it, but it's where our resistance to change lives. It's where our comfort zones live, as well as where most of our leadership blind spots emanate. Oooh, it has a lot to answer for, our reptilian brain, and it tends to shout the loudest drowning out other, more rational, voices when we try to reason with ourselves that the shadow we just saw scoot across the front lawn in the moonlight was much more likely to be a rabbit than a murderous zombie—but the murderous zombie story always wins, no matter how much we try to convince or persuade ourselves that we are being foolish and we should just bloody well grow up. We're responsible, well paid, important, and rational adults, after all; leaders of men, and very important, and what's wrong with us, anyway? Honestly! We should just put our big boy pants on and grow up.

And, despite of all of that sensible and mature rationalization, our lizard brain still compels us to race to lock the doors as well as take a baseball bat to bed...irrespective of the fact that absolutely nobody we know, or have ever met, has ever been killed by zombies—and yet we have seen rabbits count-less times with nary so much as an ensuing scratch![2]

Being such an important, well-adjusted, experienced, log-ical, well-educated, thoroughly sensible individual with lead-ership responsibilities means, of course, that you can drown out that reptile part of the brain that has you fearful and sec-ond-guessing everything, right? Wrong! Even you are subject to the vagaries of this multimillion-year-old wiring.

Which means that whenever we feel suddenly attacked or threatened, our lizard brain shuts down all other thinking and screams one of three things at the top of its lungs:

1. "Attaaaaack! Have at 'em, boys! Victory or death! Follow me! Chaaaarge!"[3]

   Fight.

...or...

2. "Take to the hills! Retreat! Leg it! Man the lifeboats. Women and children first! Discretion is the better part of valor. Run, run away!"

   Flight.

...or...

3. "Uh, now hold on, let me think for a minute. Wait. Just let me think about it. Give me a sec! Ummm. Maybe we could...uhhh, now let me see. Aaaah, no, what about? No, now...hold on...maybe...."

   Freeze.

---

2   Still, better to be safe than sorry, right? And don't get me started on murderous zombie rabbits, for pity's sake!

3   You know, all *Braveheart* and stuff!

And we all know how the highway is literally paved with squashed hedgehogs, rodents, squirrels, and so on wrestling with this kind of critical indecision, right?

But, let's be honest, we all recognize that we don't live in the prehistoric jungle anymore—we've got a corner office by the water cooler, just opposite the elevator. It's nice with a good view of downtown, and the perfect place to eat a cheesy snack at lunchtime. Not many sabretooth tigers wandering around these days,[4] so no big deal, right?

Would that it were so simple, my glorious reader.

When at work we of course know that we're never going to really feel genuinely mortally threatened—believing our life could seriously be at risk.[5] But what if we feel somewhat challenged in some sort of professional way? Like when someone thinks our new initiative is a bad one, or when someone tells us that they simply need that report by lunchtime, or when someone challenges your timeline for delivery on a project, or when your suggestion face-plants in a particularly obvious way? Well, it's still the lizard brain again, but on a slightly more professional and controlled level. While it doesn't have you literally reach for your Colt 45, running from the office as fast as your legs will carry you, or standing there open mouthed in abject shock and horror, it does have you adopt a position of defend, justify, or rationalize.

DEFEND, JUSTIFY, RATIONALIZE

Whenever we find ourselves defending, justifying, or rationalizing (either results, or outcomes, or general, non-specific criticism), it's our lizard brain feeling attacked, and it is screaming at the top of its lungs, "I don't like this…!!!!"

---

4   Well, Billy in accounts, but we don't count him.

5   Well, maybe at the Christmas party when Billy in accounts has had one or two too many and has just picked up the mic and is about to launch into "Proud Mary" on the karaoke. But, other than that, no.

Adrenaline may well be flooding your system; your heart will quicken, your mouth dries up, your blood vessels at your extremities will constrict, directing blood away from the pokey-outey-things that might get bitten off, and inwards to the central organs in preparation to, well, club them over the head, else take to the hills.

Remember, though, that this is what a normal, well-adjusted person tends to do when they feel challenged (attacked) at work—they defend, justify, and rationalize. And it's a surefire way to spot which part of your brain is driving the truck. And, whenever the lizard brain is behind the wheel, nothing good ever comes of that—it typically ends up looking like the freeway at the end of most high-action blockbuster cops-n-robbers movies—carnage.

We (our lizard brain) defends, justifies, and rationalizes whenever it feels challenged or the need to change—even if only a change in thinking. Remember, whenever any human being has to move outside their comfort zone, they have to change. If you want to change the output, we have to change the inputs. And if there's one thing our lizard brains love more than life itself it's our comfort zones, and if there's one thing it abhors more than anything at all, it's change.

CHANGE

We all know that there is one certainty in life, change.[6]

But, what about the certainty of death and taxes? Mark Twain said so, and he's brilliant.[7]

Well, yes, of course, death and taxes too.

And birth? You can't have death without birth.

Well, yes, that too. Birth, death, taxes, and change are all certainties in life.

And pain.

---

6   Except from vending machines, of course. Grrr!

7   But it may have been Daniel Defoe...or Benjamin Franklin. There seems to be some confusion, sorry.

OK, OK, it seems there are a quite a few certainties in life, including, but not limiting itself to change. Better?

Better.

Thanks.

...and injustice.

We've moved on, so shut it!

But, we don't like change do we—or, more specifically, our lizard brains don't like change, and they fight against it whenever possible.

Humans all have a standard response to change—it's a process that cannot be avoided—it's called the change curve. The bad news is that there's no avoiding it, and there are no shortcuts. But take heart, there's some good news on the way too.

THE CHANGE CURVE

Whenever a person is forced out of their comfort zone, they must transition through the change curve. I say "forced" because, left to our own devices, we tend to want to stay inside our comfort zones—they are warm and toasty and fluffy and safe and familiar and gorgeous.

But, whenever circumstances contrive to squeeze us outside our comfort zone, we must traverse the change curve path. The stimulus for change could be almost anything: an illness, a new direction at work, coming out of the supermarket to discover that someone has rear-ended you, your favorite team lost the championship game, the freezer is on the fritz, your favorite soap opera is not being picked up for another season—you get the idea...change.

There are three main stages to change: endings, transitions, new beginnings. And there are seven stops along the way: denial, realization, resistance, acceptance, uncertainty, understanding, acceptance.

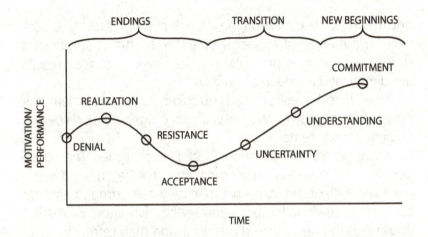

It can sometimes take us mere minutes or hours to transition from one end of the curve all the way through and out the other side, reasonably unscathed and reasonably sanguine about the whole affair.

Sometimes, though, it takes people literally years to get to the "acceptance" phase. Don't we all know someone who is still dealing with divorce after more than a decade? The other party has moved on, settled down, and started a new family while the poor unfortunate left behind is still stalking their social media, having pins stuck into wax effigies of their former spouse, and still goes around bemoaning the fact that they have been wronged in the most dreadful ways.

At the risk of sounding callous, get over it—rather, get over yourself—rather, your lizard brain should be encouraged to move on and give you some peace before the new comfort zone becomes the anger stage that you're perpetually stuck in (and have learned, rather counterintuitively, to quite enjoy—it has become the new normal). It's safe to say that we humans can be tricky to fathom at times.

Since change is 100 percent guaranteed, it is incumbent upon leaders to become expert with helping their people deal with the trials and tribulations of change. The task is a simple one: help people transition the change curve as quickly as possible, and manage it in such a way that the transition time is reduced as much as possible, and the negative consequences are diminished as much as possible.

How? Good question, glad you asked. Let's start by learning how to help ourselves. We put our own oxygen mask on before helping others, remember?

As an extra complication, Kurt Lewin argued that once people have transitioned through the change curve, if we're not ever vigilant, we can find that they can sometimes slide back again. Lewin talks about unfreezing a situation translation (moving to the new desired position), and then refreezing it so that it doesn't go back to its prior shape in the way that some materials do when they are bent out of shape and then left to their own devices...they morph back to where they started. Change management, it seems, is a leader's full-time job. How wonderful is that? ☺

We have seen that, left to its own devices, the human brain has a tendency to self-sabotage (that pesky lizard again). The question therefore is how do we reprogram that ancient wiring as well as those elements of our learned thinking that serve to hamper progress toward reaching our full potential as we embark on our journey of self-development and improvement?

IT'S A MATTER OF PERSPECTIVE.

Isn't it *always* a matter of perspective? Isn't our quality of life a matter of perspective? Isn't our attitude to change a matter of perspective? Isn't our level of gratitude a matter of perspective?

Yes, I think it is.

William Shakespeare said, "There is nothing good or bad, but thinking makes it so." YES, William, bravo!

We can all alter our perspective, alter our mindset, alter our mindset and our beliefs. We weren't born with them, after all; we have learned them along the way. None of us were born as "glass half empty" or "glass half full" people; we learned all that stuff as we transition through our lives.

Are you the kind of person who looks for solutions to every problem; or are you the kind of person who looks for problems in every solution?

HOW FULL IS YOUR GLASS?

Don't say, "Well, it depends...." That's the refuge of the coward.

Be completely honest. What's your normal default position as you hitchhike your way through life: half full or half empty? Sure, it's an oversimplification (or is it?), and it polarizes people into two camps—yes, it's too blunt an instrument, but it's just a game, so play along. You don't have to explain or justify why you typically tend to lean more towards one, rather than the other—just declare it with honesty and without reservation—half empty or half full?

If it's normally half empty:

As supportively as possible, people who believe this have a scarcity mindset. Victories, they believe, are hard won. They tend towards risk aversion. "If I win, someone else has to lose." They have predominantly negative self-talk. Challenges are seen as problems, obstacles to be overcome. They are more oriented to consider what's missing, rather than what's already given. They normally focus on lack—lack of time, or money, or resources, or opportunity. They think more of the past, than the future. They are pessimistic: "realistic," they say. Events and circumstances, they believe, are often stacked against them. They make choices with managing and mitigating loss at the forefront of their minds. They reserve and manage their energy. They worry.

They play to not lose.

If it's normally half full:

They have an abundance mindset. They manage risk and are positive about their expectations. They are optimistic and have the ability to shrug-off disappointments. Their self-talk is supportive and positive, and they are solutions-oriented. "Opportunities will find me," they think, "and I welcome them when they arrive." Quality and creativity and inspiration are born of competition, they believe. "There's plenty for everyone and, if I play the game well, the sky's the limit." They don't cut corners, and they don't cheat: "May the best man win," they say. They believe that they always have a choice, and they smile more than frown.

They play to win.

Are these two wildly different mindsets a choice, or are they somehow preordained from on high?

People (including leaders, of course) are (or will become) what they repeatedly think or believe.

If proof were needed:

> *"We become what we think about."*
> —*Earl Nightingale*

> *"If you think you can, or you can't, you're right."*
> —*Henry Ford*

More on these two later.

We become what we want to believe of ourselves, the world, and others; and we become what we decide to attract.

Or, if that's a little too esoteric for you, we become what we choose to reflect.

If you want to be a great leader, you must learn how to master your negative self-talk whenever and wherever you hear it.

Your daily Leadership Journaling practice is where you develop your positive and developmental self-talk—it's your self-talk gym.

"Thoughts become things. If you see it in your mind, you will hold it in your hand."
—*Bob Proctor*

LET'S START WITH THIS.

It's really, really difficult to have a positive life if it's filled with negative thoughts. And the problem is, unless we intentionally do something about it, we all seem to have so many of them. It's Captain Lizzardy-pants again, I'm afraid.

Recent research conducted by a team of psychology experts at Queen's University in Canada, led by Jordan Poppenk, outlines a method of isolating specific moments when a human is focused on a single idea. They describe this phenomenon as a "thought worm." They claim to be able to now track when we move from one train of thought to another separate one—when we switch between thought worms. They confidently estimate that the average human has over six thousand separate thoughts a day. This is far fewer than earlier estimates of around seventy thousand thoughts per day, but Poppenk et al. claim that we have many thoughts about particular topics at hand—and then switch on to other thoughts. So, it seems that we have around seventy thousand thoughts a day on about six thousand different topics.

That's all well and good, but here's the rather disappointing news: according to research conducted by the National

Science Foundation, around 80 percent of our thoughts are negative. Doing the simple, yet disappointing, mathematics, we reveal nearly 5,600 negative thoughts on around 4,800 negative topics—per day. While not wanting to add to the general pall of negativity,[8] that hardly sounds very healthy, right? ☹

Now that we have dropped that unfortunate truth bomb, consider this: Where do those negative thoughts come from? Outer space? The man in the corner store who always looks at you a little funny? Our parents? Our bank balance? The weatherman—he always seems rather insincere and unnecessarily jolly? And what kind of person becomes a weatherman anyway? They're nearly always wrong, and they never seem to get fired. If I was as wrong about my sales, cash, and profit forecasts as they are with such unerring regularity, I'd be fired in a hot minute! It's such a bogus job, and what's with that stupid moustache? It's not the 1970s, mister, and another thing... ahem! I digress. Sorry. Forgive the run-away negativity—I don't know where that unnecessary and unprompted rant (thought worm) came from.

No, these negative thoughts come from you. 100 percent from you! Which is rather unfortunate because there isn't anyone else but you to account for them—nobody but you to blame. Drat.

The problem with negative thoughts is that they are almost like a virus—these negative thought worms get into the system unnoticed, and before we know it, they have taken hold and are trying to take over, and it often takes an enormous amount of skill and effort to track them down and banish them. According to psychotherapist LaToya Gaines, PsyD, "Usually negative self-talk is so automatic that it happens outside of conscious awareness." We do it without even noticing.

It's really easy to be negative about things, sometimes everything. We're all (humans) really good at negativity: stink-

---

8   To quote the inimitable Bart Simpson, "The ironing is delicious!"

ing thinking. Negativity comes in a wide variety of exotic and tempting flavors: catastrophizing, polarizing, filtering, personalizing. And then, if you're after a really, really good dose of dreadfulness, you can pick and mix, and mix and match your negativity into a veritable mélange of delicious awfulness. Let's have a quick taster menu of the four main flavors and what can be done to deal with them in a slightly more helpful way:

Catastrophizing

This is a delicious one that I believe most of us to some extent fall prey to at times. It basically describes how you automatically expect the worst of all possible outcomes.

On your way to the office, you hit a traffic jam and expect to be stuck for hours.

When you watch the weather forecast and it predicts tornadoes, you race off to the supermarket to buy up all the bottled water, toilet rolls, and plywood you can get your hands on—not forgetting to fill to the brim every canister you own with gasoline.

When you stumble and twist your ankle badly, you immediately picture yourself in a wheelchair...for the rest of your life!

Catastrophizers expect this month's poor sales to extend out to the quarter, the half year, the year, and forever.

They resist the investment in the much-needed capex for fear of not being able to realize the return in the reported timescale.

They don't invest in any new product development initiatives in case there's another Black Friday like there was in 1869...and we all know how horrible that was for everyone, right? Took the world simply years to recover from that one. Wouldn't want another one of those again, no, sir. Brrrrr. Discretion is always the better part of valor, I find. These little hairs on the back of my neck have served me well over the years, and whenever they prickle like this, I find it better to sit tight, batten down the hatches, and ride out the storm

Leaders who think and behave like this not only damage themselves, they damage the business—this kind of negativity leads to massive risk aversion right across the company, and it stands in the way of change, development, and progress.

Remember, the business looks to its leaders for guidance— they're the model everyone tries to emulate, and if the leaders are running around like Chicken Little terrified that the sky will fall, they will start believing and behaving like it too.

Leaders like this have a very lopsided view of risk and reward: they predict all risk and anticipate very little reward— and it needs to be stopped; here's how.

1. Adjust Your Perspective

Take a step back.

Ask yourself, "Really, how likely is this to happen? How many times in my life have I genuinely been stuck in a traffic jam all day?"

"How many times has a poor sales month turned into a poor quarter and a poor year?"

"How many times have I twisted an ankle, only to be subsequently confined to a wheelchair for months on end?"

"Ah yes," you say, "but there's a first time for everything, right?" And to you, dear leader, I say, "Grow up."

2. Use Tools

Decision-making tools help us remain objective, rational, and more intellectual and considerate. The best decisions are normally light on emotion and heavy on thoughtfulness: the use of good decision/planning/strategy tools helps us achieve this. Conversely, the worst decisions are often based heavily on emotion and light on strategic thinking.

To combat catastrophizing, simply sit down with your journal and "scale" the issue.

A. Write a very accurate, not emotionally charged or exaggerated, Problem Statement as you currently see it—consider accurate timescales, review realistic resource-deployment, and so on. You're after an accurate and specific overview.
B. Plot this well-defined problem on a scale from 1–10.

1 = Uncomfortable

It makes you feel a little uncomfortable, but it's not really deadly...

...all the way to...

10 = Truly Catastrophic

I can't possibly see how we might be able to make it through this issue alive.

If the answer is anything less than a 6, grit your teeth, gird your loins, take some deep breaths, go splash water on your face, and just let it slide. And really, let it slide. Move on. Forget it. Hakuna Matata!

7/8/9 = Refer to the extra tools in Chapter 13.

10 = If it's really a 10: remember, almost nothing ever is; but if it really is, then it's time for extraordinary measures. DEFCON 1—maximum readiness, immediate response. Atomic solution. Drop everything else to give your full attention to this alone. It's

a twenty-car pile-up, and there are eight ambulances streaking to the ER, and you're in charge of the triage team.

Call for help—all hands on deck. Nobody eats or sleeps till this is sorted.

It's NEVER a 10! It's simply never Bay of Pigs or 9/11.

Organize. Prioritize. Review. Take a deep breath...is it really 9, or 8? ...or 7, perhaps?

3. Keep Score—every day

Think about the DEFCON analogy above.

Once we calmly start to track the DEFCON levels every day, we soon come to learn that the seriousness of the situation wavers, sure, but it almost NEVER becomes DEFCON 1. We see how incredibly rare the Dealey Plaza, Dallas, plus the sixth floor of the book repository plus the passing presidential cavalcade plus the grassy knoll plus the "magic bullet" really is.

Your Leadership Journal is the place for all three of these solutions: remember, in the poker game of leadership, intellectualizing always trumps catastrophizing.

Polarizing

This particularly tasty morsel of leadership ghastliness is similar to catastrophizing but with the added twist of more of a definite good/bad, up/down, left/right, black/white "certainty."

There's no middle ground with this kind of leader—things are either perfect, or they are a total failure. If you hit budget for twenty-three months straight, but miss a month, you start feel like you're a total fraud and have let everyone down. Really? Have you really, though?

When your people make suggestions does your brain automatically go into polarization mode? Do you find yourself thinking in absolutes: good idea/bad idea; yes/no; love it/hate it?

These kinds of leaders labor under the certain belief that decisiveness is a critical leadership skill which, of course, it is, but any and every virtue taken to excess is harmful.

Remember, it's never all things and everywhere, it's always some things, sometimes, and to some extent. We simply don't live in a black and white world—nearly every leadership decision requires operating firmly in the gray. And remember, if it were easy, clear, and obvious, well, we wouldn't need you, would we?

Everything is on a continuum. With a bit of work, every idea can be made better...or worse. What polarizing is, at its core, is a crushing lack of imagination. Blur your edges—take a step back.

Remember, too, that some you win, and some you learn. But the biggest polarizing-busting method is gratitude, plain and simple. Be kinder to yourself, your ideas, your people, and their ideas. Nothing is ever born fully cooked, fully perfect, fully operational with no kinks, no gremlins, no wriggle-room for improvement.

This kind of leadership positivity is not turning a blind eye to the unfortunate situation or set of circumstances. It's not trying to fool yourself that things aren't as bleak as they truly are. It's much more a belief that you will find a way around it, you will find a solution to it, you will come out the other end of it faster, stronger, better.

☺

Your Leadership Journal is the place to deal with polarization.

Filtering

This is when the leader seeks to magnify all of the negative aspects of a situation or plan and seeks to minimize all of the positive ones. "It's my job," they say, "to look for areas of weakness, places where things might go off the rails—to predict the 'downsides.'" This helps them deal with the eye rolls, and "here we go agains," of course.

If this is you, let me use an image that I am confident you will instantly understand: the glass is half full, OK?[9]

As soon as you notice yourself filtering in this way, race to your journal and jot down a list of all the things that have gone right lately. Things are not as bad as you could make them seem—things are never as bad as you could possibly imagine them to be.

Perspective helps with filtering. President Bill Clinton in his autobiography, *My Life*, explained the importance of not falling prey to filtering.

US presidents hold, arguably, the most important and most powerful position in the world—dealing with some of the toughest and most intractable problems on the planet. Right or wrong decisions would inevitably have extremely broad and long-term effects—perhaps for generations into the future.

Bill Clinton had a tremendously balanced perspective on such thorny issues. He recognized that he wasn't God and couldn't possibly be perfect 100 percent of the time. If he somehow averaged seven out of ten—that is seven good decisions for every three bad ones—he would be able to sleep at night hoping that the seven good ones might outweigh the negative ramifications of the three bad.

Seven out of ten is a great score line: go for seven out of ten...not ten out of ten; it's not reasonable, and it makes you grumpy and everyone around you scared. Stop it!

---

9   It's not half empty—it's never half empty. Neither do we have more glass than we need. The glass is just half full, and that's an end to it—now go figure out how to fill it some more.

Personalizing

Personalizing is the mantra of the victim leader.

"It's not you, it's me."

"It's not your fault that you failed, it's mine for not explaining it better to you."

"I understand why you don't like me. Leadership is not a popularity contest, after all. I'm may not be such a nice fellow, but I'm trying to get the job done."

"The reason this project failed is because I have been too lenient on my people. It's my fault, I allowed them to be lazy and cut corners."

If it's fake...
Stop being such a victim. Grow up. Nobody is buying your fake self-blame. Stop it: it's beneath you.

If it's real...
It's not real—take a step back, take a deep breath—you're a good person. Your friends like you because you're a good person. Your family likes you—because you're a good person.

Your Leadership Journal is the arena for personalization-busting thinking.

So, how are we to deal with all of those pesky (damaging, limiting, destructive) negative thoughts? Should we just simply stick our fingers in our ears again and chant, "La, la, la. Not listening!" with an ever-increasing sense of louder and louder desperation in our voice?

Or, are we simply to become more mindful and, once we spot the virus in the early stages, drown them out with a barrage of much more positive thoughts and optimism? Bingo!

Negativity is, like anything else we do, a habit. The great news is that positivity can easily become one too—we simply have to be intentional about it.

When you are grateful for what you have, including the opportunities that may yet come your way, rather than what you don't have and the opportunities you may have missed, life becomes much more exciting.

Negativity takes no wit, no intentionality, no creativity, and no imagination: it serves little, if any, purpose. Negativity lessens, weakens, and destroys all that it touches. To slightly misquote the inimitable Shania Twain, "Negativity don't impress me much!"

Positivity, on the other hand, takes some conscious effort. It takes some skill and intentionality. It takes some intelligence. Positivity is life-affirming.

Imagine how the world might be different if you were to take a few moments each day in order to learn to be more positive and optimistic. Imagine how the outcomes you experience will be all the more enriched.

SELF-LIMITING BELIEFS—DO WE CHOOSE THEM?

Actually, we do.

What is a belief? And why do we believe what we do? Go on, give your beliefs some thought.

Beliefs are, quite simply, a collection of thoughts that we have learned to hold as true. But, and here's the trick, are they actually empirically true? More often than not, they are not.

So, a belief is something that we hold to be true, but isn't necessarily so.

People once believed, really, really, like 100 percent believed that the world was flat.

It really, really isn't.[10]

They believed that it was impossible (not improbable) for the human frame to run a sub-four-minute mile.

It isn't. Roger Bannister showed us the way.[11]

Scientists, doctors, and medics of every persuasion believed it was impossible (not improbable) to ascend Everest without supplementary oxygen.

It isn't.[12]

When the steam engine was invented, they said that trains should be limited to speeds of less than thirty miles per hour since people would surely suffocate when traveling over that threshold.

They don't.

Some say that there are microchips in our vaccines and that the authorities are using them to track people's movements and ultimately control our thoughts.

There aren't, they don't, and they won't. Grow up.

Human history is positively replete with entirely firmly held beliefs that, it later turned out, were complete hokum. What hokum beliefs might be holding you back right now, I wonder? Hint: there are many.

Human beings are not born with the ability to read, write, walk, and talk—we must learn these skills, and some of them take literally years to learn—some of us are still learning them.

Similarly, we are not born with our beliefs all pre-baked and raring to go the second we are born; these, too, are learned—and some of them have taken years to learn. All of our beliefs are developed over the course of our lifetime—*every single one of them.*

---

10   Sorry flat Earthers, there you have it—spoiler alert! If it were indeed flat, you'd all have traveled to the "edge" by now and pointed it out to the rest of us red-faced scientists...'cept there is no edge, so you can't. Ouch! ☹

11   And no, he didn't use a special shortcut.

12   In fact, these days if you ascend Everest with bottled oxygen, you're considered a tourist climber and a bit of a sissy.

One of the best things about being human is the principle of neural plasticity: the ability to rewire the neural pathways in our brains, to learn new skills and abilities as well as relearn new beliefs, if we so choose.

Our beliefs, just like our skills and abilities, are a choice.

However helpful or unhelpful they may be, you chose your beliefs; and you can choose to re-choose them.

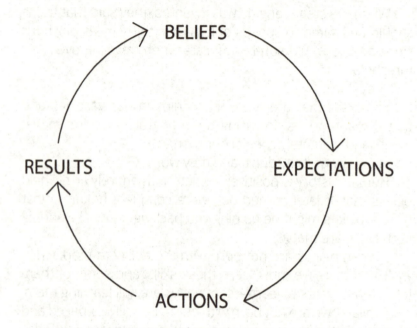

The model above determines that the outcomes of situations, positive or negative, are predicated by one's initial belief paradigm.

A negative set of beliefs and dispositions attracts negative results, and a positive set of beliefs and dispositions results in positive outcomes. These results (positive and/or negative) then feed into our original belief sets serving to further reinforce them: positively or negatively.

If, for whatever reason, you *believe* that a particular person is going to be unfriendly and rather standoffish, you would naturally *expect* them to be cold and behave cynically towards you. As a consequence of this predisposition, you would, in turn, *act* rather guarded towards them, and you would be disinclined to open up to them. You would behave in a cold and unfriendly way towards them. They would, of course, in turn, perceive your hostility, and the *result* would be that they would behave in an unfriendly and rather standoffish way towards you.

And, lo, you were right about that unfriendly person all along. QED.

Clever old you.

If, for whatever reason, you *believe* that people who work for you are not to be fully trusted, you will naturally *expect* the worst of them. You would come to imagine that your job is to act as company policeman. Your *actions* would be to spend time writing lots of lengthy and unambiguous and onerous protocols and processes regarding timekeeping, company property, reporting structures, approval hierarchies, budgetary and spending restrictions, and so on. You would "make examples" of missteps wherever they were ferreted out. As a *result*, your employees, perceiving this all-pervading mistrust from the top, quickly learn to mistrust whatever policies come from above, and they would challenge every decision, complain about every new initiative, and work-to-rule at every possible opportunity. Looking at the resulting behaviors and hostility, the leaders, in turn, would comment to each other about how the employees who work for them are not to be fully trusted and should all be kept at arm's length.

And, lo, you were right about that shifty lot all along. QED.

Clever old you.

If, for whatever reason you genuinely *believe* that your customers are the heartbeat of the business, and they are to be cherished at every turn, you would *expect* your customers to become your best supporters with record-breaking lifetime customer value. You would imagine that they would actively look for opportunities to give you testimonials, referrals, and repeat business wherever possible. Your likely *action* would be to invest in a truly customer-centric organization. As a *result* of this evangelical confidence and investment in them, your business would flourish, and you in turn would be ever more evangelical about how much you cherish your customers.

And lo, you were right about the importance of customer investment all along. QED.

Clever old you.

This universal maxim is true for what you believe of yourself too, of course. As Mr. Ford once said, "If you think you can or you can't, you are right."

Clever old Mr. Ford.

HAVE TO...OR GET TO...

If you were to write down all the things that leaders have to do, you'd quickly realize that it's a really, really extensive list.[13]

Just writing the list down all in one place would likely depress you. "I have to do this.... I have to do that.... I have to do the other...." A long list of important obligations, right?

Let's take a second to consider the principle "I have to...," shall we?

"I have to..." carries with it the weight of obligation, and responsibility, and compulsion. "Have to..." is heavy-duty stuff.

"Have to..." feels like a dangerous and restrictive postulate: it contains within it a sense of scarcity, and threat, and danger—and who in their right mind (their lizard mind) would volunteer for those things? Not I, certainly.

Obligation, responsibility, requirement, liability, encumbrance, and so on are all sufficiently loaded with indebtedness

---

13　Please don't bother, we'd be here all day—and likely well into tomorrow too.

and risk to the extent that most lizard brains would likely try to avoid them if they were given half a chance.

So, let's not give to our easily-triggered lizard brains the opportunity to create unnecessary tension—the leaders' world has enough tension already without us inviting more of it over for a nice cup of tea and a slice of cake: the danger is that it will likely outstay its welcome, ask to borrow your lawnmower, ask for a lift to the airport, and ask to borrow money—it normally does.

The antidote to "have to" is as simple and powerful and elegant[14] as "get to."

Think about all of the things that leaders "get to" do.

Remember, with power comes privilege.

Hmmmm, how lovely and crumpety-warm is that? Delicious, even.

Compare that to the sentence earlier: think about all of the things that leaders have to do.

From now on, when writing a to-do list, write a "get to do" list.

When describing what you have to do today, substitute all of your have-tos with get-tos.

"I get to...today," is so much more inviting than "I have to...today." Brrrr, no thank you.

"Have to..." is playing not to lose. It is scarcity oriented. It is risk averse. It is lizard brain afraid.

"Get to" is playing to win. It is an abundance mindset. It is gain-oriented. It is brave.

While we are on the topic...

"However" and "but" are to be substituted with "and" whenever humanly possible.

---

14   Leadership Rule: As mentioned earlier: in business, if it's simple and elegant, it's almost always right. If it's complex and cumbersome, it's almost always wrong. Remember this—it's a critical litmus test for, well, almost everything.

"I think I see what you're driving at, *however*..." we instinctively know that what comes next throws what we have just said into contrast: we're about to disagree with the notion. Roadblock. Landmine.

"I think I see what you're driving at, *and*..." is much more supportive: it builds up, not knocks down.

"I like your idea, *but*...."

Sounds better (sets itself up better for the sender and the receiver) with, "I like your idea, *and*...." Gorgeous.

"I'm supposed to be on holiday, *but* the office is calling me—it had better be important," is, by its construction, a statement of disappointment, and lack, and frustration.

"I'm supposed to be on holiday *and* the office is calling me. It's likely to be important." Delicious.

Remember, great leaders encourage, and inspire, and build. Watch your mouth—when talking to others as well as yourself—because you listen to you too.

TELL ME, TELL ME, TELL ME...

By using repetitive mental activities or instructions (thoughts) we can *literally* change the pathways in our brains—this neural plasticity is the single best thing about owning a brain. Whenever we think a thought or undertake an action, we reinforce and build pathways in our brain. If we have a positive thought, we create the ability to have easier and more frequent positive thoughts. If we have a negative thought, we increase the likelihood of having another, and then another, and then another, and then another, and then another....

But, remember, our lizard brain is naturally negatively-biased, so much effort will be required. Barbara L. Fredrickson, PhD, in her book, *Positivity*, claims that it takes three positive thoughts to counterbalance just one negative one.

Since whatever we choose to believe serves to further reinforce our beliefs (good and bad), we should spend time considering, reviewing, and shaping our belief sets: they will have a direct 1:2:1 correlation to the quality of the life that we, and those around us, live.

Where could we possibly share, record, and repeat our positive thoughts and intentions, do you think? Oh, of course! *My Daily Leadership*—what a super-dooper idea. ☺

But, what if you get tired of constructing all of this positivity (it's not quite natural—yet), and eventually will want to give up?

THE FORMULA FOR FAILURE

There is a really simple and really powerful six-word formula to guarantee failure at absolutely anything:

Don't start...

...and/or...

...give up!

How gorgeously self-contained and simple is that?

If you want to fail at anything, everything: don't start. And, if you do start, quickly give up. It really couldn't be simpler. If you don't start, you will fail. If you give up, you will fail. 100 percent cast iron guaranteed failure. Lovely.

The converse is true, of course: the absolute best way to succeed at anything is make a start and never give up despite all of your lizard brain insistencies telling you to do so!

So, what holds back our start, and what precipitates our lack of staying power? Fear and lack of conviction/resilience. It's our pesky lizard brain again.

Fear of failure holds back our good start, and lack of conviction, resilience, and determination restricts our staying power. Basically, the leader's enemy is the FUD factor.

WHAT THE FUD?

Fear. Uncertainty. Doubt.

Catnip for the lizard brain.

Growth is *never* found inside our comfort zone. If you want to be a great leader, think like a Navy Seal: get comfortable being uncomfortable. Great leadership is often uncomfortable. Remember the lizard brain loves (and I mean adores) worry. Worry, (negativity) it takes no effort and no wit. Fear, uncertainty, and doubt are as easy as falling off a log.[15]

BUT, HEY, NOBODY IS PERFECT, RIGHT?

Are any of us 100 percent perfect?

Nope. Sad, but nope.

But we all get better at leading one way or another. I mean, eventually we figure it out, right?

Not necessarily, no. Some get worse.

But what about some sort of divine intervention? If I'm a terrible leader, my God will swoop in and save me and the company, right?

Not likely.

Maybe the Ministry of Leadership Magic might feel sorry for us, our company, and our people and send someone terribly

---

15　See, I told you that log looked slippery. Best to try to avoid logs in the future, I'd say. Not just logs, but stones, steps, and anywhere icy, really. It's best to be safe. Safety first, I always say. Love, Captain Lizard.

clever from Hogwarts to come wave a magic wand and save us all just in the nick of time?

Well, I wouldn't hold my breath.

Experience has to count for something, right? Experience will make me a better leader, surely?

Nope, time served is absolutely no guarantee of leadership ability.

But what about luck, we can always count on luck, eventually, right? Luck will save us.

Sorry.

Should we go light a candle and say a prayer to the leadership gods? Maybe they can intervene to make us better leaders.

Again, no.

What if I pay thousands and thousands on a top leadership course delivered by a top university?

Well, in my experience, most people only take from these kinds of courses the things that they like the look of and that appear easy, and they dismiss the tricky things, because, well, anything is better than nothing, and the tricky things looked a bit fiddly, and you know how I abhor fiddly things, and that professor doesn't know my world like I do, and theory is one thing, but practicalities are another, and what do they know anyway? Me and my father started this company fifty years ago, and we know all that we need to know about business anyway, and I read some leadership articles when I get the chance and I'm not binge-watching something on Netflix. Sure I completely ignore them, but at least I read the thing in the first place, right?

Err...

So, let's agree to stop looking outwards (or to the heavens, or to the crystal ball, or to the chicken entrails, or to the village shaman) for help. Let's resolve to look inwards and, with a sprinkle of self-introspection, a pinch of self-awareness, a dollop of professional humility, a cup of considered reflection, and a soupcon of intentionality and determination, let's start to control the controllables and work on improving ourselves by ourselves. It's going to be a wonderful 'up and down' journey, I promise.

SELF-FULFILLING PROPHESIES

Make no mistake, all of our beliefs become self-fulfilling prophesies and serve to further reinforce themselves.

If you choose to truly expect the worst of people, the worst of circumstances, the worst of yourself, the worst of the world, and the worst of the future, guess what? People will invariably be terrible. Circumstances will be dire, the world will be difficult, and the future will be decidedly grim...at least they will in your estimation of them.

If, however, you choose to truly expect the best of people, the best of circumstances, the best of yourself, the best of the world, the best of the future, guess what? People will invariably delight you. Circumstances will play to your advantage. You will grow and develop in wonderful ways. The world will be filled with wonder and opportunity, and the future will be bright and exciting and exceptional...at least it will in your estimation of it.

Clever old you.

Your daily Leadership Journal is the perfect place to squash fear, uncertainty, and doubt and stretch comfort zones by reinforcing positive and helpful belief-sets while squashing those that will only serve to hold you back.

MEERKATS EAT SCORPIONS

Tom went to visit his manager, Bill, for his weekly catch up.

It was obvious that Tom was troubled by something, so Bill asked him what was wrong.

Tom explained that he had experienced a tough week. He'd had an argument with his dad, he felt hurt by something one of his friends had said, and he had missed out on a promotion at work.

"So, what should I do now?" he asked.

Bill looked at Tom and said, "Did you know that meerkats eat scorpions?"

"Um, what?"

"It's amazing," Bill continued. "These cute little guys attack and eat poisonous scorpions—like every day. It seems that they have been stung so often, they have become resistant to their poison, and it doesn't hurt them one bit."

"Sorry? Did you say meerkats?" Tom responded incredulously.

"Yes, meerkats."

"Oh, I didn't know."

"Yes. And then there are these beautiful little tree frogs in South America who are extremely toxic. They aren't born that way, but they get their toxins from the food they eat, and it builds up in their system until they become really dangerous to eat. Their bright colors warn potential predators to keep their distance."

Tom shook his head. "I don't think I understand. I come to you with a problem, and you give me a biology lesson."

Bill smiled.

"Look, when you experience the poison of pain, you have two choices. You can be like the meerkat and use the experience to become more resilient. Or you can become like the frog, allowing the poison to rise up in your system until you're toxic and everyone wants to keep their distance. Everyone experiences pain; how you respond is up to you.

You can choose to be a meerkat, or you can be a tree frog. Which one are you?"

MEERKAT OR TOXIC TREE FROG— IT'S A CHOICE.

One of my kids, Alice, often asks people whether today is a green-light day, or a red-light day for them. It's a decision, she contends—and she's 100 percent right.

There are, she says, green-light people, and then there are red-light people.

The green-light people are naturally buoyant—they look for positivity, optimism, and growth in every situation. They actively hunt out opportunity and productivity. They express gratitude for the positive things in the day—however small. They remark on the wonderful smell of the coffee, perhaps. They turn their face to the sun—and just revel and delight in it...and they smile. On their way into the supermarket, they take a second to pet the tied-up dog. They pass around the boiled sweets. They give the busker whatever change they have in their pocket as they walk past. They let cars go ahead of them at the junction—just to be kind. They smile and wave as they pass children. They give decent tips to servers in restaurants and hotels. They always expect the best of people—and they usually get it. Their first assumption is of the best intentions of others. They believe that people are inherently good. They look for a better interpretation of events than most.

They take time to treat themselves.

They have a mindset of abundance and gain; they are promotion-oriented.

They play to win.

Life is generally good to them.

Red-light people do the opposite—they actively hunt out worry, fear, disappointment, friction and expect and believe the worst of people, events, or situations.

They are risk averse.

They have a scarcity mindset, and they are relegation-oriented.

At best, they play not to lose.

Life is generally difficult for them.

Don't think I'm simply taking about introverts and extroverts; or optimistic people and pessimistic people; or hard-nosed people and pushovers—this red-light/green-light approach is much more sophisticated and nuanced than that.

Green-light people are not pushovers; of course, they often find themselves wanting to scream, "Get out of the bloody way!" in a traffic jam. But they choose to override their natural urge to holler when things do not go quite the way that they'd wish. They realize that the hollering only hurts themselves and others, and it does not actually make the traffic jam thin out any more quickly.

For green-light people, I'm talking about those positive folks who choose to develop and encourage self-control, and they work hard to resist destructive or unhelpful impulses. They actively, purposely build self-awareness. They are reflective and reflexive. They actively seek to learn positive lessons from every situation, not the easy, at-hand, unimaginative, witless, negative ones. Green-lightedness is a highly sophisticated sense of emotional intelligence played out on a daily scale.

Electing to have a green-light day does not obligate you to agree to everything nor does it force you to say yes at every opportunity—it's a very reckless leader who would choose to follow this principle. Green-light people recognize when they should state an emphatic "no"—they do not abrogate themselves of the responsibility of choice and consequences. Great leadership is about knowing when to say yes and when to say no—in fact, great leaders realize that they are more likely to have to say "no" much more frequently than "yes." They recognize, too, that when they say yes to something, they are likely saying no to something else and vice versa.

YOU CAN SAY "NO" ON A GREEN-LIGHT DAY.

It's perfectly OK to say no. Nope. No. *Niet. Oji.* Not now, probably not ever.

Green-lightedness does not mean that you become a pushover overnight. You must continue to say yes to the things that make sense, but it's OK to say no to those things that don't.

Intentionally say yes or no—don't just fly on autopilot saying yes or no—because sometimes your lizard brain autopilot says no a little too easily, as we have explored.

What should you intentionally say "no" to right now?

Find a gloriously enlightened space in your journal to make a note of what you should say an emphatic "No!" to right now. And mean it. Once you have made that firm and unambiguous declaration, make a few notes about why you have made that decision right now, figure out who you have to tell, and figure out how you will tell them.

Then, for balance, decide what should you decide to say an emphatic yes to—what should be given a big green-light response?

INCREASING THE WATTAGE OF YOUR GREEN LIGHT BULB.

It's so easy to increase the wattage of your green-light—gratitude. Remember, you can't have a positive life (green-light life), if it's filled with negativity (red-light).

As you read the next few lines, please try to use a fully-ironic tone of voice.

Gratitude journaling isn't for everyone, of course—especially not terribly important and serious leaders with lots of responsibility and the lives of countless families in their hands.

Now, of course, I realize that you, dear reader, are a serious, big time, terribly important leader burdened down by the heavy weight of crushing responsibility holding the lives and futures of others in your gravely concerned and troubled hands. You're ever so important, I get it. As such, default red-light approach to the world probably seems more apropos than green-light thinking. Gratitude just isn't for you.

But you'd be wrong—dead wrong. Determined and persistent gratitude is how you retrain your lizard brain.

YOU ARE THE STUFF OF DREAMS.

If you put your mind to it, I am confident that you could easily find 365 things to be grateful for. A year of gratitude will change your life for the better—heck, a week of it will, *if done properly*.

Most people, when trying to live a life of gratitude and abundance, think of something that they should be grateful for, write it down (the good ones), and then proceed with their day hoping that this single positive thought will carry them through and make things somehow magically better for them—it will not.

The trick is not to simply *think* the positive thought, it is to *feel* the thought and to remember the feeling as often as possible.

Every morning you must take a second to recognize at least one thing to be supremely grateful for, and you recognize the corresponding feeling. You should carry this uplifting and rejuvenating thought and feeling with you throughout the day—you should repeat the thought often and focus on the feeling even more often. The grateful thought and the corresponding feeling should be your mantra and your emotional anchor for the day. They should center you when things get a little tricky (and they will). They should help keep you grounded and shield you from your natural proclivity to overreact—you know you are sometimes prone to the catastrophizing that we discussed earlier.

Take a look at some of these thoughts. Do they inspire you to think again about your approach to gratitude? They should.

Your health is the stuff of dreams to those who are sick.

Your home is the stuff of dreams to those who are homeless.

Your job is the stuff of dreams to those who are looking for work.

Your water is the stuff of dreams to the thirsty.

Your books (this book) are the stuff of dreams to those who cannot read.

Your pen is the stuff of dreams to those who cannot write.

Your friends are the stuff of dreams to those who are lonely.

Your freedom is the stuff of dreams to those who are trapped.

Your money is the stuff of dreams to the penniless.

Your daylight is the stuff of dreams to those who are blind.

Your food is the stuff of dreams to the hungry.

Your confidence is the stuff of dreams to the insecure.

Your smile is the stuff of dreams to those who are sad.

You get the idea...always, ALWAYS, A-L-W-A-Y-S be grateful.
The greatest leaders are a grateful bunch. How can you do better here?
Write down just one of the sentences above that resonates most with you.
Write it in the first person.
Write down how it makes you feel. Mean it. Feel it. Smile.

Carry it with you for the rest of the day.

...look, only 364 more to go. ☺

SET A POSITIVE LEADERSHIP INTENTION FOR EACH AND EVERY DAY.

As well as an attitude of gratitude, the best leaders also set a positive intention for the day. This is something, normally just one thing, that, come hell or high water, will be done before the day is done—it will be your leadership North Star, guiding your every move for the day with nothing able to blow you off course or distract you from your goal.

QUESTION:

Do you believe that an improvement in demeanor, fueled by an attitude of gratitude, coupled with a list of critical daily must-dos, and a playing-to-win mentality inevitably leads to better decision making, better judgment, and better outcomes? Yes, I do too. These things are, after all, the objective of leadership.

Guess what? Leaders and managers are carefully observed by others—they take guidance cues from those in charge. Your people will watch what you do more than they will listen to what you say. Remember, we encourage what we tolerate in others as well as ourselves. Model the kind of person that you want others around you to want to emulate. Your daily intention will give focus to your day: your job is to live your intention. Others will see it in you and, most importantly, you will begin to see it in you.

AN INTENTIONAL WEEK

To illustrate what we're talking about, here's a week's worth of leadership intentionality to get your juices going and to get some forward momentum going. Each statement/phrase/ question represents a day's worth of intentionality, and each should represent your leadership model for the following twenty-four hours. Just imagine what a month, or a quarter, or a year could do to your goal of reaching your maximum leadership potential when you adopt this winning mentality and behavior. Big stuff.

Find somewhere suitably intentional in your journal. Every day write down one from the following list—or something similar to it that maybe fits a little better in your skin or circumstances. Your twenty-four-hour task is to then honor the commitment of intentionality that you just made to your journal, to yourself, to your development, to your company, to your people, to your growing potential, and your success.

Sunday
I will look for it.
Today I will look for an opportunity to be kind.

I will look for someone who needs help.

I will look for a kind word when a cruel one would be easier.

Today I will look for someone worse off than I.

I will look to make it better.

> *"Be kind whenever possible. It is always possible."*
> —*Fourteenth Dalai Lama*

Monday
Make things better.
I will accept whatever happens today with good grace—as if I had chosen it! What's more, I will figure out how to make it even better.

Making things better is, after all, my purpose, and I will 100 percent live this single-minded intention all day today.

Tuesday
I can take it, I promise.

I will ask for feedback and honest critique from my senior team today. This is one of the ways I can work on developing me, as well as them.

Doing this will allow us to serve our customers better—and I am blessed because today I get to discover how to do just that.

I will not try to defend, justify, or rationalize whatever they tell me—I will listen intently, and I will thank them for their bravery and honesty.

I will pay attention to their feedback and going forward I will act accordingly.

Wednesday
Shake it off.

"Take off your bedroom slippers. Put on your marching shoes," he said, his voice rising as applause and cheers mounted. "Shake it off. Stop complainin'. Stop grumblin'. Stop cryin'. We are going to press on. We have work to do."
—Barack Obama

Thursday
Be brave.

Today I will actively look for one thing that I have been avoiding due to fear, uncertainty, or doubt—and I will resolve to jump in anyway. I don't know how it will end, but the journey of a thousand miles begins with the first step—today is the day to make a positive start. I will not allow myself to be distracted from this commitment. Today is the *perfect day* for this. Chaaaaaarge!

Friday
Be bold.

Today I will be, above all things, bold.

Boldness has power and magic all its own.

My mantra for today will be, "Let's do it, let's make a start. We can correct as we go along if we have to. We might not know what to do, but we have to start somewhere."

One mustn't avoid eating for fear of choking.

Saturday
Time to laugh.

Life can get too heavy, too serious, too desperate at times. Today is not one of those days.

I will put my worries and troubles in a bag. I will lock the bag in a box. I will put the box on a very high shelf, and I will close the door—just for today. My worries will be just where I left them when I return to the high shelf in the morning.

Today I will find time to hear a good joke. I will find time to smile. I will remember what it feels like to share a laugh or two.

"The most wasted of days is one without laughter."
—E. E. Cummings

...and so on.

If you want happiness, choose it. If you want positivity, choose it. If you want to be a great leader, choose it. If you want compassion, choose it. If you want kindness, choose it. If you want strength, choose it.

Similarly, if you want struggle, choose it. If you want disappointment, choose it. If you want frustration, choose it. If you want fear, uncertainty, doubt, and worry, choose it.

We 100 percent become what we choose, and we live the life that we choose—for better or worse, *so choose wisely*.

While we're on the topic...

It would be wrong of me to leave the topic of mental wellness without giving some thought to physical wellness.

Lots of leaders bemoan the fact that they're always so incredibly busy...

(so very important)

(so dreadful at delegating)

(so awful at hiring A-players)

(so appalling at managing cash and profit)

(so ghastly at devising and implementing strategy)

(so abysmal at organizational culture)

...that they simply cannot find the time to properly look after their physical well-being. No time for the gym, they say. No time for the annual doctor's checkup. No time to destress. No time to eat properly. No time to take a real vacation. No time to turn off e-mail. No time to sleep. No time to breathe. No time to stretch. No time to spend with the family. No time to relax. No time to drink more water. No time to smoke less. No time to eat better. No time to laugh more. No time for fun. No time to tell those you love that you love them.

Find a truly sincere and intentional space in your journal and write this down in big fat letters:

> If I can't find time for my mental and physical well ness, I will be forced to find time for my sickness!

Take thirty seconds to consider that statement.

How can you truly expect to be able to lead others if you can't first lead yourself physically, emotionally, spiritually, intellectually? You can't.

Remember, there simply aren't many people who, on their deathbed, wish they had spent more time in the office. The single biggest regret that most leaders report is not prioritizing their health. Please, act accordingly.

THE HOLY TRINITY OF LEADERSHIP REGRET

How often do you find yourself living with the holy trinity of leadership regret: shoulda, woulda, coulda?

Who is 100 percent responsible for 100 percent of those shouldas, wouldas, and couldas?[16]

How you choose to spend (invest) your time is exactly that, a choice. Choose wisely, dear reader: today and tomorrow... yesterday is already over and done with, forget it.

---

16   Ouch!

We all get exactly the same twenty-four hours a day, from the lowly CEO of a global billion-dollar company, all the way up to the CEO of a tremendous inner-city not-for-profit organization: the differences between good leaders and great leaders is how they decide to invest the same daily 86,400 seconds. Time, like anything else, is a precious and non-elastic resource that all leaders need to make really smart decisions about. Are you making shortsighted choices, reckless choices, good choices, great choices specifically about the time you invest in your own wellness and happiness?

If you're not happy with the time you can invest in your wellness, the answer will NOT be found in a time management course: the answer is NEVER a time management course. There's no such thing as a time management course—we cannot manage something that we cannot control. Since we cannot control time, we cannot manage it. What we CAN manage is our own behaviors. What we decide to do with exactly the same twenty-four hours a day that we are all given—that's the measure of a great leader.

One last point. Assuming that, for all of the right reasons, you choose to make a higher priority of your wellness. What about your people and your company? What part of *their* wellness is also part of your responsibility?

> *"You have exactly one life in which to do every-*
> *thing that you will ever do. Act accordingly."*
> —Colin Wright

Find a spectacularly resolute space in your Leadership Journal:

> Write a list of nine things you choose—I have taken the liberty of putting the first two in for you, but you come up with the other seven. Use really juicy language, it helps.
>
> 1. I choose to be a truly spectacular leader.
>
> 2. I choose to look after myself significantly better.
>
> 3. I choose
>
> 4. I choose
>
> 5. I choose
>
> 6. I choose
>
> 7. I choose
>
> 8. I choose
>
> 9. I choose

Well done.

Now all you have to do if figure out what things you need to do, what things you need to believe, and what skills you need to acquire in order to be the person (not just the leader) that you now choose to be—the person that you get to be.

BUT, it's a great start.

Before the feelgood express leaves the positive intention station on the way to physical and mental well-being for you and others, here's something else I'd like to share:

When somebody says something nice about you...
When somebody complements you...

When somebody gives you a testimonial or a recommendation...
When somebody praises you...
When somebody admires you...
When somebody says that you look well...
When somebody says that you're a nice/funny/kind/ thoughtful/warm/friendly/smart/ approachable person...

...choose to believe them. ☺

> *"If you change the way you look at things,*
> *the things you look at change."*
> —Dr. Wayne Dyer

CHAPTER 10

Are you proactive or reactive?

Task-focused or people-focused?

UP AND TO THE RIGHT

Think back over the last, say, sixty days: have you been more task-focused or more people-focused? Have you found yourself being more proactive than reactive or the opposite?

Let's take a look at what that means, shall we?

Let's imagine that a leader—we'll call her Emily—has had a busy month trying to complete a lot of projects. She reports that she's been 70 percent task-focused and 30 percent people-focused. She has also been responding to an unusually high number of questions and issues from customers and has also been pulled in lots of different directions: internal meetings, new price lists to put to bed, budgets to finalize, and so on. As a consequence, she has been around 80 percent reactive and only 20 percent proactive the last couple of months. Early starts, late nights, weekends too: lots to do. Her calendar has hardly been her own these last few weeks, she feels.

This would suggest, of course, that Emily has been living in the shaded area below.

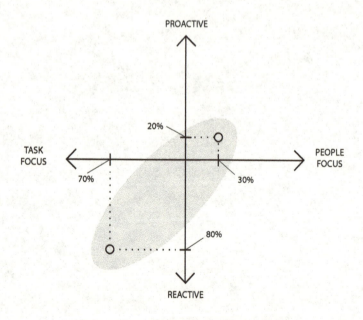

But is that where Emily *should* be living? Probably not. No, not "probably not," not.

Sure, it's OK to have a busy week or two, dealing with lots and lots of unforeseen distractions and urgent fires to put out—but every week? Every month? Every quarter?

Here's where Emily *should* be living:

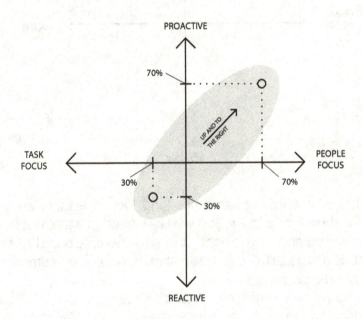

Emily, like all *great* leaders, should be consistently aiming for 70 percent people focus with 30 percent task focus, and 70 percent proactive activity and around 30 percent reactive time and attention. This is what great leadership balance looks like—mainly developing people and handling the important stuff, not just the "urgent" stuff.

Take a few minutes to plot your oval now for the last sixty days or so.

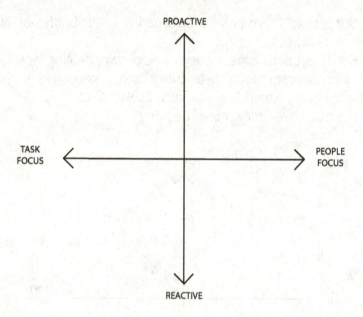

If you're anything like Emily (and lots of leaders are), if you're shooting for *great*, you will likely need to figure out how to move up and to the right...and stay there. "Up and to the right" is a wonderful daily leadership mantra, and I commend the idea to the house.

You might be thinking, "Well, it's situational, isn't it? Some months I'm in one mode, and some other months there are other priorities." You might be thinking if you didn't have two hundred e-mails a day, and if you didn't have such a demanding job, you'd *love* to live in the "great" leadership egg, but the world just doesn't work that way.

Some leaders (not you, of course) even enjoy living in the reactive and task-focused arena—it makes them feel special, and important, and in control of things, and needed. "I'm the kind of leader who leads from the front," they say. "I like to have my fingers on the pulse," they say. "I lead by example," they say.

What they don't say, unsurprisingly, is:

"I don't know how to delegate properly."

"I don't know how to manage my priorities."

"Working of lots of projects gives me an inflated sense of importance."

"I will get around to developing my people when things slow down a little."[1]

The best leaders take time to intentionally figure out how to balance *getting things done* (task-focused) and *inspiring, developing, empowering* others (people-focused).

Highly task-focused people don't seem to understand that in the mid- to long-term, slowing down to speed up is the only way. In the book *Scaling Leadership* by Robert J. Anderson and William A. Adams, they identify the number one differentiator of effective leaders is *a strong people focus*...and it's your job to figure that out.

Your job is to make your people better—they will improve results, make the business better, make your customers happier, ensure the future success of the business—not you.

Task-oriented managers think that if they don't work super intensely, they won't be successful. DOOM LOOP.

IS IT GROUNDHOG DAY...AGAIN?

Are you too busy mopping the floor to turn off the faucet? Are you too busy firefighting to spend more time in fire prevention? Are you too stuck in the tactical weeds to think about anything strategic? Are you too focused on tasks and not enough on people? Does it feel like it's Groundhog Day...again?

In the romantic comedy movie *Groundhog Day*, the main protagonist, Phil Connors, played by Bill Murray, was given the opportunity to live a day of his life over and over again until he got it just right.

---

1   Naughty.

Before being trapped in his twenty-four-hour time loop, Phil was a cynical, pessimistic, self-centered, self-serving, ego-centric TV weatherman[2]. At the end of his bizarre ordeal, he had developed enormously as a person: he learned new skills (playing the piano and speaking French, for example), he developed enormous empathy for those around him; heck, like all feel-good movies, he even got the girl.

The leadership lesson from the movie is the importance of recognizing the value of what can be learned from good feedback and increasing self-awareness.

Imagine what you could learn if you, too, were stuck in a *Groundhog Day* situation 'til you got that board meeting just right, or that personal development review, or that site visit, or that customer conversation, or that new product development meeting. Imagine what you could achieve if you, too, could relive again and again those circumstances where you were a very average C- leader till you learned what it took to become an exceptional A+ leader.

What would happen if you were to ask your direct reports some magic questions—in fact, the same questions again and again and again and again, just like Phil in *Groundhog Day*? What would happen to their thinking or their behaviors if they knew that their boss was going to ask them the same ten or so magic questions again and again and again? Would they start to change their own thinking in any way? Would they start to seek out better answers to the questions that they knew were coming? If the questions were great questions, would it change the trajectory of their days, I wonder? Would this new, more developmental, and forward-looking thinking help them achieve more, and would it affect the quality and scope of their outcomes? Would it force them towards the more people-focused thinking and more proactive behaviors?

---

2   Sounds rather like some leaders I know. Not you, of course. Other people. No, you don't know them either.

Hard to say till you give it a go, right? So, what's stopping you? Other than you, I'd say nothing.

LEADERSHIP QUESTIONS ARE SHIELDS, NOT SWORDS.

Before we explore the magic ten questions that the great leaders ask their people with enormous regularity, I first want you to recognize that these questions are to be employed not as swords but as a shields. They are not designed to be asked aggressively or with malice, or in order to hurt or embarrass or catch anyone out—don't turn this into an ego-play for you. These questions are designed to reveal chinks in your managers' armor that could potentially hurt them, your business, or you: and then give you (and them) the tools to help them to close them. They are to be used in order to keep your managers out of harm's way—safe: they are shields, not swords.

TOP 10 LEADERSHIP QUESTIONS

First ask...

"What are your top three goals this week?"

You are looking for precision and specificity in their answers.

At first, they will want to say something upbeat and positive that they imagine will buy your approval or largesse. They will likely say something like, "To beat our numbers for the month." Or, "To kill it!" Or, "To ensure that our new product gets into the marketplace quicker." You know, non-specific, optimistic, and entirely hopeful platitudes.

You should respond with a gentle smile and a firm, "No, what are your *specific goals* for this week, in *specific* detail?"

Oh dear; at first they won't like this question at all. I am sure that you can imagine why—most managers are just trying to keep their head above water and are being almost 100 percent reactive and not proactive at all—too busy mopping the floor to turn off the faucet.

If they now say anything nebulous or wooly at all, make them try again. And encourage them to be very precise and unambiguous. Unfortunately, they likely won't be. So, tell them that you will give them a few hours to come up with something a bit more specific and actionable, and that they should let you know what they come up with.

By asking this question with some regularity, it won't be too long (a few weeks, perhaps) before they start to develop very intentional and proactive thinking, and they will be able to articulate their weekly goals with enormous clarity and purpose and specificity—wonderful.

Whatever they say, remember it: write it down, even—you'll need to refer back to these goals at the end of the week.

Then ask[3]:

"Why those specific top three goals and not any others?"

There are lots of specific goals they could have chosen, of course, but there are some specific reasons they chose those particular goals—get them to share why they elected those goals, and, by inference, discounted others.

Remember, as we covered in the last chapter, when you say yes to something, you likely say no to something else: it's important to understand how they prioritize. In fact, it's really important for you, the leader, to understand how your managers rationalize and consider possible solutions to their problems (it's called solutions orientation)—they may well know some things that you do not. In fact, if they're doing their job properly, they really should.

---

3   Again, nurturingly, please.

If their reasons for the selected goals make sense, good. If not, ask them to try again.

Remember though, shields, not swords.

Then ask:

"How will you specifically measure and track these goals?"

Again, specific and detailed thinking is required.

Remember, if it can't be measured, it can't be tracked. If it can't be tracked, it can't be corrected. And if it can't be corrected, it can't be controlled. Naughty.

Then ask:

"What will you do if those goals aren't met?"

If they say anything that sounds like, "Oh, don't worry, they will be, boss." Don't accept this non-specific answer; make them be SPECIFIC about a potential recovery plan and course correction behaviors.

This will be the toughest of all of the questions that you will ask them this week. Again, lots of detailed thinking from them is required.

Remember, above all, what we are teaching them with these questions is how to think critically and with purpose. We are ultimately looking to build a high level of self-sufficiency in our teams, and that requires that we help them to learn how to think through and tackle problems.

Consider how you feel about their course correction thinking—that will tell you what to do next.

Then ask:

"What did you learn about your team last week?"

Ooooh, this is a great leadership question: clever old you.

Again, if they are wooly, or broad, or non-specific with their response, make them answer again, but ask them to be more precise.

Remember, the only advantage we have today over yesterday is what we have learned.

Again, it might take a few weeks for them to realize that learning is one of your prerequisites—they'll soon get the message and will soon pay much more attention to it.

Though it may be a little bumpy or patchy in the short term, you are helping them think more like a leader—and that takes some persistence and time.

Then ask:

"How can I help you with these specific goals?"

Another great leadership question.

You're on a roll—clever old you.

Again, ask them to explain their answer.

Wait a week or so (not much more, please), and then ask them how they went about achieving their goals for the week that just unfolded.

Then ask:

"Remind me, what were you trying to accomplish this week?"

Did they remember? Did they conveniently move the goalposts in order to ensure more wins? If they did, what do you think you should say? Remember: shields, not swords; shields, not swords.

Then ask:

"Where did you hit (or miss) your goals?"

The misses teach us more than the hits—bear that principle in mind when they recount for you the slings and arrows of this week's outrageous fortune.

Obviously, they will naturally want to share with you the touchdown plays, not the fumbles. Ask more about the fumbles: we learn more from our failures than our successes.

The manner in which you receive the news of the fumbles will determine how they report to you next week, and the next week, and the next. Again, shields, not swords, please.

Then ask:

"What caused this hit (or miss)?"

If they know which circumstances lead to good outcomes and which ones do not, they have learned a lot. If they don't, well, that's where you need to help them. Critical thinking, self-awareness, impulse control, professional humility, and so on will need some attention. Figure out which and give it.

Then ask:

"What should you start, stop, or continue to do next week?"

This is where the rubber really meets the road.

If we don't figure out how to apply what we are learning in order to make the place better for all, well, we may as well try teaching our pets card tricks.

OK, so terrific leadership-type stuff.

If you're sitting down, and up for a massive bite of a reality sandwich, read on. If you're not, then go lay down for a bit, take a good nap, gird your loins, and then read on.

Easy Question:
If these questions, or questions very similar to them, are being asked by the best of the best leaders on a (monotonously) regular basis, then what would be gained if you were to adopt the same habit? What would you learn, what would your people learn, how would things improve?

Hard to say till you give it a go, right? So, what's stopping you? Other than you, I'd say nothing.
Act accordingly.

Harder Question:
If there is something valuable to be gained by asking your people these types of questions on a regular basis, then what might be gained if you were to start to ask *yourself* these kinds of questions on a regular basis too?

Hard to say till you give it a go, right? So, what's stopping you? Other than you, I'd still say nothing.
Act accordingly.

Harder Question Still:
Rather than slavishly asking the questions above, what would be the absolute perfect questions for you to ask yourself and your people on a regular basis?

Hard to say till you give it a go, right? So, what's stopping you? Other than you, I'd still, still say nothing.

Act accordingly.

Last question—well, last question for now: Where might we record our answers to all of these pesky leadership-type questions that we ask ourselves?

Hmmmm, now don't tell me, don't tell me...let me guess... my daily Leadership Journal? BINGO!

See, you knew this was all leading somewhere, right?

A reminder:

All of these questions, and many more besides, are always available, 24/7, at www.mydailyleadership.com.

Subscribers to any of the Leadership Journaling programs will receive a weekly or monthly leadership development task such as the ones covered immediately above.

Go on, you know you want to.

By asking the types of searching, yet developmental, questions above, great leaders get to the heart of the issues holding the company (and its people—including the leadership) back, and they help highlight and explore potential solutions to issues, pinch-points, roadblocks, and speed bumps...and that's your job, after all.

Complete this exercise for a few weeks and then ask yourself: What needs blowing up?

The answer is NEVER "nothing": there's ALWAYS something that needs blowing up—blowing things up is another part of your job. Just make sure that you're blowing up the right things, for the right reasons, at the right time, in the right way.

Most of the time we don't blow things up for fear of making them worse (lizard brain). But, I promise you, it's nearly always high time to blow *something* up.

PUTTING OUT OIL RIG FIRES BY BLOWING SOMETHING UP

Paul "Red" Adair was a fiery Texan who founded his oil firefighting company, the Red Adair Company, in 1959. Red, so called because of his mop of fiery red hair, became famous for capping Kuwaiti oil wells set ablaze by Iraq. His life was the subject of a 1968 movie starring John Wayne, *Hellfighters*.

In his career, Red put out some of the world's most notoriously difficult oil rig blazes—often using high explosives!

Oil fires are particularly difficult to extinguish due to the enormous fuel supply for the blaze as well as the high pressure of the oil at the wellhead. Fires like this are incredibly dangerous, unpredictable, and can burn for years if not properly extinguished.

Red Adair became famous for extinguishing just these types of technically tricky fires using, of all things, dynamite! Dynamite is not the kind of thing that you'd imagine would be particularly welcome at oil rigs: and you'd be right, it isn't!

Controlled explosions detonated right in the heart of an oil well fire create a massive shock wave that pushes the burning fuel and local atmospheric oxygen away from the burning wellhead—a bit like blowing out a birthday candle, but on a much, much larger and more dangerous scale.[4]

It is an incredibly tricky and perilous procedure, as you can imagine, and not one that most firefighters are brave enough to attempt for fear of making the problem much worse.

Sometimes, though it might seem unpalatable, the best cure for a problem can seem to be more dreadful than the dis-

---

4   With lots less singing and clapping. And no birthday pressies or games at all. ☹

ease—but sometimes, for the greater good, you have to hold your breath and do it anyway.

Armed with the answers to the questions that you have been asking your people (and yourself) for a couple of weeks, take a look around the business—what do you creatively and intentionally and surgically need to blow up?

What's one area in your business or team that needs to be intentionally disrupted/unsettled/destabilized/disturbed?

Like the oil well fire that only resolves itself when it has been sufficiently unsettled or disturbed by radically starving it of fuel and oxygen, where in your business do you need to be like Red Adair right now and *surgically* blow something (or someone) up?

As simply as I can state it, great leaders encourage healthy conflict, healthy debate, healthy change.

Are you encouraging enough healthy conflict?

Are you sufficiently challenging the status quo?

Are you disrupting enough—not for disrupting's sake but for the sake of progress?

Like Red Adair, identify the fire, put an action plan in place to extinguish it, however unpalatable it might seem—be brave, light the blue touchpaper, and hold your breath.

BLOWING-UP IS "DISRUPTING."

As mentioned, all businesses need a certain amount of disrupting, destabilizing, upsetting. Sometimes the impetus for this destabilization is driven by conditions in the market, sometimes by innovation, or a new CEO, perhaps. Sometimes the catalyst is a new owner or new entrants into your space. Sometimes it's the wish to float or, the opposite, go private. Sometimes it's because R & D develops a better mousetrap. Whatever the reason, disruption is to be heartily encouraged—all the time. But it needs to be surgical, planned for, controlled—just like putting out the oil well fire.

Disruptions need disruptors—and, as the leader, it's your job to encourage them, if you have them; or encourage someone else to find them if you don't. Disruptors challenge the status quo. Disruptors are good at driving insight and innovation.

If you want to be world-class as an organization, you will have to figure out how to be world-class at finding and encouraging disruptors, as well as world class at targeted disruption. I'm not talking about looking for anarchists hell-bent on revolution (shit kickers): it's not the Wild West, after all. But every company needs the kinds of people who challenge things and make us look differently at things—sometimes, ourselves.

When Clayton M. Christensen first coined the now well-used term: "disruptive innovation" in a Harvard Business School paper in 1995, he wasn't just referring to completely breakthrough innovations that turn the world upside down to make good products better, he was also referring to making small but critical changes in our thinking that have us question why something has to be done one way and not another.

Think about this: when Karl Benz[5] developed the first automobile, there were no gas stations—none! What on earth was he thinking?

The first fax machine had no real practical use—there wasn't another one to send anything to. What on earth were they thinking? Look how fax machines were disruptors, and look how they dominated the market for years—mobile phones and personal computers went on to disrupt fax machines. It's the "Circle of Life," people.[6]

When Gutenberg invented the printing press in 1448, over 99 percent of the world couldn't read. What on earth was he thinking?

If only Blockbuster had listened to Netflix when Netflix asked them if they wanted to buy their company—Netflix was

---

5   No, not Henry Ford, Karl Benz. Look it up. ☺
6   Cue Elton.

convinced that streaming was the future. Blockbuster was convinced that brick and mortar and millions tied up in staff and stock and the postal system was the future. What?

If only the Encyclopedia Britannica[7] had a watchful eye on Wikipedia, they wouldn't be where they are today. Where's that? Exactly.

Airbnb figured out that P2P commerce (Peer to Peer) was the future. And it was. And it is. And it ever shall be.

Disruption is on its way to your world right now. Like it or not, something wicked this way comes. Sticking our fingers in our ears, tightly shutting our eyes, and hiding below the covers doesn't change what's about to change your world. We have to skate to where the puck is going to be...and—this is key—we have to be ready for it when we get there. Make the change, or be the change—you decide. This is what disruptors in our business give us.

Find an incendiary and unstable space in your Leadership Journal to think about this:

Here's what proactively, intentionally, but surgically needs disrupting—perhaps blowing up:

Here's why:

Here's how I intend to light the fuse...

"Whenever you see a successful business, some-
one once made a courageous decision."
—*Peter F. Drucker*

---

7   Who? Exactly!

CHAPTER 11

Is it a rabbit?
No, it's a fox.

Spotting patterns in the clouds.

HUMANS ARE ADVANCED PATTERN-RECOGNIZING MACHINES.

Around a million years ago, early humans learned how to start, maintain, and control fire. It was a big deal—a really big deal. Some say that it was the development of this singular skill that was the springboard for humanity's eventual dominance the world over.[1]

There are those who argue that the advent of rudimentary language some 150,000 years ago heralded the most important development in the ascent of mankind—and that's why we "rule the school."

Others say that it was the later development of rudimentary hand tools some 40,000 years ago that first distinguished our Paleolithic ancestors from the rest of the animal kingdom.

Some maintain that an appreciation for art and the ability to externalize an internal image around 35,000 years ago was the most significant single progression to species-dominance.

However, for all of these and countless other skills and competencies to have developed as they did, the very early humans first had to develop an acute ability for advanced pattern recognition. And it is the emergence and development of this single skill in our very early ancestors that presaged the most important survival mechanism for the entire human race—it is the reason that you're reading these very words right now. The ability to spot patterns kept us alive along enough to develop fire, tools, the wheel, art, language, tying our shoelaces, and the like. Our innate pattern recognition programing is why, when we look to the night sky, we make constellations of the stars.[2]

Pattern recognition really began when our brains started to estimate magnitudes in proportion. What started off as our

---

1 My cat seems to have a different view—especially when it comes to deciding who the couch really belongs to; but, for the sake of speed, we're going to overlook that issue just for the moment. It is my couch, though. Chairman Meow thinks differently—she thinks she's the dominant lifeform on the planet, but she's wrong. Dead wrong.

2 Quick joke. Zeus on TripAdvisor. "It's pretty good, so I give the Orion's Belt constellation three stars."

ability to estimate and plan to hunt, say, three wolves, is significantly different than the plan to hunt (or evade) thirty wolves. There are significantly different cues left by thirty wolves as opposed to three; and decisions made in response to each can determine whether or not individuals survived the encounter or became a tasty wolf snack around lunchtime.

Recognizing magnitudes in proportion quickly led to counting—appreciating the difference between "one," "two," "few," and "many" largely determines how to deal with bees, bears, and bison.[3]

Nowadays, lots of leaders take enormous pride in their ability to estimate magnitudes when looking at the monthly board pack.

Using our newly emerging pattern recognition skills helped us learn to read people's faces—mommy, friend, foe. These skills also served to help keep us as a species alive.

Lots of leaders take enormous pride in their ability to read people when recruiting, negotiating, questioning, and so on.

So, too, recognizing certain sounds, smells, and so on required pattern recognition, and these, too, allowed us to keep ahead of the game and avoid becoming a tasty snack for something stripey, sneaky, and snarly.

Lots of leaders take enormous pride in their ability to stay one step ahead of the enemy when considering strategy, new product development, infrastructure investment, and the like.

Pattern recognition wiring led to the ability to lay down and later recall memories of prior events—and connect them together, perhaps. Remember how Ug ate the red berries, made a funny noise, coughed, and then died? Must remember to avoid red berries, unlike Ug. Poor Ug.

Lots of leaders take enormous pride in their looooong and accurate memories—it's pattern recognition in play.

---

3   ...and slices of cake. Am I right?

Pattern recognition is now fully hardwired into modern brains; we don't have to go to the store to get a bag of it, it's already there. Watch how a breastfeeding child studies its mother's face: that's not something that has to be taught, it's a feature of the hardware and pre-installed software when the new baby first comes home from the new baby store. The baby is learning what its mother looks like—that way it can spot her and attract her attention when it needs something. Newborns are constantly on the lookout for patterns in everything they see, hear, smell, taste, and touch...and think—it's how they learn how the complicated and bewildering world works.

Watch older children playing in the park: they can happily spend ages looking up at the clouds[4], spotting animals galloping across the sky, or rabbits that turn into tigers with big feet, or elephants with six legs and a tail that looks a bit like their homeroom teacher, Miss Ross.

The greatest capacity of the modern human brain is the neocortex's incredible ability to consider things at a higher level of thought: to recognize and process disparate bits of information, find patterns and correlations, and create powerful and meaningful connections between them—to bring a conceptual order to things (a cognitive template/paradigm), which often, on first sight, seems chaotic, disparate, or disconnected.

So, that's the good news, Mr. Scientist smarty-pants.

The bad news is that we often get it wrong! Doh!

But that's OK, I promise. Let's find out why.

GOOD LEADERS MAKE BAD DECISIONS.

Does each decision that a leader makes have to be perfect? No. It's perfectly OK to take (considered) imperfect action and course correct along the way. Remember what Bill Clinton said (Chapter 9); he found that he could sleep pretty well at night

---

4   Or at least they used to—now there's probably an app for all of that. If there isn't, it was my idea! Copyright.

once he came to the realization that, so long as he continued to average seven good decisions out of ten, things would, on balance, be moving in the right direction.

All leaders are required to make decisions, of course—it's a prerequisite of leadership; it's what it's for. Leadership without decision-making is...well, I'll tell you tomorrow; I'm busy reading this recipe for making churros at the moment.[5]

It's as binary as this: those who can't make decisions can't lead.

Typically, those leaders who take a Taoist approach to leadership decision-making (when you don't know what to do, wait; more will be revealed) don't tend to last too long.

> "On an important decision one rarely has 100%
> of the information needed for a good decision no
> matter how much one spends or how long one
> waits. And, if one waits too long, he has a different
> problem and has to start all over. This is the ter-
> rible dilemma of the hesitant decision maker."
> —Robert K. Greenleaf, The Servant as Leader

I'd much rather leaders take what they have, describe the problem, model their options, make a decision, communicate it, and get really good at course correction. That's what the great leaders do. Pattern recognition skill is at the heart of all of those processes.

Some leaders think that time served (experience) is directly correlated to making better decisions—they've been around the block a few times, you see; they've had more time to learn more patterns, more miles under their wheels.[6]

And there is *some* truth in that supposition.

I'd rather learn that the captain piloting my flight, or the knee surgeon standing over me on the operating table, knife in

---

5   **Ba dum, Tsss!**
6   Who said "old"? Stop it!

gloved hand, had twenty successful years under their belt. I'd much rather hear that, than today was their very first day on the job, wouldn't you? However, time served (experience) is, of itself, certainly no guarantee of leadership quality.

We interview lots of leaders who claim to have twenty years' experience—when we dig deeper, however, we discover that in reality they had a good solid two years' experience early on... then all they did was rinse and repeat another ten times.

Decision-making is the ability to consider information and make choices concerning the cause and effect of multiple complex scenarios. In Chapter 13 we will explore how models help us make decisions: mental models built from our experience and training, as well as leadership and decision-making models and tools used by the best of the best. But, for now, let's consider how building up pattern-recognition skills by using our Leadership Journal helps you make better, more robust, more pressure-tested decisions.

Considering (and understanding) patterns and developing a range of possible options and outcomes is a powerful way to facilitate better (more successful) problem solving and decision-making.

Your Leadership Journal...

...provides a regular series of patter-recognition workouts for your brain.

The longer you spend looking at and studying clouds, the more patterns you see: the more able you are to connect the dots.

Leaders use their journal in the same way that artists use their sketchbooks to train their eye. Sketching (and keeping records of the sketches) helps them to see better and to build stronger, more accurate connections between eye and brain and hand. Leaders who journal do the same thing, learning how to connect the dots between problems and options and solutions.

...is your mechanism by which to examine root causes and better define problems.

As mentioned, we can't fix a problem that we can't properly understand and articulate. Thinking on paper and playing with (exploring) a variety of business models (see the next chapter for more) is the best way to figure out possible solutions to problems.

...provides a private, non-judgmental space to explore and work through issues.

Your journal doesn't judge: it's a safe space where there is no separate audience, no third-party judgement, and no fear of mistake, reprisal, or critique.

...gives you the chance to properly formulate tasks and frame issues before revealing your thinking and possible conclusions to others.

Have you ever seen the soccer coach with the magnetic counters on a big board explaining the play to the team? That's what I'm talking about.

...helps facilitate idea generation and new perspectives.

Blue-sky thinking and what-if scenarios. Developing alternatives and examining positive and negative implications in outcomes in options.

...in short, it helps you to develop and explore patterns and connections between them in order to make better decisions. Decision-making sit-ups for leaders, if you will.

WHEN YOU MAKE DECISIONS—EXPECT SOME HEAT.

As we mentioned in the previous chapter, when you make decisions (especially ones that disrupt, that unsettle, that change the status quo), you should expect resistance and friction. Resistance and moving people through the change curve (Chapter 9) takes effort and energy. Resistance, and effort, and energy, and friction cause heat—it's simple physics, people.

The bigger the change, the bigger the move, the more friction. If small moves are required, there will likely be little friction, less resistance, less heat.

The leader's job, therefore, is to consider the heat (often called "fallout") that the decision will generate—and whether or not the heat will light optimistic and excited fires within people,[7] or whether it will burn the place to the ground in an uncontrolled wildfire.[8]

Since change can't be avoided (and shouldn't be), friction, resistance, and heat cannot be avoided either. This means that leaders should consider how people will respond to the heat. Whenever a company launches a new product and service, a key part of the thinking is the customer response model and the competitor response model. Well, it's the same for internal change. There will be a reaction somewhere (it's physics again)—find it—everything has consequences. How might you lubricate the friction points? Communication, incentives, and rewards (what gets rewarded gets repeated), clearer vision, find champions, share success stories.

Big decisions need big thinking. Measure twice (thirty times, if necessary) and cut once. Blow it up, by all means, be Red Adair, but know exactly where the fallout will likely be.

As a general rule of thumb:

Slow down on the big decisions; speed up on the small ones.

---

7   Great.
8   Not great.

DECISION LOOP

Take a look at the ten steps of this really simplified decision loop:

1. Decide whether or not the decision is big or small.
2. Decide when the decision should (or should not) be made.
3. Gather the data, information, knowledge, and opinion relative to that decision.
4. Decide what good looks like (how to measure it) and what the early milestones for success would look like (and the course correction triggers and model).
5. Set a deadline to light the fuse(s).
6. Let everyone know the plan.
7. Light the fuse.
8. Measure and review.
9. Course correct, measure, and review again.
10. Go back to Step 1 and do it all again.

If you pay attention to the progress and fallout of your decisions, based on what you had planned and what transpired, patterns will emerge. They will tell you where you need to get better in your decision-making.

Your journal is the perfect place to record your plans and consider your decisions—they will help you plan better and achieve better outcomes the next time, and the time after that, and the time...well, you get the idea.

WEEDS AND FLOWERS AND BURIED TREASURE

Some flowers I just don't care for. And some weeds I think are quite beautiful. It seems that we are somehow expected to love all flowers and loathe all weeds. Who says that has to be true? Not I. And I'm quite sure the bees don't care what we call them.

Sometimes we write wonderful journal entries: insightful and succinct, profound, dazzling, and downright earth-shattering; gorgeous, sweet smelling, bountiful beauties.

Sometimes we write what can only generously described as absolute drivel: hogwash.

Sometimes these profound entries flow, take no effort, and almost write themselves. Sometimes it's almost impossible to write just a few words—every one of them drags its backside down onto the page.

There are times when we are supremely inspired, and there are times when we are just not feeling it today. On days that we are just not feeling it, it's easy to say, "I'll skip it today and pick it up again tomorrow—I'd probably just write drivel, anyway." Write anyway! It's important to write every day—even if it's drivel. Drivel is to be preferred to nothing.

Don't overanalyze nor be too critical of what you put down on paper—we already know that you're not William Shakespeare; it's not a love sonnet from one star-crossed lover to another, it's not going to win a Pulitzer Prize, we get it: so, don't try to be too clever—just think and write.

Sometimes you will reveal weeds and sometimes flowers... and sometimes when we're journaling what we really do is discover buried treasure—so just think, and write.

It's often difficult to write; we're not even sure what we're looking for. We get all muddy looking for it, and when it emerges it often looks grubby, misshapen, and not worth very much. But then, when it's washed by the subconscious, given a little time, and mulled over a little more, the real treasure emerges. Remember, the subconscious is doing all the heavy lifting—it always is. So, just write.

Guess what, Post-it notes were a mistake. Spencer Silver was trying to make a super-strong adhesive for 3M. He made the complete opposite but noticed that when the adhesive was removed, it left no marks. He could easily have thrown the idea in the trash, thinking it a weed, but instead he spent time trying to figure out what this unsticky glue could potentially be used for when, hey, presto, buried treasure! There's hardly a building in the developed world that doesn't have a pack of Post-it notes in a drawer somewhere.

So, too, Scotchgard—a mistake. Patsy Sherman was trying to develop rubber that would not be degraded by jet fuel.[9] She dropped some of her experimental chemical onto one of her shoes and noticed how, over time, that part of her shoe remained cleaner and brighter than the rest. It's a good job that she took great notes in her journal because, eureka! Buried treasure!

So, too, penicillin, chocolate chip cookies, potato chips, the pacemaker, Silly Putty, microwave ovens, Corn Flakes, x-rays... and a veritable cornucopia of other world-changing ideas—all of these "treasures" were all made by mistake—none of them were intentional.

And my all-time favorite, the Slinky. Richard James, a naval engineer, was trying to design a meter to measure power consumption on naval vessels. He was designing the mechanism in his journal when, by accident, he knocked one of his super-long, low-tension springs off his desk and noticed how it bounced around quite unusually. Ta-daaaah![10]

Just go for it. Just write.

Sometimes a weed is the winner of the rosette in the show. Sometimes, that "dumb" idea can lead to your biggest ever insight or growth moment. What's the message? Just write. Every day. When you look back in three months or so, you will be surprised how the really smart stuff seemed dumb, and the random meanderings of a tired, stressed, and half-drunk mind became the stuff of legend. Sometimes the weeds outshine the flowers, and sometimes the buried treasure, when you rub the detritus and sh*t off it, reveals something of unimaginable value.

---

9   It doesn't matter why—just go with it.

10 Where would we be without the Slinky? The world would be a much-impoverished place without it, I'm sure you agree. Unthinkable.

Find a magnetic space in your journal to consider this for a moment or two. Let's see whether or not you can sniff out some dots to connect or some new patterns to notice.

If I were to run my leadership metal detector over all of the parts of the business, searching for where some buried treasure might be lying unnoticed, maybe in plain sight, I think the best places to start would be...

There is treasure hidden in every problem: it's your job to find it.

"Trust that the treasure we look for is hidden in the ground on which we stand."
—Henri Nouwen

CHAPTER 12

· · · · · · · · · · · ·

You don't know what you don't know.

You are on a learning journey.

Here's one thing that we all know—we all know that we don't know what we don't know.

We do know that there's stuff that we don't know, but we don't know what that stuff might be, neither do we know how useful the stuff that we don't know might be to us. This means there could be one thing: just one single thing that, if we did know it, it would make us significantly better leaders. Trouble is, we don't know what that one thing might be.

Drat.

What we do know for absolute certain, however, is that we don't know everything that there is to know. So, we need to figure out how to come to know those things that we need to know—but how?

Tricky.

Well, we also know that we can wait patiently for it to appear to us in a dream, perhaps. Or it could arrive in a flash of inspiration while doing the gardening or some other activity.

Maybe we can even wait aggressively for it—all tense like a coiled spring, ready to pounce on it the moment it somehow magically appears.

Unlikely.

Here's the point, though: Are we to wait passively for this pearl of infinite wisdom to arrive from outer space, or are we to actively seek it out?

Decisions, decisions, decisions.

Most managers and leaders (the decent ones, at least) have a pretty clear development path for all of the individuals who report to them. They can articulate with reasonable clarity which gaps their direct reports need to work on: gaps in knowledge, skill, attitude, application, and so forth.

These gaps are often formalized, recorded, and tracked.

Nice.

The good managers and leaders can also, when asked, define with some clarity what poor performance looks like from their direct reports.

You might even want to take a few moments to carry out that exercise now—it's an enlightening exercise.

Pick a person one rung down the hierarchical tree in the organizational structure and write ten bullet points or so on what poor performance for that person and role looks like. Give it a go; it's a really valuable exercise and pretty easy to do.

Great.

Now then, construct another list—a trickier list. This list is called, "What poor performance from *me* looks like...."

Ouch.

Remember, we did this whole exercise already in Chapter 8. But let's develop it just a smidge.

If you've been honest, two of the items on the, "What poor performance from me looks like..." list will definitely include:

Not developing my people.
Not developing myself.

And here's the thing, many leaders, while they have a development plan for all of their people, don't have their own formalized development plan for themselves.

Gasp.

As mentioned in various ways throughout this book, the only real advantage that any of us have today over yesterday is what we have learned—otherwise we are just another day closer to dead.

A sobering thought.

What we are talking about (and what journaling is all about) is lifelong learning—continuous professional development, remember?

I wonder what you would write if I asked you to define in some detail what your personal leadership development plan should include. Most leaders, when we ask them this very specific question, really struggle to express it with any intentionality or any purposeful clarity. Why? Well, that's because most leaders don't have one.[1]

Sure, they tell us that they really want to get better at leading. "Great," we say. "Tell us, how is that going to happen?"

"Well," they reply, "you know, I read a lot of articles and stuff. And I talk to other leaders. I'm in a terrific mastermind group—we share ideas all the time. You know, I'm always learning stuff."

"Wonderful,'" we respond. "Tell us about the last leadership article you read, what it taught you, and how you modified it and applied the principles in real life scenarios. Also, tell us how you found the article in the first place—was it a happy accident, or did you intentionally seek it out?"

"Uh, it was about leadership."

"Yes. And?"

"Well, I was thumbing through (insert: *Wall Street Journal*, *Forbes*, *The Times*, *The Economist*, and the like), when I happened upon a terrific piece on employee engagement. Did you know that we are facing a crisis in employee engagement right now? A crisis, I tell you."

"A crisis? Right-oh then. And what have you done differently as a consequence of reading the article?"

"Well, I passed it on to my HR team, of course. I e-mailed it the very same day—to the whole team. They all said how terribly interesting it was."

Beaming smile.

Pat on back.

Appropriate and knowing nod.

Clever old me.

To spare everyone's blushes, let's move on.

What we see (all over the place) is that most enlightened leaders ensure that each person on their team, and in the business, has an annual personal development review. Each person has a formalized learning and development plan. The

---

1   Gasp!

good ones even review the plan with their people more than just once a year—usually around salary-review time, and on the occasion of their anniversary with the company.

Groan.

When we ask the leader to show us *their* latest performance review, as well as their own current personal development plan, guess what we typically see when we go to the training and development tab of their own employment file? *Nada*. Nothing. Zip. *Rien*. *Nichts*. *Walla*. *Nowt*. Put simply, we see moths fly out—that's what we see.[2]

"Do as I say, not as a I do."

I get it.

Nice.

Not!

Let's take a look at what your own personal development plan should look like. It's six things: a 6-R model.

Well, it's five Rs and a W, but who's counting, Captain Pedantic?

Let's take a look.

THE 6-R SELF-DEVELOPMENT MODEL

They are:

Write—Read—Reflect—Record—Refine—Reveal.

Let's take a peek:

Write.[3]

No surprise here, of course.

---

2   Remind me, how do we spell "hypocrite"?

3   Yes, I know it's a "W", but it *sounds* like an "R"—and that's what makes it more fun. No? Look, just go with it, Catpain Pedantic, we have bigger fish to fry.

Complete your daily Leadership Journal—Morning Momentum and Evening Evaluation. It the start of your reflective and reflexive practice.

Just write.

If it's guided journaling (as we strongly recommend), great, just follow the prompts (www.mydailyleadership.com). If not, that's fine, too, just write.

Writing allows you to organize and develop your thoughts—and thoughts are the leaders' stock-in-trade.

Just write.

Every day.

You'll be amazed how, before too long, you will feel that you simply must write in order to understand and address a situation—and when that happens, you'll finally be on the path. ☺ You're very welcome.

Read.

Leaders are readers. The secret here is intentionality.

Don't read for reading's sake—who on earth has got time for that sort of nonsense, not I...and likely not you either.

Reading does more than simply keep your mind entertained or sharp; it also teaches you things that you didn't know—and how wonderful is that?

I know lots of companies who have a wonderful policy on reading. If someone in the company buys a book, and they like it, and pass it on to another member of your team with a recommendation of some sort, the company will reimburse them for the book. A million-dollar idea can often be found in a twenty-dollar book—if it's the right book.

Notwithstanding the requirement to reread your own journal entries, your external reading selection should include these considerations. Ask yourself these questions before you dive headlong into a new book:

First question: Is it relevant?

This is a go/no-go gate, people.

Is it possible that a beautiful golden nugget of an idea for leadership development is to be found hiding in a cookery book on filo pastry and the virtues of preparing a decent millefeuille? Yes, it's possible—unlikely, but possible. Let's play a bit smarter with the odds and elect instead to read anything by Marshall Goldsmith, Simon Sinek, Malcolm Gladwell, and the like. The chances of striking gold in them thar hills is so much more likely.

Be precise and intentional with what you choose to read. Your reading material should be specifically targeted to close specifically identified gaps in your personal development plan.

Second question: Will it likely teach me something new?

Again, play the odds here. We are trying to close gaps. If you're considered a bit of a whizz at Excel, why read another book about it? If you're already tremendous at fifth level root cause analysis, you'd be much better off reading about how to have difficult conversations (if that's an important skill but critical gap in your armament).

There's just limited value gained from *overgilding* a lily, after all, right?

Third question: Will it likely help me to move the flag further down the beach?

Does it challenge you and encourage new thoughts and behaviors? Is it part of your intentional self-development plan? If not, see you later.

Here's how to figure out the answers to these questions. Have a plan and measure those questions against the plan. Easy.

Every leader should be working on improving and learning more about three things/issues/topics at any particular time. The topics can change over time, of course, but they should select three things to be highly intentional about learning more about.

Shiny Purple Squirrels

The added benefit of this sort of intentionality is that it keeps us from losing focus and getting distracted by the shiny purple squirrels that always seem to contrive to pull our attention away from our plan.

To illustrate:

Let's imagine that my three intentional learning topics are:

Leadership
Coaching
Helping people deal with adversity

These three things take precedence over all other (sometimes alluring, oftentimes distracting) topics.

When someone says to me, "Hey, Antonio, you should read this great book I just read—it's all about time management. Here's a copy, you'll enjoy it."

I think to myself, time management? Is that directly related to my three chosen topics? No, no it's not. So, I thank them, and I put the book on the "Maybe Later" pile. It's a shiny purple squirrel.

In six months' time, maybe when it's time to swap out one of the topics, I'll come back to the time management book; but for now, it's not my priority.

Here's the other great thing, once we declare with this kind of intentionality (to ourselves [our subconscious], as well as to others), we start to see articles, YouTube videos, TV programs, books, blogs, websites, social media posts, and so on about our chosen areas of investigation *all over the place*. It's amazing how this happens.[4]

If it challenges you and teaches you something new, and it's on your intentional learning path, and it looks interesting, go for it. If not, don't. Ever.

Back to the six Rs list (well, five Rs, and a W which sounds like and R—but again, who's counting?)

Reflect.

Once you've digested the new material, think about it.

Mull it over. Run it around in your noggin. Try to figure out whether the thing you just studied could link to another thing—chances are it could, especially if it's on a closely allied topic (which it is...remember? No shiny purple squirrels here, remember?). What's being developed here? Pattern recognition! Yes! Top of the class.

Record.

I wonder where on Earth we could possibly record (write down, with a pen, on paper) a summary of what we have just learned, as well as some of our thoughts about this new idea. Any idea? Yes! Top of the class again.

Refine.

When you read, then reflect, then record your thoughts, you naturally let them marinade (our pesky subconscious at work 24/7 again), and you will find that you will come back to your

---

4   It's actually your subconscious looking for those things, as well as all of the really smart AI algorithms that spot what seems to interest you and contrive to serve you more and more of it. Again, both are topics for another book, I think.

conclusions and refine them. A tweak here and there. A dash of inspiration. A sprinkling of supposition. A dusting of intuition. A cup of insight...and BOOM! A whole new mental model of the world emerges. Look, you just learned something new, and adapted and adopted it and slotted it seamlessly into your intentional leadership toolbox.

And now for the fun part:

Reveal.

Use it, discuss it, reveal what you are thinking and reveal what you have learned, and *teach it to others*. In the revealing and teaching of it to others you inevitably come to understand the issue much better, think about it on a deeper level, as well as share and learn another person's view on the topic, as well as learn how to more expertly articulate and apply the valuable learning points. YES!

In short:

> Commit to a personal development learning plan.
>
> Reflect and evaluate what you're learning every day.
>
> Determine how you can apply what you're learning.
>
> Adapt and adopt.
>
> Apply and teach.
>
> Rinse and repeat.

What the great leaders, the legends, continue to think (every day), is some version of, "I'm *always* trying to improve. There's *always* more to learn. I'm on a *daily* journey of incremental improvement. The only advantage we have today over yesterday is what we have learned. Let's learn our lessons and share them."

And to those glorious few lobsters, we salute you.

That's how in sports you win the gold medal, the yellow jersey, the big cup, the silver platter. And that's how at work you win the admiration, trust, and respect of those you lead.

DRIFTERS, SURFERS, PADDLERS, SAFE-HARBORERS, AND NAVIGATORS

Remember my coach, the ex-commander of a nuclear submarine? He often speaks about five different types of people: drifters, surfers, paddlers, safe-harborers, and navigators.[5]

Drifters, he argues, are content to go where the weather, the tides, and currents dictate. They hope things work out well, and sometimes they do. But, when things don't work out so well, well it was out of their hands—they don't control the vagaries of the tides, after all. Life gives them what it gives them, and they do their best to make lemonade when lemons are on the menu.

Surfers are a different breed of animal. These individuals travel the globe in search of the next big thing, the next big thrill, fad, trend, or good idea. They are determined to believe that the next big wave will be the one to satisfy their need for their adrenaline rush; and, if it's not this one, it will certainly be the next, or the one after that, for sure. They flit from place to place, idea to idea, job to job in search of the next big idea that will be "the one." It's almost never the one.

Paddlers are different again. They know that there's fun to be had in the water, but, just to be safe, they roll up their trouser legs and only risk going up to their knees in the sure and certain knowledge that, if things start to look a little tricky, they can always easily backtrack to the safety of the shore. Look, but don't touch. Touch, but don't taste. Taste, but don't swallow.

Safe-harborers satisfy (fool) themselves that they are "all-in"—they are fully in the water, of course, and ready to set

---

5   His stories and coaching sessions are, as I mentioned, nearly always nautically-themed, unsurprisingly enough.

sail at a moment's notice, just as soon as the weather improves, or the crew shows up, or the destination becomes clearer. They know what they like, and they like what they know. They manage risk so assiduously that they never quite leave the safety of the harbor walls.

Navigators have a clear and unambiguous, single-minded goal. They make sure that the whole crew is aware of the importance and significance of it as well as the challenges they might face on the way. They chart a clear course and set their sights on the destination, and they pursue it doggedly—despite the weather, the traffic, the circumstances, the currents, or the tides. Sure, they course correct as they go, but go they do. These individuals keep a daily journal: a captain's log.

So, with all that being said, which one of these individuals are you? Hint: if you want to be a great leader, it's the last one. So glad we cleared that up.

Leaders navigate.

They navigate themselves, what they are learning, how they are developing...and they help others do the same. They fix themselves and others to a bright and shining star, and they don't allow anything or anyone to distract them from it.

LEADING A BUSINESS IS NOT LIKE LEADING A COUNTRY.

Question: Do the best businesses run along democratic lines?[6]

No, right?

In fact, quite the opposite.

In the West most of us grow up believing that democracy is inherently a good thing—it's how we have run the best countries of the world for two thousand plus years, after all.

There are, though, a few key shortcomings with the principle of democracy. Even Plato, the brilliant philosopher of ancient

---

6   Before you answer: the answer feels like it should be "yes," but it's quite emphatically "no."

Greece, knew there were some serious concerns with electing leaders and running countries along democratic principles.

Running a state, Plato argued, takes particular expertise, and not everyone is suited to it.[7] What's more, having skill at being elected (popularity and energy), is no real reflection of someone's skill in running a country (strategic acumen and diplomacy). We wouldn't, after all, choose our pilots, surgeons, architects, or dentists this way, would we? Or any professional, for that matter. Well, I know that I wouldn't, at any rate.

That being said, democracy is the best that we have discovered so far for running things on a large scale.

So, if it's the best way we have devised so far in terms of running a country or a state, why doesn't the same principle hold true for running businesses?

Good question.

Democracy relies on this foundational principle: a large number of voters and a small number of options. This is the way that most people get what they wanted or voted for. QED.

Businesses, however, are usually facing the exact opposite issues: there are usually a small number of voters and a large number of options.

This way most people tend to get what they didn't vote for—with all the subsequent vexation, trials, and tribulations, of course. Problem.

This means that the best leaders have to learn how to make directional decisions for themselves, their team, and their business—and good ones, at that, oftentimes entirely on their own. Sure, they should council the thoughts of the leadership team, but, in the end, when all is said and done, the buck stops with the leader. And the buck really does stop with them. It is, after all, their submarine, remember? ☺

So, confer with a wide council, of course: consider a broad view, take a long position, evaluate the options, consider the

---

7   Ring a bell?

consequences...and then point everyone at the star. It's not a democracy, it's a benign dictatorship, I'm afraid.

Deal with the consequences, and course correct as you go, but go you must. Leadership means leading—deciding and leading. Decisions have ramifications; recognize that, take a breath, hold your nose, and plunge into the icy waters of uncertainty—it's sometimes a bracing but invigorating dip.

Figure out:

1. What needs to change.
2. Why that thing and not other things.
3. How to make a start.
4. When to make a start.
5. How to explain it.
6. How to involve others.
7. How to measure it.
8. How track it.
9. How to course correct.
10. What's next.

MAKE A SWITCH.

As mentioned, many times, if you want to change (improve) the output, you must first change (improve) the input.

The problem is, we humans tend not to like change—look, it's the old lizard brain again. But, change we must, since there is no growth without change and some discomfort—look, it's the old lobster again.

Also, there is no leadership greatness without bearing some battle scars...with an optimistic and positive expectation for things to improve—look, it's the old meerkats again.

On our way to leadership greatness, we must likely change many things. For those who really like to keep score, here's a great list that you'd do well to add your own favorites to:

Switch problems with challenges.
Switch "I have to..." with "I get to...."
Switch failing with learning.
Switch illness with wellness.
Switch busy with productive.
Switch red lights with green lights.
Switch me with us.
Switch efficient with effective.
Switch tactics with strategy.
Switch good with great.
Switch time with energy.
Switch TV for books.
Switch indecision for certitude.
Switch manage with lead.
Switch direct with coach.
Switch react with respond.
Switch ego with self-awareness.
Switch tell with ask.
Switch data with insight.
Switch goals for potential.
Switch "it's not about me" with "it's 100 percent about me."
Switch affirmations with afformations.
Switch externalize with internalize.
Switch delegating tasks with delegating results.
Switch directed authority to guided discovery.
Switch cooperate with collaborate.

> *"A ship in harbor is safe—but that is not*
> *what ships are built for."*
> *—John A. Shedd*

Jim Rohn said that you cannot make progress without first making a decision.

Find an intentional and changeable space in your Leadership Journal:

There are some things (lots of things) that I need to change, to switch. We put some in to give you a start.

The top ten things I need to figure out how to switch are:

Switch _____ drifting _____ for _____ navigating _____

Switch _____ for _____

Switch _____ for _____

Switch _____ for _____

Switch _____ for _____

Switch _____ for _____

Switch _____ for _____

Switch _____ for _____

Switch _____ for _____

Switch _____ for _____

So, decide to make it so. ☺

"Choices are the hinges of destiny."
—*Edwin Markham*

CHAPTER 13

Thinking on paper.

Modelling your way to success.

A4 BEFORE...

Since they're not running a democracy, leaders must make decisions. The success of their enterprise will rely largely on the quality, wisdom, and appropriateness of those decisions. So, how to make better decisions?

One of the most powerful and yet underused problem-solving (decision-making) tools that leaders have at their disposal is as simple as a blank piece of paper. There are some pieces of blank paper right now in your journal, I expect, just itching for something remarkable to do, something remarkable to hold, and something remarkable to reveal.

You cannot keep every thought in your head at all times—you just can't. Things (some potentially GREAT things) are falling through the cracks—get them down on a piece of paper, keep them, refer to them, work on them—and model them.

FOR THE WANT OF A NAIL...

Remember, writing down your targeted thoughts/musings/ramblings with a pen on a piece of paper is a very powerful way of setting a solutions-oriented intention for your subconscious. It tells it to start to understand things in a more organized way. It's one of the key premises of this whole journaling enterprise, of course. The intentionality of organizing and categorizing a series interconnected thoughts in this way tells you that you're working on an issue, and you're going to understand it better.

Clearing your cluttered mind in this way frees it from all of those noisy mental loops that are clogging up and jamming up your intellectual information superhighways.

Once we commit our thoughts to paper, we develop the habit of reviewing and prioritizing and sorting and developing them.

Visual maps (see Mind Maps below) are a very time-efficient way of transitioning from data, all the way to impact.

While it's entirely subjective and unprovable, I tend to agree with Brian Tracy when he claims that for every minute in planning, we save at least ten in execution. I'm quite prepared to believe that "thinking on paper" has at least a ten times return on investment—not bad RoI and not bad odds.

Things that find themselves committed to paper tend to get done: things that are bouncing around inside our noggins tend not to. How many genuinely world-changing ideas have been completely lost for not having completed the very simple process of writing them down and developing them a little further, I wonder.

> For the want of a nail, a shoe was lost.
> For the want of a shoe, a horse was lost.
> For the want of a horse, a message was lost.
> For the want of a message, a battle was lost.
> For the want of a battle, a king was lost.
> For the want of a king, a country was lost.
> ...and all for the want of a nail.

A FREUDIAN SLIP...OF PAPER

At risk of appearing a little too Freudian for anyone's tastes (including mine), using free association to solve business problems is a very powerful leadership tool and habit to develop. If you've not used it before, give it a go—I promise it will surprise you in unexpected and remarkable ways. Try it, just once. If it doesn't work for you (and it will), don't do it again (but you will).

Free association is a great way to quickly figure out what's going on, and it draws on the genius of your subconscious, deep down. Remember, your subconscious is where all of your creativity and problem-solving skills really lie—although it doesn't always feel that way, that doesn't make it not true.

Let's give it a go: start by writing down a problem (at this stage we don't necessarily need a fully defined Problem

Statement, as explained in Chapter 8); a broad-brush issue will do for a start. We will use what we come up with here to add into our fully-considered Problem Statement later.

Then, by a process of free association, write on that topic for three to five minutes. No evaluation. No judgement. Just write, not type—use a pen. Let the thoughts come by themselves and let them take you where they want to go. Blank paper is better—don't constrain your thinking by straight lines and bullet points and lists—generate thoughts fast. Speed is the key. Mind Maps are great (see below). Arrows, colors, and NBs are to be encouraged. Put some things in clouds. Write some things in bold. Underline important things. Keep going fast 'til the five minutes is up. Keep referring back to the Problem Statement and keep asking yourself, "Yes, and...?" "Yes and...?" is a wonderful leadership question for yourself as well as others.

Then, once the initial five minutes is up, take a short rest. Review your thoughts by rereading them and circle three different thoughts, ideas, and observations.

To each of these three "germs" (germs of an idea, not germs in the biological sense), spend another two to three minutes each on a separate piece of paper. Fast. Free association. No evaluation. Just go.

You'll be staggered where your imagination and creativity might take you.

What new perspectives or thoughts or meanderings has the exercise offered you? What should you now do? What should you now discard or embrace? Who should you talk to?

Modeling problems allows the (great) leader to think about their issues in a much clearer and cohesive way, as well as help them enormously in getting their thoughts over to others in a clear way by referring to the model and guiding others through it.

Most leaders do not normally model their problems, relying more on intuition, experience, or brute force—don't be that person, I implore you.

MIND MAPS

Anthony "Tony" Buzan, author of over eighty books, educational consultant, and winner of countless business awards, created a method of unlocking the decision-making potential of the brain: Mind Maps.

Developed in 1970, Mind Maps utilize the full range of cortical skills in order to fully explore, explain, examine, and expand connections and options. Leaders who simply employ words to explore and explain issues are limiting themselves by not also including images, rhythm, logic, space, color, spatial awareness, and so on—all of the qualities that Mind Maps can express much better.

Journals are simply wonderful vessels for Mind Maps. Mind Maps are critical tools for the intentionally developing leader. Mind Maps are used by millions of leaders who are interested in capturing the power of whole-brain thinking.

According to the Tony Buzan Learning Center, Mind Maps have a variety of uses: and all fall into the leader's remit, do they not?

> Learning. Overviewing. Concentrating. Memorizing. Organizing. Presenting. Communicating. Planning. Meetings. Training. Thinking. Negotiating. Brain Blooming and so on.

This is entirely unsponsored. If you are a leader, you need to learn how to construct and use Mind Maps. Problems and challenges are rarely linear; they are chaotic, unstructured, and difficult to capture—constructing the solution(s) to them is similarly nonlinear and organic, and herein lies the power of Mind Maps.

Bill Gates said of Mind Maps, "...(they) can be used to help connect and synthesize ideas and data—and ultimately create new knowledge."

I urge you to give them a go—they firmly belong in your leadership toolbox, and they have the potential to uncover solutions to extremely difficult challenges.

WHAT'S IN YOUR TOOLBOX?

Ask any builder, mechanic, or carpenter, and they will tell you that there is a minimum number of key tools that any (every) toolbox should include: hammer, saw, pliers, a variety of screwdrivers, mallet, tape measure, spirit level, socket set, adjustable square, utility knife, plane, chisels, adjustable wrench, hammer, cordless drill, as well as glue, penetrating oil, rope, and duct tape. Phew.

With these key tools, someone could probably make short work of 95 percent of the typical jobs around the house.

Of course, there are thousands of other tools that could be used—a trip to a large DIY store will stand testament to the fact that there a myriad of amazing tools, gizmos, and contraptions in all shapes and sizes: maybe once-in-a-lifetime tools of enormous specialty and specificity, but the list above covers most jobs most of the time.

When you hear hoofbeats, think horses and not zebras.[1]

---

1   A leadership lesson for us all.

THE LEADER'S TOOLBOX

Here are the leaders' key tools—they cover 95 percent of all of the typical business/leadership issues.

» To understand and deal with the issues in the competitive environment:
- o PEST analysis
- o Porter's Five Forces
- o Diffusion of innovation curve

» To better understand the organization:
- o USP analysis
- o Core competence analysis
- o SWOT analysis

» To better understand potential strategic options:
- o Porter's Generic Strategies
- o Ansoff's Matrix
- o Bowman's Strategy Clock

» To better understand options, and creative solutions:
- o BCG four-box model
- o Kepner-Tregoe Matrix
- o SCAMPER model

Remember how earlier we agreed that we don't know what we don't know? If you don't know any of these tools, I urge you to take time to learn them and their application(s).

There are literally hundreds of business and strategy and modeling and leadership tools—if you're a leader, you must understand them—they are the tools of the trade.

For more of these critical leadership tools, and for explanations of how to use them with your daily leadership journal, visit www.mydailyleadership.com/resources

MAKING A CABINET AND CHANGING A SPARK PLUG

If you were to try to make a cabinet with rusty and blunt and mediocre and broken tools, what might that cabinet look like? Gorgeous? I suspect not.

If you were to try to change a spark plug without a swivel head spark plug socket wrench, how would it go? Would it go well? I strongly suspect not.

You don't use a sledgehammer to crack a walnut. You don't try to pound in nails with a screwdriver. The message? Use the appropriate tools for the task at hand.

> *"It is essential to have good tools, but it is also essential that the tools be used in the right way."*
> —*Wallace D. Wattles*

As mentioned earlier:

The scale model is useful—especially when dealing with catastrophizing.

A problem well defined (by a model) is half solved.

Each business tool has a different use and application. But all tools are the single best way to deal with confirmation bias and systemic noise.

We can't leave tools behind without talking about everyone's favorite, the Balanced Scorecard. Is Balanced Scorecard also part of the answer? Let's see.

BALANCED SCORECARD?

The Balanced Scorecard is a tool developed to help managers and business leaders measure and monitor progress towards goals in an holistic and "balanced" way. According to the *Harvard Business Review*, Balanced Scorecard leadership is one of the most significant business ideas of the last seventy-five years. According to the Balanced Scorecard Institute, Bain & Company listed it as fifth in a list of the ten most widely used business tools around the world.

Wow. Aren't we building up a pretty cool leadership toolbox? I think we are.

In short, Balanced Scorecards help connect the dots between the current state and some future (more desirable) state. Lots of leaders swear by the efficacy of the tool, and they base the management of their business around the four different perspectives it focuses on:

Financial good stewardship.
Customers and stakeholders.
Internal processes.
Organizational capacity for learning and growth.

All extremely laudable perspectives, of course.

But, like any other tool (Leadership Journaling included), its use should be appropriate to the issue at hand.

QUICK HEALTH WARNING

At the risk of contracting myself, please don't go too overboard on tools and models—they are not the sole refuge of the enlightened leader.

Tools tend to measure things, and rank them, and try to connect between them, and explore options arriving from them. But sometimes, the most important things are not measurable: happiness, contentment, engagement, imagination, creativity, authentic relationships, potential, and so on.

As usual, moderation in all things. Even virtues, if used to excess, can become vices.

WHAT THE VUCA IS GOING ON?

Being a leader can often be a lonely and thankless task: multiple decisions to be made, often at speed, and often with obvious (and not so obvious) gaps in information.

The US Army War College coined a phrase in the late 1980s—VUCA. It was a way of encapsulating how difficult circumstances are in the heat of battle and how unpredictable outcomes unfold as a consequence of (multiple) decisions made. The principles of VUCA apply just as well to the commercial environments that leaders face on a daily basis as they do to fighter pilots in the middle of a dogfight.

VUCA stands for environments that are Volatile, Uncertain, Chaotic, and Ambiguous.[2]

And you don't have to be a fighter pilot or the CEO of a multibillion-dollar organization to know how a world filled with VUCA feels, right?

Colonel John Boyd was an F-86 pilot in the Korean War and later a commander in the Vietnam War responsible for improvements in one-on-one fighter combat situations. He later worked as a consultant for the Pentagon where he developed his theory of "energy maneuverability." The idea behind this concept is driven by the principle of agility—Boyd argues, "Whoever can handle the quickest rate of change is the one who survives." A little like Charles Darwin's principle we discussed earlier.

Boyd's argument regarding the importance of agility applies just as well to directing a battalion in battle as it does to directing a business. His model later became known as the "Boyd cycle"—the OODA loop.

The OODA acronym stands for:

Observation — of the situation.

Orientation — in as much as meaning is given to the situation.

---

2   Can I get an "Amen"?

Decision — to be made as a consequence of the above.

Action — as required to fulfill/satisfy the decision.

The principle is that whichever fighter pilot, general, and the like can execute their OODA loops more quickly will triumph. Again, the similarities with running businesses are obvious. In fact, the principles developed by Boyd regarding VUCA and OODA have been utilized successfully in the business world by preeminent brands such as Disney, Dell, General Electric, Southwest Airlines, and Toyota to name but a few—and if that isn't enough evidence for you, then likely none will ever exist.[3]

Why not give it a go right now—see what can be accomplished in just a few minutes using these two models. You never know, you might surprise yourself.

Find somewhere rather fab and groovy in your journal and finish off these thoughts:

> Choose a single situation in your organization that right now is filled with VUCA. Something that's Volatile, Uncertain, Chaotic, and Ambiguous. Define the problem as well as you can under the VUCA headings. Maybe one hundred to two hundred words in total:

If that problem is important enough to resolve, set about dedicating some organizational resource to the Boyd cycle: OODA.

---

3   Just sayin'.

Observe

Information gathering.

Decide which is good/reliable information and which is not.
What information is missing or incomplete.
What circumstances seem to be unfolding.
Where there is uncertainty.

Orient

Where are you now?

Make sense of the information.
What models would be appropriate to explain what you observe.
Should be versus what is—the brutal truth of it.
Analysis of the information.

Decide

What path should you take?

Decide what to do next.
Decide what the measurement criteria and frequency will be.
Define the early milestones of success.
Outline course correction options.

Act

Action plan.

Plan the resources, timing, and execution.
Test and evaluate.
Loop back to Observe.

JUST BEFORE I GO...

We mustn't leave the section on business tools without also mentioning the power of using tools in order to empower and develop others.

Once a leader uses a tool to explore a particular situation, issue, or problem, and then uses that very same tool to describe to others the process followed in reaching a decision as well as the rationale behind the decision, they are, at the same time, teaching self-sufficiency to their teams.

Tools help explore, they help understanding, they help explain, they help teach, they help execute, they help measure, they help review, they help report, and they help course-correct.

By using strategy and planning and decision-making tools, leaders develop themselves, their business, and their people. The message I hope is clear: learn how to use more tools.

"Leaders need to provide strategy and direction and give to their employees tools that enable them to gather information and insight from around the world. Leaders shouldn't try to make every decision."
—Bill Gates

CHAPTER 14

How's the weather today?

Are you more interested in the weather or the climate?

HOW WELL DO YOU WEATHER THE WEATHER, WELL?

With the world becoming increasingly concerned about climate change, it's important to spend a few moments considering how this principle applies to leadership.

> Question:
> Are you the kind of leader who is more interested in the weather, or are you the kind of leader who is most interested in the climate?

To answer that, let's first consider what the differences are between *the weather* and *the climate*.

The weather is the weather today and tomorrow. Is it raining now? Will it be sunny tomorrow? What shall I wear this afternoon?

That's the weather.

There's not much "wit" to the weather.

Here's how you tell the weather using only a small stone and a short piece of string.

> Tie a piece of string around a small stone and hang it outside your kitchen window. When you come down for a coffee in the morning, take a glance at the stone.
> If the stone is wet, it's raining. If it's dry, it is not.
> If the stone casts a shadow, it's sunny.
> If the stone is white, it's snowing.
> If the stone is moving, it's windy.
> If the stone is hard to see, it's foggy.
> If the stone is jumping up and down, you're having an earthquake—take cover.
> If the stone is gone, it's very, very, very windy—take cover.

That's the weather.

Interesting? Important? Sure.

The climate, however, is much more interesting and much more important to the leader.

The climate is the weather over time, and takes an enormous amount of wit and skill to manage.

Managers busy themselves responding to the weather while leaders are more concerned about controlling the climate.

Tactical leaders (and most businesses) almost exclusively occupy themselves with the study of the weather. What's happening today? How are we set up to deal with what's happening today? Do we have the right clothing for the weather tomorrow? Are we all safe at the moment? Are we having a good month? Did we hit our monthly target?

The problem with this approach is that subtle changes over time can significantly alter the competitive landscape to the extent that eventually their business and commercial offering becomes irrelevant. Think black and white TVs. There was a time, I promise, when all TVs in the world were black and white.[1] Manufacturers spent their time designing and building the very best black and white TV that they possibly could—they busied themselves with the very latest thinking regarding lean manufacturing and mass-production techniques, agile and flexible construction processes, well-organized purchasing, and robust distribution footprints. Efficient. Well-constructed. Fairly priced. Gorgeous.

...and then, one fateful day, thanks to the clever old chaps at RCA Laboratories, suddenly, along came the color TV.

In but the blink of an eye, black and white TV manufacturers were in trouble—serious trouble. Some manufacturers, of course, moved quickly to the new world of color, investing millions and millions in the brand new technology. Some other,

---

1   I don't mean that the TV itself was black and white, I mean that the screen only showed images in black and white—shades of gray. And, there were only one or two channels on TV, and they all shut down at midnight! I know! Madness. If you don't believe me, look it up. *Plus ça change*, the French say.

less perspicatious manufacturers, however, decried the quality of the new-fangled color reception, explaining that the picture was grainy, the sets were outrageously expensive, the cameras were too unreliable and unwieldy, and that it would just never catch on—to say nothing of the fact that consumers would have to invest thousands in yet another TV while they had a perfectly serviceable black and white apparatus already in the corner of their living room, which most were still paying off, by the way.[2] Sticker-shock and picture-quality, they surmised, would save them all.

It did not—not even nearly.

Before too long the black and white brigade was looking to improve further the efficiency and effectiveness of manufacturing—driving down costs in order to pass on reduced pricing to the consumer.

A price war broke out.

But the color steamroller rumbled inexorably on.

Eventually the black and white guys, in a desperate attempt at relevancy and distribution footprint, were practically giving their sets away with jumbo-sized cereal boxes.[3] The black and white guys started to go out of business. The market for black and white TVs went into catastrophic terminal decline along with the countless manufacturers who refused to move with the times and commit to the wonderful world of color. Why? They didn't think enough about the climate; they concerned themselves only with the weather.

Same, too, Woolworths, Blockbuster, Toys "R" Us, Ask Jeeves, and the like.

Same, too, milkmen[4] and lamplighters. Coal men. Switchboard operators. Town criers. Telegram delivery boys.

---

2   Nero: "Pass me my fiddle, can you?"

3   Not really, but I can imagine the conversation happened at some point in some desperate marketing meeting.

4   Yes, a real thing.

And before too long, librarians, travel agents, interpreters, truck drivers, and...you get the idea.

Human beings have spent two hundred years thinking too much about the weather and not enough about the climate; and look where that has gotten us—we'll lose Miami before too long if we're not careful, and I have family living there, to say nothing of Tokyo, New York, Shanghai, New Orleans, Mumbai—basically, any low-lying city. The prospects are simply too gruesome to consider. But consider them, we must.

It's fair to say that the world has had too many managers and not enough leaders.

Strategic leaders (and world leaders, I trust) should be more interested in understanding the climate. How are they set up for the weather next year, three years down the road, five years down the road? Thirty years down the road? Great businesses spend time future-proofing the business—not all the time, but critical time, nonetheless.

As a leader, your job it to future-proof you, as well as your business. Does your journal help you do this? You betcha. How? Glad you asked.

"I SKATE TO WHERE THE PUCK WILL BE."

Wayne Gretzky, of hockey fame, said that the reason he was such an outstanding player is because he skates to where the puck will be, not where it is, nor where it has been. The reason he was so adept at this was because he was a student of the game, and he realized that his job was to *anticipate*, not to *react* to events as they were unfolding. Great leaders do the same—they respond with intentionality, they don't react with urgency.

In your business it can be described this way:

> What's happening right now, today, tomorrow, next week, next month is the weather.

What does the P & L sheet look like? What does the sales forecast look like for Q2? What does the cash flow forecast show for next month?

Our core values and vision statements and recruiting policy are much more interested in defining the climate.

The weather is tactical, short-term planning and execution. The climate is strategic, more long-term forecasting and analysis.

It's important to be interested in the weather, of course, but great leaders recognize that it's more important to think about the climate.

Your journal helps you to understand the past and anticipate the future.

Leaders should be regularly asking themselves (in their journal, of course) is this a weather issue or a climate issue—and then respond accordingly.

If it's a weather issue, OK, knuckle down, wrap up warm, it'll pass. Winston Churchill said that if you're going through hell, keep going. That's the weather.

But, if what you're dealing with is a climate issue, we need a different approach. "Just get on with it," and "Apply yourself!" aren't going to work in the mid- to long-term.

WHAT'S WORTH FIGHTING FOR?

Sometimes the problem is that you're the one who's creating the dangerous climate—and it doesn't look sustainable over the mid- to long-term.[5]

I imagine that you're a rather busy and clever and important sausage, right? Lots of critical and highly time-sensitive things

---

5   Politicians, take note—please!

to do. Lots of vital things to accomplish. Lots of terribly urgent things to start and lots of even more crucial things to finish.

I imagine that your calendar for the week looks chock-a-block, simply packed as tightly as a sardine tin, or as busy as one of Santa's elves on December 24th checking the naughty and nice list for the millionth time. Busy, busy, busy. Places to go, people to see, deals to be done, things to sort, projects to deliver.

Ooh, it must feel wonderful to be so important, and so necessary, right?

How do you possibly fit it all in while remaining creative and effective?

Newsflash: over the long-term, you can't; so, stop trying. Because in the trying you will likely lose yourself, you loved ones, and your quality of life. And, since we only get one life, don't ruin it by trying to be all things to all people all of the time—you'll surely fail.

The much smarter question we should be asking ourselves is, "What should I fit in, and what should I leave out?" Be intentional with your life—it's your life; it deserves intentionality.

Steven Covey, of *The 7 Habits of Highly Effective People* fame, reminds us that we shouldn't figure out how to prioritize what's on our schedule, rather we should figure out how to schedule our priorities. Wise words indeed.

Decide the few important, really important, things and then figure out how to get those things done to the exclusion of all else.

Most leaders (well, the unenlightened ones, at least) tend to spend their lives in a stressful and thoroughly horrid box: Quadrant 2 of the Eisenhower Decision Matrix[6] below—ugh.

If you live, more often than not, in Quadrant 2, you're simply not doing a good job of allocating resources to better resolve conflicts. You're not doing a good job of managing yourself,

---

6   You know, the 34th US president, that one. The Dwight D. one.

your time, and your business—you are not being an effective leader. You should make a priority to figure out how to live almost all of the time in Quadrant 1, doing really important but not urgent stuff at a thoughtful and efficient pace.

	LOW IMPORTANCE	HIGH IMPORTANCE
HIGH URGENCY	Quadrant 1 **DECIDE IT** Schedule a time to do it—thoughtfully	Quadrant 2 **DO IT** Do it right now—quickly
LOW URGENCY	Quadrant 4 **DELETE IT** Eliminate it—completely	Quadrant 3 **DELEGATE IT** Nominate the right people—judiciously

Take a look below at some other gems the inimitable Mr. Covey gave us: What could the intelligent leader do with these wonderfully enlightened musings when attempting to transition themselves out of all of the other quadrants in the exclusive favor of Quadrant 1?

The main thing is to keep the main thing the main thing.

Live out of your imagination, not your history.

You have to decide what your highest priorities are and have the courage—pleasantly, smilingly, unapologetically, to say "no" to other things. And the way you do that is by having a bigger "yes" burning inside. The enemy of the "best" is often the "good."

If you're a leader, you often have to fight for what's important. That's what great leaders do, after all.

That necessitates deciding what's important first—otherwise, how can you fight for it? Tricky.

...and, if you don't stand for something, you'll fall for anything.

Great leaders prioritize the climate over the weather. Managers prioritize the weather over the climate. And that's how it should be.

Find somewhere a sparkling and gloriously combative space in your journal and complete this extremely critical thought:

Here is the short list of what is supremely important to me...important enough to prioritize, and important enough for me to fight for:

1.
2.
3.
4.
5.
6.

NOW, ACT ACCORDINGLY.

WORK LIFE BALANCE

Another story.

I once worked in a large open plan office. On my floor, there were around twenty people all working at drawing boards with large pieces of paper and pens and pencils and rulers, me included. Yes, the days before AutoCAD had even been dreamed of or was even a twinkle in Mr. John Walker's eye.[7]

The team had been working really hard for about six months straight—most of us putting in lots of overtime, including weekends, in order to complete a very large project with unfeasibly tight deadlines.

One day, our boss came out of his office and stood in the middle of the room, asking for everyone to put down their pencils;[8] he needed everyone's attention for a few moments.

"We have become a little concerned," he began.

I'm not sure who the "we" he was referring to was, but I let that one slide.

"Concerned about the level of work that we've been putting in these last six months."

"We" again. I don't ever remember seeing you in your office over the weekend, pal.

"It has been a really, really busy time with all hands to the pumps. And I want you all to know how much we appreciate your hard work and dedication to the cause."

Oh, OK, then. "We" seems to have noticed at least, I thought.

"But we've got good and some bad news, I'm afraid."

Oh ohhh. By the tone of his voice, it sounds more like "bad" than "good."

"We've just learned that we've been fortunate enough to have been awarded the very large Luna contract that we've been chasing for the last year or so. And we're all very excited about it."

---

7   According to the good Mrs. Google, he and a team of fifteen others invented AutoCAD—apparently.

8   I know. Don't rub it in.

Again, who is "we"? I'd love to meet them and shake their hand one day.

"This means that we're all going to have dig even deeper...."

Really, I'm serious. Who is this "we"?

"...and do all that we can to now get *both* projects delivered on time. We're looking for new designers, of course, but it's going to be tough for a few months. And..."

Here it comes. Waaaaaait for it.

"...because we're worried about how this extra work might affect us all..."

I'm going to strangle someone if he says "we" or "us" just one more time!

"...we're going to have to ask you all to stay behind this evening. We've arranged for you all to attend a seminar that we've arranged..."

Aaaargh!

"...on 'Work Life Balance.'"

...

He *genuinely* didn't see the irony of it. Kill me now.

"Thanks again. Great stuff. Everybody. Really great. And sorry, you know...again."

?

And with a slightly apologetic shrug, he was back off to his office in the corner.

...and "we" were all brushing up our resumes before the end of the day.

I'M TOO BUSY MOPPING UP THE FLOOR TO TURN OFF THE FAUCET.

Is this you?

At the risk of mixing our weather-based metaphors again, you can't possibly get around to doing anything about the climate when there's just sooooo much weather to contend with right now.

It's a prioritization issue—most important leadership issues are, after all.

Most leaders struggle to properly prioritize. Prioritization, and time management, are tricky. Books have been written about them, seminars are given on them, industries have been built around them, and coaches get rich from them. Heck, the whole of the drawing office I worked for was sent to a rather fancy seminar on the topic. Money very well spent. NOT!

Most leaders are no better. They work hard—too hard. They work long hours—too many long hours. When they're at work, they're working hard and wishing they were home; and when they finally get home, they're thinking about how to find more time to finish all the work they have to do.

Am I simply saying that you should give yourself permission to occasionally "take a day off and go do something just for you for once, and things will surely improve"?

No, I am not.

Am I saying, go, enjoy; smile, eat the ice cream, smell the roses, roll up your trouser legs, and go for a lovely little paddle? It'll all be waiting patiently for you when you get back.

Again, no.

Am I giving you permission to goof off once in a while and rediscover your inner child and prior zest for life?

Absolutely not.

What I'm saying is, you're the leader, start leading better. Organize things better, MUCH BETTER, so that you don't have to beg and steal and hour here and thirty minutes there in order to treat yourself, or to go see the kids in the school Christmas play. You should be able to do this whenever you want without having to work in overdrive the next two weeks just to catch up—else let a customer or a prospect or an employee or a project down. [9]

---

9   Honestly, the play isn't going to be that good. It's not worth the stress. Spoiler alert #1: all the kids will get their presents on time. Spoiler alert #2: nobody is going to win an Oscar for the performances.

Honestly, what an outrageous state of affairs you've let yourself fall prey to.

And, if you're the one really in charge, shame on you.

You're supposed to be the smart one, the clever one, the resourceful one, right? You're the one people come to in order to get things fixed, right? Well, if you're so smart, so clever, so resourceful, and the fix-it guy, fix this climate change issue, Mr. Fixer!

"But," I hear you cry. "Antonio, we're building a business here. You can't make an omelet without some friendly fire in the eggs department. Sacrifices have to be made in the short-term. Short-term pain, for long-term gain."

OK, but how long is the short-term exactly? Five years? Eight years? Ten years? That's not short-term, bub, that's long-term; that's your life, and it's turning out not to be such a good one.

As succinctly as I can state it, there aren't many people on their death bed wishing that they'd spent more time in the office!

Hillary Clinton, former US Secretary of State, warned in her Howard University Commencement Speech of 1988 that we shouldn't confuse having a career with having a life.

Bravo, Mrs. Clinton.

CONFLICT RESOLUTION AND RESOURCE ALLOCATION

If it helps with conceptualizing for you, why not approach the climate like any other tricky leadership challenge that you face on a fairly regular basis?

Imagine that your work-life balance, and urgent-important, and life-career, and weather-climate issues are a set of problems and issues that are adversely affecting the effectiveness and efficiency of the leadership and, as a consequence, the company as a whole. You shouldn't have to stretch your imagination too far, because it is.

Among leaders' key tasks are conflict resolution and resource allocation.

> Conflict resolution is defined as methods and processes designed to achieve the optimum solution for all sides in the event of disagreement between them. The conflict may be between individuals, or between departments, or between the company and its customers. The conflict may be between goals and resources. It may be between nice-to-haves and need-to-haves. You get the picture. Conflict.

> Resource allocation is how the leadership distributes company resources in order to best resolve the conflict(s) mentioned above. Resources include: time, effort, energy, people, money, and so on.

Typically, the trickier and the more intractable the problem seems, the greater the conflict. The greater the conflict, the more imaginative the resource allocation needs to be in order to solve or alleviate it. Well, that's good, because you do enjoy a good head-scratching challenge, after all.

As we mentioned all the way back in Chapter 1, here it is now in Latin for a little variety: *Medice, cura te ipsum*.

Zing!

HOW TO LAND A PLANE

Commercial airline pilots will tell you that when they register a flight plan with the relevant authorities advising them of the route that they intend to take, including starting point and end point, what they are really thinking about is the big picture—how to get from point A to point B on a macro-scale—big maps, large scale, big picture stuff.

Once the plane has taken off and reaches cruising speed and altitude, pilots must course correct constantly because of weather, prevailing wind, traffic, instructions from control towers on the ground, and so on—a thousand tiny adjustments, none of which were specifically predictable on the macro-scale when they first plotted their desired route, but were entirely expected on the micro-scale when they began to fly it.

Let's imagine that the flight has gone very well (just as planned). Eventually, the time comes when the pilot needs to start thinking about landing the plane safely. This is where pilots now start to scale their thinking.

As you consider this list, try to imagine a leader executing a new initiative or a strategic plan that requires some coordination and larger-scale change.

First the pilot starts to think at a thirty-thousand-foot scale:

How do I get this plane from thirty thousand feet safely to the correct airport?
Are we approximating the right speed, direction, and altitude to broadly get us to where we need to be?
What does the traffic and weather look like around, below, and ahead of us?
When do we need to start thinking about the situation at ten thousand feet?

Then at the ten-thousand-foot scale:

Have I announced my intention and requested permission to land at the airport, and have I asked for preliminary guidelines and advice?
Have I advised the passengers and crew what's coming?
Have I started to prep for the landing and begun appropriate checks and procedures?

When do I need to start thinking about the situation at two thousand feet?

Then at the two-thousand-foot scale:

Am I close to where I should be?
Is everyone (and the plane) making the right preparations to land?
Is everyone aware of where I am and where I am intending to be?
Am I aware of where everyone else is and where they are intending to be?

Then at the five-hundred-foot scale:

Are we oriented correctly?
Are we well set up for some final go/no-go decisions?
Have we consulted our critical checklists?
Are we all laser focused on the specific and imminent goal?

Then at the one-hundred-foot scale:

Are we fully committed, or do we opt for a go around?
Is everything and everyone ready inside the cockpit, plane, and airfield?
Focus, trust the process—adjust.

Then at the ten-foot scale:

Fine adjustments.
Land safely.

Notice how, as the pilot gets closer to the goal, the number of tasks reduce, but each becomes much more targeted and specific and requires more focused application.

Remember, while all of these scales are important, the last few feet are kind of really critical, right? The correct runway, the correct orientation, permission to land, clear air ahead, and so on are important, of course. But without a safe landing (at the micro-scale) even if it's on an empty highway or field, all other considerations throughout the whole flight were kind of superfluous. The safe landing is a definite need-to-have. You could argue that the fine detail is the most important part of the whole enterprise since if the landing goes badly (a crash), all of the other elements of the flight were nice-to-haves, at best.

Here's how most leaders normally mess up: they tend to want to only think at the thirty-thousand-foot scale: the overarching goal, the big vision, the bright new initiative, the big and shiny idea, the stretch objectives...and then they leave the *messy details* to others. "I'm more of a 'big picture' kinda person," they say in a very dramatic, over exaggerated, and self-effacing[10] sort of way. "I leave all of the finer details to those who understand these things much better than I."

What they really mean is that the detail is hard and dangerous, and where most plans fail...so I'd rather not have to think about that stuff.

The good leaders think at the thirty-thousand-foot scale and the ten-thousand-foot scale, but the great ones think all the way right down to the ten-foot and one-foot scale—right down to the point when the plane is landed, and all passengers are safely at the gate and off the plane, and the engines have been shut down, and all the paperwork completed.

The devil is in the details, right? Of course it is. But the details are not normally something that most leaders want to bother with—they want to involve themselves in the bigger-picture stuff, the exciting stuff, the "directional" stuff, the "vision" stuff, the flight-plan stuff...and leave the pesky details, like the landing, to others! MISTAKE!

---

10   Some might say "foppish." Not I.

If it helps to think of it this way, think of golf.

They do say that you drive for flash, but you putt for cash. Or, if you prefer; you drive for show, but you putt for dough.

This means that, sure, the drive from the tee is all full of power and speed and controlled brute force. It's where the crowds gather. It's where most of the theater takes place. Driving technique is studied and emulated. Driving gets you where you need to be broadly, directionally, quickly; but if you then four-putt from twelve feet out, what's the point of the super-dooper flashy-as-you-like drive? No point—that's what.

Remember how earlier we said that two of the main roles of the leader are conflict resolution and resource allocation? It might help to think of it this way:

Conflict resolution:	Pilot:	Registering the flight plan.
	Golfer:	Driving from the tee.
Resource allocation:	Pilot:	Landing the plane.
	Golfer:	Putting.

TAKE A LOOK AT YOUR CRITICAL INSTRUMENTS.

While we're on the subject of piloting and landing airplanes: Have you ever seen images of the cockpit of, say, a modern 747? Complicated stuff, right? It's all switches, and gauges, and levers, and computers screens—even a small single-engine propeller plane cockpit seems like a very daunting and complex space to the untrained eye.

Despite all of the dials and instruments and charts and switches and knobs, there are only six really critical instruments that most pilots pay most attention to most of the time, and these are normally arranged front and center right in the pilot's field of vision directly below the windshield—this cluster of instruments is often referred to as the pilot's six-pack, for obvious reasons.

The other instrument just mentioned, of course, is the windshield.

Together, these seven critical instruments receive most of the pilot's attention because they help the pilot answer the seven most critical issues of avionics.

1.	Windshield	What can I see around me?
2.	Compass (Heading indicator)	Where are we headed?
3.	Altimeter	How far from danger are we?
4.	Airspeed Indicator	How fast are we going?
5.	Artificial Horizon	How are we currently oriented relative to 'normal'?
6.	Vertical Speed Indicator	Are we climbing, stable, or sinking?
7.	Turn Coordinator	What is our direction and rate of change?

Think about all of those from a business and leadership perspective, if you will. Interesting, right?

With those six instruments (plus one—the windshield), pilots can navigate from any point on the map to any other. Depending on the size and complexity of the aircraft, there are also banks of other gauges and instruments, of course, showing a variety of temperatures and pressures and levels (fuel levels, for example—that's pretty important, right?). There are aircraft collision systems, global positioning systems, communication instruments, automatic direction finders, automatic pilots, ice detectors, and so on. There are visual and auditory alarms, and warnings when things stray from normal/expected.

At the root of it, all of these instruments and gauges advise the pilot about a range of relationships: the relationship of the plane to points on the ground, the relationship of the plane to the horizon, the relationship between available resources and the goal, the relationship and distances to obstacles and difficulties.

The six-pack, plus the windshield, plus the other gauges tell the pilot whether or not they are on plan, and whether they have the resources and wherewithal to continue the flight and/or course-correct. Importantly, all of these instruments and gauges also tell the pilot whether or not the plane is in balance (or, for the qualified pilots reading this: whether the plane is in sufficiently controlled imbalance[11]).

HOW'S *YOUR* SIX-PACK LOOKING?

What are your six or seven critical instruments that tell you whether or not you're in balance (or at least controlled imbalance) telling you? Is your business in balance (or properly controlled imbalance), and are you personally in balance (or properly controlled imbalance)?

---

11   Deep.

Find a suitably balanced space in your journal. Copy and complete the following critical, critical, critical[12] relationship table:

	Balanced	Controlled Imbalance	Imbalanced
My relationship with my significant other and family			
My relationship with my team and peers			
My relationship with my myself			
Now choose three or four critical others:			
1.			
2.			
3.			
4.			

(IM)BALANCE IN ALL THINGS

Pilots are generally more interested in the weather than the climate—at least on the plane they are currently flying, right?

Leaders need to pay attention to the climate generally (strategy and vision), but the weather more specifically (plans and projects). Yin and yang. Big and small. Loose and tight. It's tough.

Balance and controlled imbalance are tough. Work-life balance, for example, is much tougher to get right with any level of consistency than most people (leaders) think.

Things can become unstable and unbalanced very easily. Try standing on one leg for long enough, and you'll come to

12   You getting the picture?

realize that balance beyond the very short-term takes focus and effort—it is not naturally the order of things.

The natural order of things is not balance and harmony and structure: the natural order of things is entropy. Entropy is in every system and, since everything, even an atom, is a system, entropy is in everything.

Entropy dictates that there is a tendency for all things (yes, all things, all systems, all processes, all relationships) to decline and degrade into more complexity and increased disorder. Unchecked and unmanaged, the disorder of any and all systems ALWAYS increases with time.

Your job as a leader is to increase order and harmony and balance (or controlled imbalance, like the pilot in order to effect change) because, if left alone, things get shaky, frayed at the edges, and critically imbalanced remarkably quickly.

The best leaders realize that balance at work AND balance with their own private life is NEVER an "either, or" situation, it's both.

Less well-defined leaders seem to try to swing between one or the other, taking turns with their priority—sometimes, they say, work must take priority, and sometimes home should take priority. And they vacillate and wrestle their time and attention between the two. Normally work wins this fight.

They are like the pilot saying, "It doesn't matter which direction we fly in just so long as we're at thirty thousand feet, right? I mean, there's nothing we can collide with at thirty thousand feet, right?"

"Yes, but you're over the ocean and two hundred miles from the nearest land, and you only have two minutes of fuel left."

"Uhhh..."

How well are you balancing your work and your life? Seriously? The answer to that question likely lies in the answer to this one:

Can you take a day or two off?

Dumb question, right?

"Of course I can," you probably replied. "...just not right now."

Take a minute and complete this quick exercise:

The Top 5 reasons that I can't take more time off *right now* are...

1.

2.

3.

4.

5.

You have likely written something that includes or sounds like:

✧ The business needs me more than ever right now.

✧ We could lose critical business if I take my foot off the gas at the moment.

✧ Nobody does it better.[13]

✧ I expect a high work ethic from myself and my people— and I was always taught to lead by example.

✧ We are underresourced right now, and everyone needs to multitask—and that includes me.

✧ We have some super-tight and super-important dead-lines at the moment.

✧ We lost some good employees recently, and we haven't managed to replace them yet.

---

13   So, you think you're James Bond now? Nice.

None of these types of answers are the answer that great leaders give—because they are not the balanced situations that great leaders engineer—in fact, they are the situations that thoroughly crappy (imbalanced) leaders engineer.

If you're chief cook and bottle washer, you're likely running a crappy restaurant—it certainly isn't Michelin-quality, that's for sure. Don't build a crappy restaurant—you should be a three-star Michelin chef, working almost exclusively on people-development, menu-development, and maintaining quality at the pass.

Let the bottle washer wash bottles, not you. Let the waiters wait, not you. Let the bartenders tend, not you. Let the cleaners clean, not you. Let the valets valet, not you.

How close to burnout are you?

How stressed are you?

How far away are you from the person your significant other fell in love with?

How long can you sustain your level of current load and stress?

How often do you have to apologize at work or at home for not being there?

Take a day off; it won't kill you.

...But eventually the stress might if you don't. Ouch.

Set things up so that your people can cope while you're not around, because they can. Expect the best of people; they normally deliver it.

HOW LONG BEFORE YOUR WINDSHIELD WIPER MOTOR DIES?

The windshield wiper motor in your car is not designed to last a lifetime. Think about why that might be the case.

When a car manufacturer sells a car to a dealer, they make much less money than you might imagine. Let's say a couple of thousand dollars only. How, then, might the manufacturer (and the dealer) make more money? Parts, spares, and repairs. There's a terrific market, markup, and margin on parts and spares.

If the windshield motor, and the cam belt, and the drive shaft, and the light bulbs, and the radiator all lasted forever, the manufacturer would certainly go broke. It's in the manufacturer's interest then that the windshield wiper motor happily operates, say, two hundred thousand times (enough that the car doesn't attract the moniker of unreliability), but not much more than that.

This is called "designed obsolescence"—the tires have seventy-five thousand miles in them, but no more; the windshield motor operates two hundred thousand cycles, but no more; the spark plugs fire for forty thousand miles, but no more. What about refrigerators, are they designed in the same way? What do *you* think? Surely not cell phones, though...or software...or ink cartridges...or light bulbs...or batteries...or insurance...or watches...you get the picture. *Nothing* is designed to last forever, least of all, you.

How do you know whether or not you're designing obsolescence into yourself? Think about how well you are developing your people. Think about how well things run when you're not around for a few weeks. If you go on vacation, is it important that you check-in every day or so? "Just to see how everyone is, you understand?" Suuuuuure.

I'm sure you've heard the expression that the best leaders work to make themselves redundant—this is what it looks like. This is how they develop themselves (and others), and how they (and others) are able to move up to bigger and better things—bigger challenges, helping more people, making a bigger and better impact.

When you go visit the best leaders of all, if you were to follow them around for a day, it's often very hard to tell they're in charge at all—think about that for a sobering moment or two.

Find a buoyantly optimistic and somewhat redundant space in your journal and complete the following sentence—it will help you get much more balance in your life:

> The most fun thing about being a leader is arranging things so that I don't have to oversee/manage/decide/run everything. Here's how I am going to start doing just that:
>
> 1.
>
> 2.
>
> 3.

I do hope that you mean it.

"The trick to balance is to not make sacrificing important things become the norm."
—*Simon Sinek*

CHAPTER 15

A memo to the CEO.

From one leader to another.

HINDSIGHT IS 20/20.

Unlike the movie *Groundhog Day*, mentioned earlier, we don't get any do-overs in life; and, unfortunately, we can't predict the future either—at least not with any actionable accuracy—more's the pity.

We can only see what's behind us—we all go through life only being able to look in the rearview mirror. Once circumstances have revealed themselves, and the implications of prior decisions become clear, it is super easy to know what it was that worked and what didn't work, the consequences of what we did and said, and what else we should have thought, done, and said. Grrrrr.

Hindsight, they say, is 20/20, but isn't it frustrating that foresight isn't also 20/20? How easy would everything be if it were?[1] Foresight is trying to predict and plan for events that haven't yet unfolded. But, are there ways to increase our foresight in order to get to perfect 20/20 vision here too? Well, sadly, no. But there are some things that leaders can do in order to help them make a more handsome fist of the future than they have done in the past.[2]

Here's a tricky little list to get your foresight spectacles on:

1. **Increase self-awareness.**
   Be honest about what you're making excuses for and why you're stalling. Move past your fears. Acknowledging your speed bumps, roadblocks, limitations, and pinch points gives you clearer forward momentum.

2. **Be very clear about what you want to achieve.**
   The more clearly you can describe your short-, mid-, and long-term goals, the clearer the plans for achieving them become.

---

1   I'd have next week's lottery numbers, for a start.
2   Don't overthink that one, it will hurt.

3. **Create a mindset and environment for success.**
   You can't make progress without having a positive mindset and setting yourself up for success. Read, learn, establish positive habits, find people and processes to support you in your goals and your growth.

4. **Take action.**
   Action orientation always wins. Take imperfect action, if necessary, but get moving. Make a start and never ever give up—if you need an accountability partner to keep moving and on track, great, get one. Or commit to your journal—it amounts to the same thing if you have the correct mindset.

5. **Look in the mirror as much as you look through the windshield.**
   My driving instructor told me this on our very first lesson. It's great advice for life too.

   Yes, foresight is about looking forward, of course, but if you don't actively look backwards, too, you can't possibly learn what worked and what didn't. How can you possibly know what to do more of and less of? Remember, wisdom comes only from evaluated experience.

TAKE ADVICE.

Take advice, sure—but be careful whom you ask it of.

If I wanted to learn how to train to run a marathon,[3] I'd exclusively seek the guidance and council of someone who has successfully trained and completed a marathon.

If I wanted to learn how to be a great leader,[4] I'd seek the guidance and council of someone who has successfully led.

---

3   And I really, really, really don't!
4   And I really, really, really do!

It stands to reason, right? Of course.

Why, then, do some people seek the advice of entirely inappropriate people? Sure, they trust them, and they value their general opinions, I get it; but you know what, I'd ask a successful brain surgeon to perform my brain surgery, a successful plumber to do my plumbing, a successful mechanic to service my car—you get the idea.

I don't think I'd ever ask my maternal grandmother her thoughts on a particularly complex segment in a multimillion-dollar M & A contract—she was a seamstress all her life. But I would most certainly ask her opinion on my grandson's rash on his neck: she has six grandchildren and eleven great-grandchildren, after all.

While we are on the topic of advice, don't canvass the opinions of too many: don't cast too wide an advice net. Counselling advice from too many sources oftentimes serves only to confuse and confound us even further.

The Chinese have an expression when it comes to advice:

> If you have a watch, you know the time. If you have two, you're never quite sure.

Find an expert—but just one. Make this single expert someone who has been where you are and has successfully transitioned ahead of you (recently)—ask them for advice, and, once you have asked for it, pay attention to it—all of it, not just the bits that you like. For "like," read the bits that are easy and seem quick—those things will almost certainly not get you where you need to be.

If you want to know what it's like to be the president of the United States, it's probably best to ask the president of the United States.

Finally, and perhaps most importantly, never forget to ask advice of yourself—you almost always know just what to do if you take time to ask yourself, and, more importantly, if you take the time to listen to the answer.

WHAT US PRESIDENTS SAY TO OTHER US PRESIDENTS

Talking about presidents, there is a wonderful modern-day tradition in the United States.

The soon-to-be ex-president leaves a private letter of advice for the newly inaugurated president. They leave it in the Oval Office, in the Resolute Desk, to be precise.

These letters are traditionally handwritten, and they typically offer best wishes, hope, and critical advice from one commander-in-chief to another.

What can we (leaders) learn from some of these wonderful letters, I wonder?

Well, let's check out some passages from some of them and then take a second to consider what you think about each of them. Try not to think of the politicians or parties or personalities involved (for obvious reasons), rather you should concentrate more on the messaging and what lessons they might teach us about leadership.

From Barack Obama to Donald Trump:

Dear Mr. President,

Millions have placed their hopes in you, and all of us, regardless of party, should hope for expanded prosperity and security during your tenure.

This is a unique office, without a clear blueprint for success, so I don't know that any advice from me will be particularly helpful. Still, let me offer a few reflections from the past 8 years.

First, we've both been blessed, in different ways, with great good fortune. Not everyone is so lucky. It's up to us to do everything we can (to) build more ladders of success for every child and family that's willing to work hard.

Second, American leadership in this world really is indispensable. It's up to us, through action and example, to sustain the international order that's expanded steadily since the end of the Cold War, and upon which our own wealth and safety depend.

Third, we are just temporary occupants of this office. That makes us guardians of those democratic institutions and traditions—like rule of law, separation of powers, equal protection, and civil liberties—that our forebears fought and bled for. Regardless of the push and pull of daily politics, it's up to us to leave those instruments of our democracy at least as strong as we found them.

And finally, take time, in the rush of events and responsibilities, for friends and family. They'll get you through the inevitable rough patches.

Michelle and I wish you and Melania the very best as you embark on this great adventure and know that we stand ready to help in any ways which we can.

Good luck and Godspeed,

BO

From George W. Bush to Barack Obama:

Dear Barack,

Congratulations on becoming our President. You have just begun a fantastic chapter in your life.

Very few have had the honor of knowing the responsibility you now feel. Very few know the excitement of the moment and the challenges you will face.

There will be trying moments. The critics will rage. Your "friends" will disappoint you. But, you will have an Almighty God to comfort you, a family who loves you, and a country that is pulling for you, including me. No matter what comes, you will be inspired by the character and compassion of the people you now lead.

God bless you. Sincerely,

GW

From Bill Clinton to George W. Bush:

Dear George,

Today you embark on the greatest venture, with the greatest honor, that can come to an American citizen.

Like me, you are especially fortunate to lead our country in a time of profound and largely positive change, when old questions, not just about the role of government, but about the very nature of our nation, must be answered anew.

You lead a proud, decent, good people. And from this day you are President of all of us. I salute you and wish you success and much happiness.

The burdens you now shoulder are great but often exaggerated. The sheer joy of doing what you believe is right is inexpressible.

My prayers are with you and your family. Godspeed.

Sincerely,

Bill

From George H. W. Bush to Bill Clinton:

Dear Bill,

When I walked into this office just now, I felt the same sense of wonder and respect that I felt four years ago. I know you will feel that, too.

I wish you great happiness here. I never felt the loneliness some Presidents have described.

There will be very tough times, made even more difficult by criticism you may not think is fair. I'm not a very good one to give advice; but just don't let the critics discourage you or push you off course.

You will be our President when you read this note. I wish you well. I wish your family well.

Your success is now our country's success. I am rooting hard for you.

Good luck --

George

From Ronald Reagan to George H. W. Bush:

(On stationary that reads, "Don't let the turkeys get you down" with an illustration of an elephant surrounded by turkeys.)

> *Dear George,*
>
> *You'll have moments when you want to use this particular stationary. Well, go to it.*
>
> *George, I treasure the memories we share, and I wish you all the very best. You'll be in my prayers. God bless you & Barbara. I'll miss our Thursday lunches.*
>
> *Ron*

Whenever we consult with a new leader, we have them perform a similar exercise.

We have them write a short memo to the new CEO—as if today were their last day in office, and somebody new will be sitting where they have been sitting for the past few years. We ask them to consider the legacy they will leave behind, as well as give some inspiring thoughts to the new incumbent.

Write a list of four or five thoughts and/or pieces of advice that you would likely give to your successor if they were to sit at your desk tomorrow.

Find a suitably presidential spot in your journal and take a few minutes to finish off how this letter to your successor starts:

To the new _____ (insert role),

Congratulations, you have been given a wonderful opportunity to make your own indelible mark on this astonishing organization.

Before you begin on this privileged journey, here are some thoughts that I share in order to help you succeed in your first one hundred days:

1.

2.

3.

4.

5.

Be sure to date the letter too—that way, when you look back on this, you will be able to figure out whether or not you have taken your own advice![5]

On an allied, but slightly grizzlier theme, let's turn our thoughts to your inevitable, eventual, demise.

WHAT IF YOU DIED TODAY?

Here's another way of looking at the principles covered above.

Without wanting to alarm anyone, it could come to pass that you actually die today, right? This very day! Later on today. Perhaps in the next hour or two.[6]

---

5   Ouch!

6   I mean, you almost definitely won't; but, statistically, you could. A sobering thought, *n'cest pas*?

If you did expire today, God forbid, what would your replacement likely prioritize in the next 30/60/90 days? What would a fresh pair of eyes, unencumbered by historical cultural norms, with no hint of "not-invented-here" syndrome, and with absolutely no sacred cows to desecrate, what would they immediately focus on? What different approach would they take? Which things would they prioritize differently from those you are currently paying attention to? They almost certainly would change something fundamental: but what?

Imagine that a tip-top, brilliant, world-class, driven, capable, experienced, successful leader[7] were to assume your role first thing tomorrow morning, without any warning or preparation.

Imagine them sitting behind your desk—with it looking exactly as it looks right now: your pen will be where it is right now. The screen will be exactly where it is right now. The half-drained coffee cup will be exactly as it is right now. You get the picture.

Imagine them booting up your computer and looking at your inbox, calendar, and recent sent items.

Imagine that they spent the rest of the day interviewing the board one by one. Imagine that they even spoke to your top ten customers. Imagine that they finished the day reading the minutes of the last six months' board meetings, and imagine that they took time to talk to your other key leaders, staff, and stakeholders.

Now imagine that they had no fear.

Then imagine that they got out their pen and started some blue-sky writing.

When their new plan emerged in a day or two, what do you imagine that they would prioritize?

How would they allocate resources differently?

---

7   ...and probably terribly good looking with enormous poise and charm. Let's not forget, windswept and interesting too. If you're thinking Sean Connery as James Bond in *From Russia with Love*, or Aubrey Hepburn as Holly Golightly in *Breakfast at Tiffany's*, you're probably on the right path.

How would the immediate goals of the organization change?

Would they be interested in revolution rather than evolution, I wonder?

If you answer, "No, they would probably do exactly as I am doing right now," you'd be really missing the point of the exercise, and Captain Ego would need to go sit on the naughty step for a while to think about what it just said.

Honestly, what are you not addressing properly?

What needs more urgency attributed to it?

Which initiatives need to be squashed and which need a vitamin boost?

Which of the team needs a wake-up call?

How relevant is the current vision and mission?

Take a few moments to think about it and write down what you just realized about current directions—do you need a course correction? A client of ours uses a great expression that I think fits in exactly here: "Are you doing the work, or are you simply phoning it in?"[8]

> Here's where I'm (we're) currently phoning it in…

Great. So, guess what?

…Right!

I'M ON A MISSION—WHO'S WITH ME?

Why is it that the board almost never writes a memo to the brand new CEO advising him/her what kind of leader that the board expects the new incumbent to be, and some of the

---

8   Thank you, Martin. ☺

things that they hope the new leader will be able to accomplish? Crazy, right? It seems such an obvious and developmental thing to do, after all, doesn't it? Is it because they don't want to presume? Is it because they don't want to offend? Is it because they're worried about future ramifications? Whatever the reason, I'm on a mission to fix this cultural commercial black hole—who's with me?

As a gorgeous twist, why not include this memo in the recruitment process? If there's a headhunter in the process, why not show it to them before they start to look? Why not assess the core values of the prospective candidates? Why not ask the prospective new CEO to grade themselves against the list? Why not tell all employees and customers and suppliers that this is the list that you're using as the basis of your search? Why not base the new CEO's bonus on performance against this list?

You get the idea—the idea is "Live the List!"

If you're wondering what this memo/list might look like, why not give this fictitious example some thought:

Cristina,

On behalf of the board and management team, welcome aboard—we are genuinely excited to be working with you over the next critical phase in the history of the company. As you know, some of us were involved in your appointment, and, as a group, we do look forward to learning how we might best support each other through some of the inevitable challenges ahead.

As a management team, we thought it might be useful to set out the kind of organization we are building: this way we can explore how to build it better together.

We share with you some of the core values that we as a board hold in highest regard—during the selection process we have come to believe that you believe in them too. We are excited to discover the ways that we can collaborate to do things even better in the future.

1. We are a learning organization. The best advantage we have for tomorrow is what we have learned today. It's our job to develop our people—to help each of us reach our full potential.

   Support us in doing that.

2. There are those in the company who bring money in the front door; there are those who stop it leaking out the back door; and there are those who make it work harder for us while we have it—here, we treat each the same.

3. Every time we have to fire someone in the business, it's our failure. But a company with no turnover is in as much trouble as one with high turnover. We work hard to figure out those who are hard-working, as well as those who are committed to the cause: we value commitment over work ethic.

4. We hire and develop and retain A-players. We take personal development reviews very seriously, and we approach the performance grading system that we use with enormous integrity. We should be honest with our people regarding their performance, and we should be ever vigilant of it. Whenever we fire someone, it should never be a surprise to them. Whenever someone leaves us, it should never be a shock.

5. A collaborative organization achieves significantly more than a cooperative one. Fostering a collaborative culture is one of our non-negotiables.

6. Self-awareness is key—whatever a person's role, from top to bottom, left to right. We will ask you for regular

feedback including ways that we can improve, and we expect you to be brutally frank with us. We trust you will understand when we return the compliment.

7. No company (or person) can ever promise to never make a mistake—the value of each is measured by what it does about owning and resolving those mistakes.

8. We believe that culture eats strategy for breakfast. But strategy and tactical execution are critical too.

9. We never forget why people choose to work here—and the reasons are not the same as ours. Work-life balance is important. Quality of life is important. Having fun is important. Everybody needs to feel safe, and valued, and trusted because the chain is only as strong as its weakest link—and chains can only be pulled, not pushed!

10. Defend everyone as sure as we will defend you. If we fail, it's our fault, not theirs!

11. Accountability is key—it's where success lies. We encourage what we tolerate. And we don't tolerate laziness, silos, self-promotion, prejudice, protectionism, or leadership ego.

12. Wherever possible, we...

    ...delegate results, not tasks

    ...coach, not manage

    ...ask, not tell

    ...don't wait for the next big thing to float on by, we swim out to it.

13. Shit happens. We deal with it in a high-quality and kind way. We reward high quality and kindness wherever we find it—and we look for it.

14. We encourage a culture of insight and innovation. We are brave but not reckless. We are creative but also ruthlessly consistent. We are generous but not foolish.

We are lighthearted but not lightweight. Trust is earned in inches and lost in miles.

Help us to learn how to balance these things better.

15. We always tell ourselves, our people, our customers, and our suppliers the truth.
16. We work for them, they do not work for us.
17. We are building a world-class organization. "World-class" means world-class.

> Welcome aboard.
> Your team.

Consider:

This list could just as easily be written right now, as opposed to part of a high-level recruitment process. There's really no need to wait for your next position. It can be anonymous if it needs to be—from the board or the management team as a whole. If only their leader (you) would have the *chutzpah* to encourage it from them—with absolutely no negative consequences, ramifications, or private or public floggings.

Just sayin'.

Feeling brave?

If so, ask them.

Find an outstandingly selfless space in your Leadership Journal:

If I were to write a memo to my imaginary replacement, it would probably urge them to consider prioritizing these Top 4 things:

1.

2.

3.

4.

Congratulations!
Great list.
Maybe some things need addressing differently—but you just haven't gotten around to them yet: act accordingly. ☺

*"Doing the right thing isn't always easy—in fact,
sometimes, it's real hard—but just remember
that doing the right thing is always right."*
—*David Cottrell*

CHAPTER 16

. . . .

Get your mind right.

Ready to make an intentional start?

MIND YOUR MINDSET

All successful people have a successful mindset. It's obvious, right? We've alluded to it dozens of times already.

Also:

> All successful leaders have a
> successful and winning mindset.

> All successful _____ (insert role) _____
> have a successful mindset.

> Anyone who has overcome _____ (insert adversity) _____
> has done so as a consequence of
> having a successful mindset.

Everyone who is intentionally and successfully growing and learning and developing has a successful mindset.

As succinctly as possible: successful mindset is a growth-oriented mindset, not a fixed mindset.

Stanford University psychologist, Carol S. Dweck, PhD, in her book *Mindset: The New Psychology of Success*, argues that those with a fixed mindset (those who believe that abilities are locked-in and fixed) are less likely to succeed than those who believe that attitudes and abilities are there to be developed—those that have a growth mindset.

Does this mean, therefore, that if you have one, you're a shoo-in for rip-roaring success, and everything that you ever dreamed of, while if you have the other you are doomed to failure, struggle, and mediocrity? Not a bit of it![1] You are the author of your own mindset—if it isn't serving you well, you can 100 percent change it. You changed your mind about that wallpaper in the dining room fifteen times, after all. Changing your mindset is the same as changing your mind—and you do that twenty times a day, probably.

---

1   Phew! What a relief.

Take a look at the two lists in this table. Be honest with yourself. Which list more closely describes your belief set right now?

LIST 1	LIST 2
Intelligence is largely determined by our genes.	Intelligence can be developed.
It is important to look smart.	It is important to constantly learn.
Difficult challenges are to be managed.	Difficult challenges are to be sought out.
Some obstacles are too difficult to overcome.	Every failure teaches us something new and valuable.
I put in the right amount of effort for the task.	Effort leads to mastery.
Negative feedback is unhelpful: criticism is likely sour grapes.	Critique leads to learning.
Success requires discomfort.	Success in others inspires me.
I am near my full potential.	I am a long way from all that I will achieve.

So, which list is more like you? It's a tricky exercise and, if you overthink it, you can easily find completely logical and rational arguments to justify your position in each list, right? So, don't overthink it, don't try to over intellectualize it, quickly, look again: List 1 or List 2?

List 1 is a fixed (red light) mindset individual, while List 2 is a growth (green light) mindset individual.

List 1 people—I have some bad news for you:

You will not likely stick to your daily Leadership Journaling, since deep down you believe that abilities and intelligence and capabilities are largely static: so, what's the point?

Self-awareness? I already have it.

Self-improvement? I already get better every day.

Vision? I already see further than most.

Sure, you might give it a go, all enthusiastically journaling for ten days or so, then give up (or kind of forget, or get busy, or re-prioritize—which all amount to the same thing)—as you likely have done with so many things before.

You will likely not reach your full potential.

List 1 people are often in denial. They sometimes say that their life is good, they're doing OK, things for them are better than things for most. They are, in fact, in denial. They think that if they admit their life is flawed, they admit that they, too, are flawed—and that will never do. Why? Because they're fixed in their mindset and List 1 people. QED.

If the paragraph above challenges you, or disappoints you, or inspires you, you're actually a List 2 person. Congratulations! There's hope yet.

If the paragraph does not challenge or disappoint you, it's maybe time to try something else—another new initiative, another quick-fix solution. Leadership Journaling is probably not going to be a good fit for you—it's maybe going to be a bit too much like hard work. I hear hypnosis can sometimes work wonders, or those chilly cryotherapy tanks—why not give those a go? And if they don't work, well, why not give something else a go? Another seminar, perhaps? Giving things (lots of different, sometimes desperate, things) a go till you (hopefully) find something useful (relatively easy) is a really great self-development strategy, and very List 1 thinking, right?

Those who live in List 2 will almost certainly persist at their daily Leadership Journaling since they recognize that, by persisting in the struggle to improve, they will assuredly reach higher and higher levels of success and achievement. Given enough time and determination, they will eventually reach their full potential.

List 2 people recognize that their life and level of success is not perfect. They have goals for growth—and they persist, and they reach them—and that's why they succeed.

PLANS, PLANS, PLANS

Some people don't see the value of having a clear plan.

Naughty.

Some people see the value of a clear plan, but they don't create one.

Very naughty.

Some people create a clear plan that they don't carry out.

Despicable.

Some people create a clear plan that they carry out, measure, and course-correct.

Gorgeous.

Those who tend to carry out a plan, tend to carry out most of their plans.

Very gorgeous.

Those who tend to not carry out a plan, tend to not carry out most of their plans.

Very naughty.

Those who tend to carry out their plans tend to have a concrete vision and a detailed and specific intention for them that plays out in the present or near.

> At three o'clock today I will...
> Tomorrow, as soon as I get up I will...
> Here's how I will complete this project...
> To succeed at that, I must first learn this...

In other words: they have a vision, they create a very detailed plan to achieve the vision (including how, and when, and where, and who, and so on), and then they just do it! Every day! Action orientation at play. One step at a time. One day at a time. One thing at a time. Deliberately. Relentlessly. Intentionally. Purposely. They have, you might say, the action-orientation, energy, and mindset of a champion.

THE LEAD HUSKY SETS THE PACE.

When you see a pack of huskies pulling a sled, the lead husky does more than just run as fast as she possibly can, for as long as she possibly can, and by pulling as much weight as she possibly can. There's much more to it than first meets the eye.

Let's consider the lead husky's role.

First, her job is to carry out the wishes of *her* leader. Where does that leader sit? In the sled right at the back of the pack—not the front.

The lead husky is responsible for getting herself and her team closer to the goal—safely, together, and with a single purpose and intention.

Lead dogs are often not the biggest dog, nor the strongest dog, nor the fittest dog. They are normally the most determined. They set the right pace, and they keep the other dogs from going off the trail. They respond quickly to unpredictable circumstances, and they make decisions that are best for the pack rather than those that best suit the leader alone.

The lead husky does not do any of this by threat or intimidation or coercion. The lead husky is the dog that the other dogs *choose* to follow.

The lead dog is the example that all the other dogs try to emulate and try to live up to.

The leader carries with himself/herself not only their own mindset, but the mindset of the team, the department, the division, the enterprise.

THE MINDFUL MINDSET OF CHAMPIONS

Champions do not achieve a positive mindset by a single, one-time-only proclamation.

They do not make one single grand declaration: "We declare these truths to be self-evident, that all champions are made differently, they are endowed by their Creator certain unalienable gifts, among these are determination, talent, and the pursuit of greatness...."

Positive mindsets are as a consequence of a mindful and intentional journey, not a single, one-time, one-size-fits-all sweeping declaration.

Champions make a decision.
They plan for success.
They execute the plan for success—day by day by day.
They learn from failure.
They ask for feedback and help.
You, too, can develop a champion's mindset.

If you fail to plan, you plan to fail.
If you fail to communicate the plan, you plan to fail.
If you fail to work the plan, you plan to fail.
If you fail to learn from failure, you plan to fail.
If you fail to track and correct the plan, you plan to fail.
If you fail to be mindful of the plan, you plan to fail.

Ooof.

When you do things, sometimes new things, your brain makes new connections. These connections, if not reused and reinforced, degrade over time. But, if you do them again, the tiny connections reform, and, if you do them again before they have chance to degrade, the connections multiply and become stronger, and the number of connections increase, and the ability to access them increases too. The more the connections increase, the easier it is for the brain to do those things. The easier it is for the brain to do those things, the more the connections multiply and grow stronger...and so it goes on. It's exactly the same for executing a new plan, learning how to play the piano, learning a new language, origami, making asparagus risotto.

Remember the downhill skier we met in Chapter 6.

Remember how she focused all of her attention exclusively on controlling the controllables? Everything that was inside her sphere of control received 100 percent of her attention, and everything outside her control received none of her attention.

She had the mindset of a champion.

What do you notice when you see champions preparing to launch the toboggan down the hill, kick the penalty, serve the first ball, swing the club, jump the first fence, set themselves into the blocks? They first empty their minds. They completely purge themselves of all unhelpful, distracting, and doubtful thoughts. You've seen them do it a thousand times. They set their face (their mind) to the immediate task—the next thing: the first stride, the next swing, the first three yards, the first spring—as Linford Christie, the British Olympic 100 m runner would say, "All I think about is the starter's pistol, and I go on the 'B' of the bang."

Champions decide what to focus on, what to not focus on. What thoughts to listen to, to amplify, to visualize, and which thoughts to eradicate or ignore.

They do say that the race is won or lost before the first step is taken, and it is, in the mindset of the victor.

Champions first empty their mind—then they decide (intentionally, deliberately, with purpose) what to fill it with: the vision of them crossing the tape first, the route they will take down the course, the wrist-snap of the serve, the ball landing right by the pin.

At My Daily Leadership we develop the same habits: Morning Momentum.

After the race is run, the javelin has been thrown, the bar cleared (or not), champions decide what to learn from their successes (however big or small) and failures (however big or small).

At My Daily Leadership we develop the same habit: Evening Evaluation.

When the chips are down, what few thoughts/beliefs/intentions/visions of success will you fill your mind with *to the exclusion of all else?*

Determination
Optimism
Creativity
Strategy
Humor
Grit
Kindness
Service
Wisdom
Strength
Flexibility
Stamina
Gratitude
Insight
Courage
Solutions-orientation
Collaboration
Fortitude
Resilience
Confidence
Adaptability

It's time to decide.

Find a suitably decisive page of your journal and resolve now the three things you will fill your mind with (every moment of every day) in order to guarantee success:

In order to guarantee success, I will (remember to) focus (almost exclusively) on:

1.

2.

3.

4.

BEWARE "THE CIRCUMSTANCES."

Own it: whatever it is, good or bad.

Don't ever accept it when you hear yourself say something like:

"Hey, listen, under the circumstances, we're not doing so bad."

"We're not doing so bad, I suppose—you know, under the circumstances."

"We're doing OK, in spite of all of the confusion and uncertainty in the world today."

"Compared to the competition, we're not doing too badly, you know, all things considered and under the circumstances."

"Taking everything into account, and under the circumstances, we're not doing too badly, I suppose."

"We've done pretty well, under the circumstances."

"Under the circumstances..." and, "In spite of..." is stinking thinking—it's fixed-mindsettedness.[2]

"Under the circumstances," and "taking all things into account," and "all things considered" is settling. These are the thoughts of those with a fixed mindset, a mindset of limitation and lack of imagination. Don't fall into the trap of giving yourself a medal for participating. Don't settle for settling.

This is "at least" thinking, or, "in spite of" thinking:

"At least we had a go."
"At least we tried."
"At least we made a start."
"At least..."
"In spite of..."

Don't be an at-leaster, nor an in-spiter!

Instead of saying, "Well in spite of that..., we at least achieved this...."

This kind of thinking lets you off the hook. It gives you sufficient margin for failure before you've even begun. It mollifies the pain of failure—it's the Ibuprofen of the "nearly" person. We almost did it—we nearly did it.

Own it. The good, the bad, the ugly.

Instead, say, like Edison, "We learned another way not to make a light bulb," and mean it...and learn from it...and next.

SUCCESS IS THE ENEMY.

How counterintuitive is this concept?

How can success possibly be the enemy? If we're trying to achieve something great, surely the enemy is failure, not success, right? If we don't get to where we want to be, that's failure, surely?

---

2   Yes, I realize it's not a word. It should be. It is now.

Well, the truth is that we don't ever learn the really valuable lessons from our successes; we learn them from our failures and difficulties. We get to improve only when we learn and apply something new.

Leaders (heck, everyone) should expect more difficulties than not. More rejections than approvals. More difficult waters than smooth sailing. More rocky roads than sandy beaches. More failures than victories. More storm clouds than clear skies. You will upset at least as many people as you delight. You should expect to hear more "no" than "yes."

If you are only shooting for victories for fear of the damaging effects to your already bruised self-esteem by more failure and difficulty, then perhaps leadership is not for you.

Failures, not successes, force you to up your game, to develop a better strategy, to face up to weaknesses in planning and execution.

If you don't learn from failures, nor learn how to deal with failures, you're simply not going to be able to be the leader you have the potential to be. Once you start to torture yourself with every failure or misstep, it's only a hop, skip, and a jump till you're blaming your team too. And that's only a short bus ride to dissatisfaction, fear culture, and the blame game. And that's only a short walk across the park to staff turnover, a shitty culture, and someone looking at the fine print of your employment contract and having a headhunter keeping an eagle eye out for your potential replacement.

At the start of this book, I said that good leaders help people be better at their job while great leaders help people be better at life. This is where great leaders do just that—where they and/or their people fail.

There is no such thing as a mistake-free plan, a mistake-free market analysis, a mistake-free assumption, a mistake-free response-model, a mistake-free execution of the plan. This means that mistakes, missteps, misalignments, misappropriations, misunderstandings[3] are inevitable—they should be expected. Mistake-free, error-free, pain-free is the prison cage of the fixed-mindset leader.

High standards, a nurturing approach, and a learning mindset are critical if you are going to succeed. I once had a CEO who constantly told his board that they will likely know when they're on the right road to success, because it will all be uphill. Genius.

Things of value should require effort—it helps to give them value.

Don't be interested in failure, be fascinated by it. Be intrigued by it. Be riveted by it. Be enchanted by it. Be enthralled by failure and from the wonderful lessons it teaches you. Be engrossed by learning and developing everything you can from every misstep or miscalculation.

You learn significantly more from failure. Failure is good. No, failure is wonderful. Failure is to be encouraged. Failure is inevitable. Failure makes success even more sweet.

"If you're not terrified going through the corners," said race car driver Mario Andretti, "you're simply not going fast enough."

BUT, WHAT TO SAY TO THE TEAM?

Leaders with a fixed mindset say, "Hey, we missed the plan, people. I told you that failure is totally unacceptable. We must try harder, work harder. Apply yourself better. Work your teams harder. I will not accept failure, and neither should you! Failure is not an option. I didn't get where I am today by accepting defeat. Our shareholders are counting on us, and if they can't, I'm sure that we're all replaceable. Defeat is not in my vocabulary." And so on, and so on, and so forth. Drone, drone, drone. Threat, threat, threat. Stuck, stuck, stuck.

This is what judging, and scarcity, and bullying, and really ineffective, creativity-crushing leadership sounds like.

---

3   "Mis…" is much misused at times. **Bad da boom!**

Leaders with a winning mindset say, "Hey, we missed the plan, people. What can we learn from it? How shall we fix it? What should we do differently next time? How could I have supported you and the plan better?" And so on, and so on, and so forth.

Learn, learn, learn. Fix, fix, fix. Build, build, build.

This is what responsibility, maturity, and coaching should like.

The best leaders are not bullies; they are coaches. They build people up when the stakes are high and the chips are down.

READY TO MAKE AN INTENTIONAL START?

Just before we finally get around to our daily journaling practice, let's first talk about and understand the purpose and the power of our daily afformations.

Affirmations?

No, afformations—it's a totally different thing. Keep an open mind; you're going to love it: afformations are genuinely life changing. We're *not* talking about manifesting or telling the universe what you want (see it, feel it, imagine it) and wait enthusiastically for it to be magically delivered on a silver platter before tea time or the end of the month at the outside. I don't hold much truck with that kind of overly optimistic and naive thinking. Afformations are a completely different concept.

As we have mentioned, the human brain is programmed to look for patterns, to solve problems, to figure stuff out: all we have to do is to give our brain the right kinds of problems to figure out.

Typical affirmations look something like:

*I am wealthy and enjoying my increased wealth
every day.*

...or...

Today I am positively brimming with energy and over-flowing with joy.

...or...

My thoughts are filled with positivity, and my life is plentiful, and I am prosperous.

...or...

I am a wonderfully helpful and successful leader.

At its root, affirmations are statements we *want* to be true. The principle is that if we say these kinds of things to ourselves with enough frequency, with enough emotion, and with enough conviction, and enough of a clear visualization, then these things will supernaturally come to pass—eventually. Maybe. And if they don't, it's your fault for not believing or visualizing it with sufficient intention or sincerity.

The main problem with these affirmations or visualizations or manifestation strategies is that they are, unfortunately, entirely self-defeating, and they can make the situation that you're trying to improve worse, much worse.

Whenever you say something to yourself like, "I am wealthy beyond my wildest dreams," your subconscious says to itself, "Wealthy? Ummm, no! You're not wealthy, pal, not a bit of it. Last time I looked, you're living in a one-room walk-up, with no money, an empty refrigerator, a maxed-out credit card; and when you open your wallet, dead moths fall out."

And then, a little later in the day, you say it to yourself again; and again, your subconscious says, "Um, I thought we talked about this. Open your wallet, go on. See, dead moths!"

And, to make matters significantly worse, the more you say the "I am wealthy..." or, "I am losing weight..." or, "I am a great leader..." the more your subconscious says, "I don't think so, mate!"

In other words, the more you say that stuff, the more your subconscious digs its heels in and fights it. Your subconscious basically reinforces and strengthens its belief in the exact opposite of what you're going for! It's almost as if you're trying to convince yourself of something that you know is actually a lie. Nightmare.

To be clear, I do not have any issue with positive thinking; on the contrary, it is to be encouraged—but, by making a tiny, yet powerful tweak that turns subconscious resistance into subconscious challenges, things can get so much better, so much faster; these new super-powered intentions (affirmations) are called afformations.

Leaders with a developmental and growth mindset recognize their weaknesses and set to intentionally address them.

FIX, NOT RESIST.

Noah St. John, the recognized creator of afformations, argues that by changing a positive statement that our subconscious resists (affirmation) into a positively stated question that our subconscious can set its energy into resolving (afformations), we can close the *belief gap*. The *belief gap*, St. John argues, appears when we state something positive about ourselves and/or our situation and/or our circumstances that we clearly know is not based in reality.

Afformations, therefore, are exactly the opposite of affirmations.

Afformations get your subconscious figuring out how to *fix* the issue, not how to *resist* the issue.

Smashing.

Put simply, when you claim something to be true that patently isn't, your subconscious *resists the issue*. Ask yourself a question, however, and your brain starts to go to work to try to figure out the answer—your subconscious tries to reduce the discord; it looks for ways to positively *fix the issue*.

Our brain has an in-built search function. It tries to find answers to the questions it asks itself. Psychologists call it "embedded presupposition." Ask yourself a really intriguing question, and you'll be amazed the lengths you will go to in order to figure it out—that's your subconscious driving the bus—and your subconscious runs in the background 24/7/365 and *never* gets tired.

Read the statements/questions in the short table below. As you do, take notice how your brain seems to say, "I don't think so, pal" to the first list, and "Ooooh, good question, let's figure it out" to the second list.

Try it.

AFFIRMATION	AFFORMATION
I am super-success-ful in business.	What things am I doing to be significantly more successful in business?
I always do today's work today, and I never, ever procrastinate.	How am I becoming more intentional with my time ensuring the most important things routinely get done?
I am lovable.	What are the many ways I am becoming more inter-esting and lovable?
I am happy and healthy.	Why am I so happy and why do I live such a healthy lifestyle?
I am strong and unstoppable.	Why am I so amazingly strong and unstoppable?
I am a super-suc-cessful leader.	Why am I so determined to be the very best leader I can possibly be?

Repeating column one, affirmations, every day won't actually change much in your life—other than make you increasingly frustrated.

Repeating column two, afformations, every day invites your subconscious to get ever more creative and determined to resolve the puzzle—and pretty soon you'll be making decisions and solving problems to take you closer and closer and closer to where you're intending to be.

As you continue your daily Leadership Journal, you will begin to include daily afformations on a variety of topics. We will start to get our amazingly powerful subconscious working for us rather than against us—and won't that make a refreshing change? A morning afformation that we will live by for the day and all subsequent days since your subconscious never ever, ever, switches off.[4]

AFFORMATIONS—THE BASICS

Afformations should be...

> ...framed as a "why" question: Why do I...? Why am I...?
> ...positively stated: be focused on what we want, not what we want to avoid.
> ...emotionally juicy: use language that gets your emotional juices going.
> ...brief: brevity is key—short is much better than long.
> ...stated and grounded in the present: get your subconscious on the task right away, not tomorrow, not next week.

Here are bunch of leadership-type afformations[5] to get you going, but don't worry, you're smart, you'll figure how to create a bunch more for yourself as you move through the

---

4   No, not even on national federal holidays and birthdays.

5   Disclaimer: other afformations are available.

year—or at least your super-creative, super-busy, super-stubborn, super-subconscious will. ☺

Why is it so easy for me to commit to my daily Leadership Journal?

Obviously.

Why do I love the responsibilities of my job so much?
Why does my work give me such a deep sense of satisfaction?
Why does my job give me so much freedom and choice in life?
Why do I truly enjoy helping others develop so much?
Why do success, health, and wealth flow so freely to me and the others I serve?
Why do I respect the people who work for me so much?
Why do I give my best every single day?
Why am I learning so much about leadership?
Why does my team admire and appreciate my leadership style?
Why do I always create such healthy relationships at work?

Why not write a few more here just for you, just to get you going, just for practice, and just for fun:

1. Why _____
2. Why _____
3. Why _____
4. Why _____

Finally, remember that the journey of a thousand miles begins with the first step—we all know this, right? Well, guess what? It's time to begin—and start at the perfect spot, exactly where you are right now. One step, then another, and then another. Sometimes you will take two steps forward and one step back. Sometimes you will feel stuck. That's all OK and perfectly normal, so long as every day you make some effort for some movement forward—however small.

Be patient with yourself, but don't tolerate laziness. Every day, at least one step, and then tomorrow at least another.

READY TO BEGIN?

Are you ready?

Are you excited to discover the leader you were meant to be?

You know what, who cares?

Let's begin.

Ready or not, who cares?

Let's begin.

You may not be quite ready; heck, you may never be ready. Who cares?

Let's begin. Imperfect action is infinitely better than no action at all.

You're not quite feeling the love for it today?

Who cares? Let's begin.

You're a bit busy right now?

Who cares? Let's begin.

You're feeling a bit tired at the moment?

Who cares? Let's begin?

Get the picture?

It soooooo easy to find reasons not to start today:

Tomorrow the weather will be cooler.

Tomorrow the weather will be warmer.

Tomorrow the fridge will be fuller.

Tomorrow the day will be quieter.
Tomorrow the stars will align better.
Tomorrow the ironing basket will be empty.
Tomorrow...

...and so on and so on ad nauseam.
Who cares?
I don't, and neither should you.
Let's begin.
Just begin. Be brave. In spite of the obstacles, be bold.
Or, to put it another way by paraphrasing the inestimable Johann Wolfgang von Goethe:

Begin it.
Be bold.
Boldness has magic and power all its own.

CHAPTER 17

Putting it all together.

A month of daily leadership development prompts.

EVER SET A NEW YEAR'S RESOLUTION YOU DIDN'T KEEP?

Lots of us have—almost every one of us, I'd guess. Why? When we set the resolution, didn't we really mean it? Again, I'm guessing, but I'd wager that we did mean it—like, really seriously. Why, then, did we not follow through and eventually give up thinking there's always next year, or summer, or next month? Some failed because of lack of clarity, some for lack of specificity, some for lack of planning, some for other more pressing distractions—a whole host of reasons (excuses).

The following pages are a sample of a month's Leadership Journaling prompts—your first month only, of course.

Your aim is to interact with your journal every single day for the next thirty-one days—yes, including Saturdays and Sundays. Ideally, every single morning (Morning Momentum) and every single evening (Evening Evaluation). Remember, leadership is about action bias, energy, commitment; so, too, is leadership development, so, too, is Leadership Journaling.[1]

However, before we begin in earnest, let's talk about the elephant in the room.

There is a mountain of data to suggest that if you embark on this new regimen (any new regimen) that requires your attention for thirty days or more, you are statistically unlikely to succeed—it simply seems like too big and steep and difficult a hill to climb. If, however, you make a different commitment, your likelihood of success rises dramatically.

A DIFFERENT COMMITMENT: A MINIMUM STANDARD

Here's the commitment that really works—just make a start today and promise you'll keep going till the end of the day—two entries, that's all: just two. Then, at the end of the day, make a

---

1   Remember the rats from Chapter 3?

new commitment to do the same tomorrow but for tomorrow only. Then make a new time horizon of Friday. On Friday make a new commitment that extends only until Monday. Then on Monday, promise to keep going till Saturday. Then on Saturday, set your horizons no further than a few days out. And so on and so on and so forth.

The best way to eat the elephant in the room is, after all, in bite-sized elephant nuggets.

Every day, make a fresh commitment to starting that day (that particular day only) by completing your Morning Momentum and your Evening Evaluation—and that's it, no more, and no less. You don't need to make a promise any more extravagant than this; just today, it's your minimum standard. But, as a minimum standard, it simply MUST be done. It's the MINIMUM—the *minimum!*

Your Morning Momentum will give you something for your brain to chew on for the rest of the day—a new thought, a new mentality, a reinforced attitude, an augmented belief, a new insight, perhaps.

Your job is to answer the question by writing down your thoughts (yes, with a pen—look, we've gone over this already) and carry it with you throughout the day: try to honor it, stay true to it, live it—just for today. Keep it at the forefront of your mind and, if you lose it, recognize that it has been lost and come back to it—no harm, no foul. In fact, recognize that you had lost and rediscovered a diamond—well done.

Then at the end of the day, take a few moments to review (reflective and reflexive review) how well you managed to live up to the principle(s) covered in that morning's kick start. Just reflect. Give yourself a score from F all the way to A+. Jot down where you could have done better that day. Your brain will most assuredly chew on it while you sleep.

Then, close your journal and off you trot to dreamland,[2] in the sure and certain belief that you're another day forward on your journey of improvement and leadership greatness.

The next morning, make a firm commitment to that day only—to the morning and to the evening.

Before you know it, it will be the end of the month. At the end of this first month, you should then look back at all of your entries with enormous satisfaction and pride—you will have made a truly wonderful start of eating the elephant in entirely manageable nuggets!

Experience tells us that at the end of thirty days, you will likely be genuinely amazed at the progress you will have made in terms of leadership thinking and insights. You will have started to form a wide range of new business initiatives, advances in commitments, and insights. New thinking, new habits, and new theories of leadership will have started to germinate.

There will be some things in either your business, your team, or yourself that now magically appear a little shaky, and some things will have emerged more solid than ever—both are OK.

So, let's go: grab a cup of something deliciously hot, grab a good pen, and start today: not tomorrow, not next Monday, not on first of next month, not on the first day of the next quarter, not on January 1st, not next year, not on a quieter week: today. *Hoy. Täna. Hoje. Simera. Oggi.*[3]

You can elect to write on/in this book, or you can copy the questions down in your journal, or you can download this list by visiting: www.mydailyleadership or you can subscribe to receive a handmade leather journal including an exclusive carbon fiber fountain pen and ink with a daily prompt printed on sumptuous paper containing all of these questions and more every day for the next two years at least.

Just sayin'.

---

2   Or, if you're feeling thoroughly British today: up the wooden stairs to Bedfordshire.
3   RFN, if you follow me.

Let's commit to today—today only. Tomorrow can worry about itself. TODAY is our minimum standard. Let's go...

Day 1: Morning Momentum
What do you really, really want?

Think about what you really, really want.

You can answer this on a personal basis or on a professional level—I would much prefer personal.

Declare the things that you are working towards.

Your answer should include a broad sense of timing too, please.

Your answer should be around sixty to eighty words, and it should start with these words:

What I really, really want is...

Evening Evaluation:
Today's Leadership Report Card:
A+ A A- B+ B B- C+ C C- F

Because...

Tomorrow I will do better.

Day 2: Morning Momentum
Why do you want those things?

Think about your response to yesterday's question and formalize what the drivers are behind your answer.

Understanding your why will significantly improve your chances of achieving your what.

Your answer should be around one hundred words, and it should start with these words:

Here's why I really, really want these things...

Evening Evaluation:
Today's Leadership Report Card:
A+ A A- B+ B B- C+ C C- F

Because...

Tomorrow I will do better.

• • • • • • • • • • • • • • • • • • •
Day 3: Morning Momentum
What's standing in your way?

Warning: there are some very tough challenges ahead. You maybe can't see them right now, but they are surely coming—and you need to be ready for them by the time they arrive.

Think about the roadblocks, speed bumps, and blockages that are preventing you (or slowing you down) from achieving what you really, really want.

Be as honest as possible with the issues—do not be in solutions-mode at this point—that stuff will come later.

Provide a list of internal and external issues that need to be resolved in order for you to get closer to reaching your maximum potential in the next quarter.

Your answer should be no more than thirty words, and it should start with these words:

Here are the main internal and external issues that are currently impeding my progress...

External Issues Blocking Progress

Things outside you, outside your control

Internal Issues Blocking Progress

Things that are your own creation (beliefs, mindset, past experiences, and the like)

Evening Evaluation:
Today's Leadership Report Card:
A+ A A- B+ B B- C+ C C- F

Because...

Tomorrow I will do better.

. . . .
Day 4: Morning Momentum
How can you fix/address/mitigate those things?

Put the issues/answers from yesterday's journal entry into a priority list starting at number one (the easiest to fix), all the way down to the most difficult to fix/address. For each of the top five issues listed, think about a mini-plan of things that you could implement/develop to resolve the things that are potentially standing between you and your personal goals.

Your answer should be around one hundred words, and it should start with these words:

> *Here are some of the things that I could implement to mitigate/remove these blockages...*

Evening Evaluation:
Today's Leadership Report Card:
A+ A A- B+ B B- C+ C C- F

> *Because...*

> *Tomorrow I will do better.*

• • • • • • • • • • • • • • • • • •
Day 5: Morning Momentum
What gifts and talents do you have that will help you achieve your goals?

While you develop as a leader, you will need to develop new skills and competencies, of course. However, take a few moments to recognize the things that are already propelling you positively towards your goals.

Your answer should be around seventy to one hundred and twenty words, and it should start with these words:

> *Here are some of the gifts and talents that I currently have which are sure to help propel me towards my goals...*

Evening Evaluation:
Today's Leadership Report Card:
A+ A A- B+ B B- C+ C C- F

Because...

Tomorrow I will do better.

. . . .
Day 6: Morning Momentum
What kind of legacy do you want to leave?

Think about how you want to be remembered by the people who know you, as well as those who will work with you in the next couple of years.

Think also about your answer to yesterday's question. Think, too, about how you might expand your influence/reach to better utilize your gifts and talents.

Don't answer this like you're about to die, answer it as if you had to suddenly leave your current role.

Your answer should be around fifty to seventy-five words, and it should start with these words:

> *The legacy I wish to leave after I am*
> *gone can be described thus...*

Evening Evaluation:
Today's Leadership Report Card:
A+ A A- B+ B B- C+ C C- F

Because...

Tomorrow I will do better.

- -
Day 7: Morning Motivation
What is your Purpose Statement?

The answers to the last few questions should now be pointing you towards your own personal leadership Purpose Statement.

This is a clear, concise statement expressing what it is you are trying to achieve and the reasons behind this wish.

It should inspire and motivate you every day to reach your maximum daily leadership potential.

Your Purpose Statement will become your personal daily compass—it should become the driving force behind your daily choices, intentions, and leadership actions.

Your answer should be around fifty to one hundred words, and it should start with these words:

My Leadership Purpose Statement is...

Evening Evaluation:
Today's Leadership Report Card:
A+ A A- B+ B B- C+ C C- F

Because...

Tomorrow I will do better.

Day 8: Morning Momentum
What is your leadership message?

If you could define your leadership style/message into your personal ten leadership tenets (rules, guidelines), what would they be?

These rules should incorporate much of the content of your answers over the last week.

My personal leadership message could be summarized in this list of 10 Golden Leadership Rules...

1.

2.

3.

4.

5.

6.

7.

8.

9.

10.

Evening Evaluation:
Today's Leadership Report Card:
A+ A A- B+ B B- C+ C C- F

Because...

Tomorrow I will do better.

. . . .
Day 9: Morning Momentum
Did you do anything last week to be proud of?

Did the things that you did last week (from a management and/or leadership perspective) get you any closer to where you are trying to get?

Specifically, what things did you do over the last seven days at work that you are proud of?

Your answer should be around fifty to seventy-five words for the first section and the same for the second, and they should start with these words:

Last week I did these things that I am proud of...

And I am proud of them because...

Evening Evaluation:
Today's Leadership Report Card:
A+ A A- B+ B B- C+ C C- F

Because...

Tomorrow I will do better.

- - - - - - - - - - - - - - - - - - - -
Day 10: Morning Momentum
What are you specifically working on to become a better leader?

Newsflash:

You're not a perfect leader; nobody is a perfect anything. But we are all on a journey of self-improvement (or we should be).

We all have weaknesses that need to be addressed. But we can't fix anything until we first admit that the problem exists.

What do you need to get better at over the next three months?

> *Over the next three months specifically, if I want to be a better leader, I had better bring some focus and attention to the following three or four critical issues:*

    1.

    2.

    3.

    4.

Evening Evaluation:
Today's Leadership Report Card:
A+ A A- B+ B B- C+ C C- F

Because...

Tomorrow I will do better.

· · · · · · · · · · · · · · · · · · ·
Day 11: Morning Momentum
Honesty time—what things really need fixing in your world?

Take a long hard look at the things that need fixing that are under your control, but that you are hoping might just go away all by themselves.

Or, maybe you're already working on some things, but you need to step up the pace.

Or, maybe you know exactly what needs to be fixed, and you're on it perfectly already.

Let's declare a list of things that need attention in your world that are under your direct control.

A list of the top five things that need fixing under my control:

1.

2.

3.

4.

5.

Also include some critique/analysis of how well you are currently fixing them, please.

Evening Evaluation:
Today's Leadership Report Card:
A+ A A- B+ B B- C+ C C- F

Because...

Tomorrow I will do better.

. . . .
Day 12: Morning Momentum
What should your boss know that he/she doesn't?

What are you avoiding telling your boss for fear of reprisal, headache, hard work, or receiving instruction on?

I am not asking you to tell your boss anything...but if you could, what should he/she know?

If you could write a 100 percent anonymous magic note into his/her inbox that kept your identity entirely hidden, and that he/she would pay serious attention to, what would you say?

Your answer should be at least one hundred well-chosen words, and it should start with these words:

I wish my boss would pay more attention to...

...and here's why...

If you don't have a boss, and the buck stops right at your door, then today's prompt is:

What part of your business needs the biggest push?

Evening Evaluation:
Today's Leadership Report Card:
A+ A A- B+ B B- C+ C C- F

Because...

Tomorrow I will do better.

. . . .
Day 13: Morning Momentum
Lost Opportunity

Where did you fail to celebrate?

Thinking back over the last month, were there any opportunities that you failed to celebrate either alone, with your team, or with your family and friends?

Even if the answer to the last question is "not really," what small thing could you create to give someone some praise for, if you had wanted to?

What small goal could you create that you know will be achieved...purely for the purpose of being able to celebrate?

List three things that you could have celebrated...if you had been sufficiently inspired.

If I had really wanted to, I could/should have celebrated...

Today I will actively look for something to celebrate with others—even if only by e-mail.

NB: Don't do it by e-mail.

Evening Evaluation:
Today's Leadership Report Card:
A+ A A- B+ B B- C+ C C- F

Because...

Tomorrow I will do better.

• • • • • • • • • • • • • • • • • •
Day 14: Morning Momentum
If you could redo the past week, what would you do more, or less of?

We all find ourselves reacting to people and/or events—but we know that we should be less reactive and more proactive.

What things did you do last week that were focused on the short-term (or immediate-term), rather than the longer term?

Who, or what, did you allow to hijack your calendar?

Where were you in the "urgent, not important" box this week and why?

If you had your chance to manage your time better last week, knowing what you know now, what would you have done differently?

Your answer should be around one hundred words, and it should start with these words:

If I had my time again the last week, I would not have allowed myself to get sucked into...

Here's why...

Evening Evaluation:
Today's Leadership Report Card:
A+ A A- B+ B B- C+ C C- F

Because...

Tomorrow I will do better.

• • • • • • • • • • • • • • • • • • • •
Day 15: Morning Momentum
What have you learned over the last two weeks of journaling?

You are now two weeks into your new Leadership Journaling regimen—what have you learned?

Your answer should be around at least one hundred words, and it should start with these words:

Here's what I have learned over the last couple of weeks with the help of My Daily Leadership *reflections...*

Evening Evaluation:
Today's Leadership Report Card:
A+ A A- B+ B B- C+ C C- F

Because...

Tomorrow I will do better.

. . . .
Day 16: Morning Momentum
If your staff could e-mail you anonymously, what would they likely tell you?

Look back to the question a few days ago. What do you imagine would appear in your inbox if your staff could e-mail you anonymously?

Would they be right, or would they be wrong?

Imagine they were right, though. Do you think you would react well to their telling you? Do you think you could learn something from this?

Are people afraid to tell you what you should hear, maybe?

What if your people are not telling you something because you have never asked them, or worse, because they are afraid?

Instead of simply asking, "How could I help?" or, "What's the one thing I could do to help?" what better questions could you ask them?

Your answer should be around seventy-five to one hundred and fifty words, and it should start with these words:

Here's my strategy to try to get to the truth from my team specifically about my leadership style next week...

Evening Evaluation:
Today's Leadership Report Card:
A+ A A- B+ B B- C+ C C- F

Because...

Tomorrow I will do better.

● ● ● ● ● ● ● ● ● ● ● ● ● ● ● ● ● ●
Day 17: Morning Momentum
How good a coach have you been last week?

Look back on the last week—how well did you develop someone in your team who really needed the help/guidance?

What conceptual issues did you identify in your team?

Your answer should be around eighty to one hundred words, and it should start with these words:

> *Last week I was a rock star coach*
> *when I specifically noticed...*

I noticed it because...

And I did this to help fix it...

I will review it again on this date...

I will know that things are improved when I see...

Evening Evaluation:
Today's Leadership Report Card:
A+ A A- B+ B B- C+ C C- F

Because...

Tomorrow I will do better.

. . . .
Day 18: Morning Momentum
How's your team doing?

1. List all the people who report directly to you.

2. Next to each name write, "Our business benefits from this person because they are great at...."

3. Next to each name write, "Our business would do better if this person would do more...."

4. Next to each name write, "Our business would do better if this person would do less...."

5. Next to each name write, "If I can't coach this person's weaknesses by (insert date), I will get them more help."

6. Next to each name write what skill they need to be trained in, or developed, or what they need coaching in.

How happy are you with your answers to these questions? What do these answers say about your skill as a great leader?
Your answer should be around fifty to seventy-five words, and it should start with these words:

I am determined to fix the following people issues as a matter of priority because...

Evening Evaluation:
Today's Leadership Report Card:
A+ A A- B+ B B- C+ C C- F

Because...

Tomorrow I will do better.

· · · · · · · · · · · · · · · · · · ·
Day 19: Morning Momentum
Confidence and Courage

Leaders are courageous, and brave, and confident. Are you?
If you had 50 percent more confidence, what would you be doing differently?
Your answer should be no more than twenty words, and it should start with these words:

If I had 50 percent more confidence in my leadership ability, my people, and my business, I would immediately...

...so, take a deep breath, be a brave soldier, and go figure out how to do exactly that thing. ☺ But give yourself some very firm deadlines too, please.

Evening Evaluation:
Today's Leadership Report Card:
A+ A A- B+ B B- C+ C C- F

Because...

Tomorrow I will do better.

Day 20: Morning Momentum
How can you delegate better?

Let's imagine that you could be even better at delegating than you currently are. I wonder why you don't delegate more. I wonder how much faster your team could go if you could delegate better. I wonder how clearly you delegate. I wonder if you can make the necessary change to you style.

It's delegating day—get the message?

Decide which things you could delegate. Play to the strengths of your team. Ensure you also give good support and the right level of authority. Allow for failure (learning). Be patient. Measure. Stay close to it. "Delegate" does not mean "abrogate."

Leverage your position as little as possible. Delegate a lot more. At the very least start saying, "You know what, I'll let you decide."

Your answer should be around one hundred to one hundred and fifty words, and it should start with these words:

> *I am determined to start delegating better,*
> *and here are the specific things I could include*
> *and the specific people I have in mind...*

Evening Evaluation:
Today's Leadership Report Card:
A+ A A- B+ B B- C+ C C- F

Because...

Tomorrow I will do better.

· · · · · · · · · · · · · · · · · · ·
Day 21: Morning Momentum
What has been the toughest question so far?

Here we are, three weeks in already—which question has been the trickiest so far? Why?

Your answer should be around one hundred words, and it should start with these words:

The question that I found tricki-
est these last three weeks was...

Because...

It tells me...

Evening Evaluation:
Today's Leadership Report Card:
A+ A A- B+ B B- C+ C C- F

Because...

Tomorrow I will do better.

• • • • • • • • • • • • • • • • • •
Day 22: Morning Momentum
What are you scared to admit?

This is a big one.

Your answer should be at least fifty words long, and it should start like this:

I'm scared to admit...

Well done.

Evening Evaluation:
Today's Leadership Report Card:
A+ A A- B+ B B- C+ C C- F

Because...

Tomorrow I will do better.

• • • • • • • • • • • • • • • • • •
Day 23: Morning Momentum
What are you gonna do 'bout it?

Look at yesterday's answer to a very BIG question. If you were honest with yourself, it was likely a very significant answer.

Something should likely be done about it, but what?

Your answer should be around eighty to one hundred words long, and it should start like this...

I really need to...

Well done, again.

Evening Evaluation:
Today's Leadership Report Card:
A+ A A- B+ B B- C+ C C- F

Because...

Tomorrow I will do better.

• • • • • • • • • • • • • • • • • • •
Day 24: Morning Momentum
What small act of kindness can you perform today?

Your answer should be around ten to twenty words long, and it should start like this:

I'm going to make someone's day today by...

Evening Evaluation:
Today's Leadership Report Card:
A+ A A- B+ B B- C+ C C- F

Because...

Tomorrow I will do better.

• • • • • • • • • • • • • • • • • • •
Day 25: Morning Momentum
JFK wasn't wrong, was he?

JFK said of leadership, "Effort and courage are not enough without purpose and direction."

Where are you most lacking: effort, courage, purpose, or direction?

Your answer should be one well-considered presidential word. _____

Just for today, act accordingly.

Evening Evaluation:
Today's Leadership Report Card:
A+ A A- B+ B B- C+ C C- F

Because...

Tomorrow I will do better.

• • • • • • • • • • • • • • • • • •
Day 26: Morning Momentum
Challenges make changes.

If it doesn't challenge you, how can it possibly change you? In ten words or less, finish this sentence:

My single biggest challenge right now is...

Great. Go fix it.

Evening Evaluation:
Today's Leadership Report Card:
A+ A A- B+ B B- C+ C C- F

Because...

Tomorrow I will do better.

· · · · · · · · · · · · · · · · · · · ·
Day 27: Morning Momentum
Put your hat on.

When doing your job, which "hat" do you typically wear?

Edward de Bono (in 1985) proposed that all leaders should look at their operational challenges from six different perspectives. He codified his model in terms of colored hats. He argued that we each wear one main hat (our standard personal perspective and thought model). We tend to measure all problems/challenges against our personal standard way of thinking. This limits us, he argues, since our habitual thinking does not create new/better results, and we should try to look at issues from all angles before making firm decision.

White Hat Thinking
When wearing this hat, you tend to focus on data, information, and trends.

Red Hat Thinking

The person who wears this hat looks to his/her intuition, gut, and emotions to fix issues.

Black Hat Thinking

Black hat wearers make decisions trying to avoid negative outcomes—they approach problems cautiously and defensively, looking for fatal flaws and possible problems.

Yellow Hat Wearers

These people are determined to always think positively and optimistically. They look for opportunities and possibilities in all situations.

Green Hat Thinkers

Wearers of this hat naturally work hard to look for creative solutions to problems believing that a freewheeling approach leads to better outcomes.

Blue Hat People

These people need to keep control of the situation preferring to ensure that every detail is well managed and organized.

Your answer should be around eighty to one hundred words, and it should start with these words:

My natural default hat color tends to be...

This likely limits my thinking because...

I should try to wear the _____ *colored hat more often, because I recognize that I need to try to....*

Evening Evaluation:
Today's Leadership Report Card:
A+ A A- B+ B B- C+ C C- F

Because...

Tomorrow I will do better.

. . . .
Day 28: Morning Momentum
Abracadabra

If I only had a magic wand...

There are probably a few (good) reasons that you're not quite where you want to be yet. There are some reasons that your team or department or business isn't quite where you want it to be yet. And, yes, it's all your fault, of course...BUT it takes strength to realize the one, single, main thing that you have yet failed to do, or yet failed to get sufficiently great at...yet.

Your answer should be no more than twenty words, and it should start with these words:

*If I had a magic wand, I'd make
myself instantly better at...*

Great, so, now that you have declared it, off you pop to go and figure out how to fix it.

Evening Evaluation:
Today's Leadership Report Card:
A+ A A- B+ B B- C+ C C- F

Because...

Tomorrow I will do better.

. . . .
Day 29 : Morning Momentum
How do you feel?

Evaluate your emotions.

Sit still. Clear your mind. Take a moment. Look inward. Notice how you're feeling about stuff. You're likely feeling a number of emotions right now. Go through this list quickly and underline the ones that resonate with how you're currently feeling. Do not overthink it. There's no limit to how many you can underline.

Ready?
Steady?
Go!

Energized—Patient—Absorbed—Relieved—
Confused—Fearful—Sad—Nervous—Loved—
Satisfied—Heartbroken—Compassionate—Happy—
Noticed—Amused—Troubled—Joyful—Excited—

Proud—Rich—Lonely—Lost—Jovial—Resigned—
Uncomfortable—Miserable—Fulfilled—Bitter—
Desperate—Impotent—Sanguine—Stressed—
Desperate—Grateful—Horrified—Unable—
Friendly—Unyielding—Pleased—Elated—Dominant—
Relaxed—Insulted—Poor—Vengeful—Kind—Strict—
Jolly—Contrary—Driven—Peeved—Disturbed—
Withdrawn—Confused—Violent—Comfortable—
Ignored—Occupied—Threatened—Interested—
Tickled—Fascinated—Bored—Unfulfilled—Thrilled—
Entertained—Wanted—Liked—Needed—Chosen—
Soothed—Compassionate—Lessened—Cheery—
Lucky—Eager—Impatient—Potent—Romantic—
Fierce—Dominated—Intense—Effective—Haunted—
Regretful—Able—Eloquent—Severe—Austere—
Questioning—Difficult—Terrible—Distracted—
Healthy—Slight—Rushed—Merry—Frisky—Roguish—
Subdued—Enigmatic—Chatty—Witty—Manipulated—
Glamorous—Captivating—Appealing—Ugly—Athletic—
Connected—Prepared—Fixed—Robust...other.

Do you need to talk to someone?

Are you hoarding something?

Do you need to take action?

Are you fixating on anything?

Do you need to fix something?

Do you need to forgive someone?

Do you need to forgive you?

> *Now make a firm "emotional" commitment.*
> *Write it here:*

Evening Evaluation:
Today's Leadership Report Card:
A+ A A- B+ B B- C+ C C- F

Because...

Tomorrow I will do better.

· · · · · · · · · · · · · · · · · · ·
Day 30: Morning Momentum
Meaningless or Meaningful?

Looking ahead—what do you have to do to make this year a really meaningful year?

Time flies by so quickly, doesn't it?

Do you sometimes think that the days go slow? So much to cram in, busy, busy, busy. But, counterintuitively, the months seem to fly by at an alarming rate, don't they?

This is not a dress rehearsal. Life does not have a press "Control+Alt+Delete," more's the pity.

This is it.

No do-overs.

No "take two."

No kidding.

No "time-out."

So, let's make a good start.

Your answer should be around two hundred to three hundred words, and it should start with these words:

To make this a really meaningful year, and in order to be a better leader, I am absolutely determined to...

Evening Evaluation:
Today's Leadership Report Card:
A+ A A- B+ B B- C+ C C- F

Because...

Tomorrow I will do better.

• • • • • • • • • • • • • • • • • •
Day 31: Morning Momentum
Who or what are you taking for granted?

A moment's introspection for a simple, yet critical question. Your answer should be around ten to fifteen words, and it should start with these words:

> *Lately I have been taking the following*
> *for granted, and it stops today...*

Evening Evaluation:
Today's Leadership Report Card:
A+ A A- B+ B B- C+ C C- F

Because...

Tomorrow I will do better.

And how about a lovely, juicy, fluffy, moist, and pink bonus day, just 'cause I love you. You can finish this one while you are subscribing at www.mydailyleadership.com. Look, stop being all coquettish and coy, it's beneath you and it's unbecoming—just get your credit card out, already. ☺

• • • • • • • • • • • • • • • • • • •
Day 32: Morning Momentum
The Power of Purpose and Belief

An apocryphal story.

After the great fire of 1666 that leveled London, the UK's most famous architect, Christopher Wren, was commissioned to rebuild St. Paul's Cathedral.

One day in 1671, Christopher Wren observed three bricklayers on a scaffold, one crouched, one half-standing, and one standing tall. All were working very hard and fast—cathedrals don't build themselves, you know.

To the first bricklayer, Christopher Wren asked the question, "What are you doing?" to which the bricklayer replied, "I'm a bricklayer. I'm working hard laying bricks to feed my family." He then asked the second bricklayer the same question. The second bricklayer responded, "I'm a bricklayer. I'm building this enormous new church." But the third bricklayer, when asked the same question, "What are you doing?" replied, "I'm a bricklayer. I'm helping build this wonderful new cathedral to help bring people of the world closer to their God."

In no more than twenty words, describe what this tale tells you about the power of purpose and belief.

To what extent are you, a leader, responsible for the sense of motivation and purpose and passion that your people feel?

Evening Evaluation:
Today's Leadership Report Card:
A+ A A- B+ B B- C+ C C- F

Because...

Tomorrow I will do better.

Hats off to you, clever clogs! Somehow, you made it all the way to the end of the month.

I wish there was some way I could give you a big shiny medal and wrap you in one of those shiny space blanket, tin-foil-looking things, and give you a big high-five and an energy-ball...but I can't. Well, not physically, at any rate. But mentally, I'm doing that right now. ☺

"Congratulations!
Today is your day.
You're off to great places.
You're off and away!"
—Dr. Seuss

"Follow effective action with quiet reflection.
From the quiet reflection will come
even more effective action."
—Peter Drucker

POSTSCRIPT

· · · · · · · · · · · ·

Some final thoughts...

LOOK, YOU MADE IT!

Look at you, you great big smarty pants, you: you reached all the way to here, all the way to the end! Well done!

I cannot possibly ever find the words to adequately express how supremely grateful I am that you persisted. Finishing a book, any book, is an exercise in determination and stoicism, so, well done. Finish a book like this, one that doesn't pander to the reader and one that delivers some difficult and challenging home truths at times, is no easy task; at times it would have been much easier for you to put the book down and never pick it up again, but you didn't. You should be thoroughly, thoroughly impressed with yourself and should be feeling suitably smug. I hereby give you permission to be terribly superior and haughty—just for the rest of the day.[1]

JOURNALING IS NOT JUST WRITING, IT'S ALSO READING.

Reading something written by another person forces you to think thoughts that aren't originally really yours; they are the writer's. Look, I'm doing it to you right now with these very words.

And here again: hippopotamus.

---

1   But don't overdo it—nobody likes a smart-arse, after all. ☺

As if by magic, the thought of a hippopotamus was just somehow shoehorned into your brain outside of your conscious will or beckoning.

Skyscraper—and there again.

Rose petal.

Apricot jam.

Monkey on a bicycle.

You get the idea: my written-down words become rather like a burglar, breaking and entering into your mental home, perhaps even uninvited. But my thoughts do not have the same potency for you as the wonderful thoughts that you yourself create—the new and sparkling thoughts that you have personally given birth to.

All journalers need is a solid framework that gives them a series of gentle nudges and suggestions to tip them in the right direction. See www.mydailyleadership.com for examples.

But, here's where the real magic happens—when you return to read your own journaled thoughts a few hours, days, or weeks later. The regular practice of rereading your earlier entries—thoughts that were entirely created by you—explode into life like a virus overtaking a host. Please don't forget to go back to reread your earlier entries. That's why journaling is not just writing, it's also reading. Keep writing and keep going back to read your wonderful words—there is real transformational magic in them, I promise.

Picture a single domino given a gentle nudge falling into another slightly bigger one, and then another slightly bigger one, and then another slightly bigger one after that—a cascade gathering speed and momentum and power. The first tiny, insignificant domino, if set up just right, can set off a cascade that could eventually topple buildings or mountains.

"Give me a lever long enough, a fulcrum on
which to place it, and I shall move the world."
—Archimedes

Your journal is your lever.

Sometimes, given just the right set of circumstances, and the gentlest of nudges in the right direction, things as small and inconsequential as snowflakes can become an avalanche.

Take time now to go back and review everything you've written down in your journal to date—look how extraordinarily far you've already come.

WHAT'S YOUR TRUTH?

What's your single truth? What is true about you that nobody can take away? Something that no amount of adversity can diminish. You need to know what it is in order to properly protect it, no matter what.

Finish this thought, this truth...

Above all things, I am _____

Figure out how to protect, project, and promote that.

SPREAD THE LIGHT.

Share and share alike.
Tell others.
Spread the word.
Pay it forward.
Evangelize.

> *"No matter what happens in life, be good*
> *to people. Being good to people is a*
> *wonderful legacy to leave behind."*
> —Taylor Swift

> *"There are two ways of spreading light: to be*
> *the candle, or the mirror that reflects it."*
> —Edith Wharton

TO BE, OR NOT TO BE?

At the risk of upsetting the Bard of Stratford, here's a really short list of things you can choose to be, and things you can choose not to be:

Be kind.
Especially to those who can appreciate it.

Be generous of spirit.
Especially to those who demand high standards in quality and delivery.

Be contagious.
Especially with the principles of excellence.

Be forgiving.
Especially with those who you will be wanting it from too one day.

Be warm.
Especially with those who need your support the most.

Be approachable.
Especially to those who understand boundaries.

Be curious.
Especially with those who trade in truth.

Be trustworthy.
Especially to those that need your trust.

Be lighthearted—but not lightweight.

Great leaders are not tough and demanding and focused and driven and goal-oriented...or rather, they are, but in a *good* way. For "good," read "kind." For "kind," read "self-aware." For "self-aware," read the above.

> *"You don't build a business, you build people,*
> *then people build the business."*
> —Zig Ziglar

Leaders build themselves, and then they build their people.

Leaders are in a position of power and authority and influence.

Be kind to yourself.

Be kind to your people.

Choose to be extraordinary...and kind.

Namaste.

www.mydailyleadership.com
concilio et labore
Creating the world's best leaders one day at a time.

ACKNOWLEDGMENTS

· · · · · · · · · · · · · · · · · · · ·

There are simply too many people to thank for the part that they played in the making of this book: to all of you, a sincere and heartfelt thanks.

That being said, there are a few especially delicious people that simply must get a separate mention, because without their help, guidance, and support, this book would never have seen the light of day:

Alice and Grace:
Two too smart, and two too gorgeous.

Lori:
Remember, this is all your fault.

Heather, Debby, and the Post Hill team:
Thanks for your patience, persistence, and professionalism. But mostly, thanks for your enormous patience.

Carlos:
Thanks for your critique. As ever, smarter than the average bear: much.

Crystal:
You saw it better than I ever could.

...and, for their part in everything else:

Dad:
I too would rather be the head of a mouse, than the tail of a lion. As ever, muchisimas gracias.

Mum, Effie, and Yaya:
If you knew them, you'd know why.

ABOUT THE AUTHOR

· · · · · · · · · · · · · · · · · · ·

Antonio Garrido has over twenty-five years in leadership positions with world-class businesses. He is expert in building
high-performance leaders and blends his own vast commercial
experience with proven techniques to embed a unique brand
of leadership development. He is also a serial entrepreneur,
successful business coach, speaker, and leader from small private businesses, up to Fortune-60 size.